The Moral Economy of Labor

The Moral Economy of Labor

Aristotelian Themes in Economic Theory

James Bernard Murphy

Yale University Press   New Haven and London

Designed by Sonia Scanlon.
Set in Times Roman type by
Marathon Typography Service, Durham, North Carolina.
Printed in the United States of America by Edwards Brothers,
Ann Arbor, Michigan.

Library of Congress Cataloging-in-Publication Data
Murphy, James Bernard, 1958–
The moral economy of labor : Aristotelian themes in
economic theory / James Bernard Murphy.
p.   cm.
Includes bibliographical references and index.
ISBN 0-300-05406-8
1. Labor—Moral and ethical aspects.   2. Work ethic.
3. Aristotle—Views on labor. I. Title.
HD4905.M87   1993   92-45689
306.3'6—dc20

A catalogue record for this book is available from
the British Library.

The paper in this book meets the guidelines for permanence
and durability of the Committee on Production Guidelines for
Book Longevity of the Council on Library Resources.

10 9 8 7 6 5 4 3 2 1

To Kirsten
fide, spe, caritate

Contents

Acknowledgments

Every work of scholarship is the product of a chemical reaction generated by the confluence of myriad persons and ideas. Nonetheless, some individuals usually play a more catalytic role than others. From Rulon Wells I learned how to distinguish Aristotle's official logic from his logic-in-use. From Robert Dahl I learned to appreciate the political dimension of economic organization. From Philip Mirowski I discovered the pervasive role of the concept of nature in economic theory. I must acknowledge a profound intellectual debt to these three men.

During the precipitation of this book, I received invaluable assistance from various readers, notably Louis Dupré, Steven B. Smith, Douglas Rae, Joseph Hamburger, and Larry Arnhart. I am also very indebted to my many conversations with John L. Murphy, Elliott Mordkowitz, Jahan Ramazani, Philip Chmielewski, Rogers Smith, and especially Roger Masters—all of whom have taken a lively interest in my work and have made keen observations about it. Ian Shapiro and Russell Hittinger must be singled out for their enormously helpful criticism and suggestions during the process of crystallization. Since this book is about productive labor, it would be remiss of me not to mention all the help I received from Yale University Press editor John S. Covell and manuscript editor Susan Higginbotham.

Financial assistance came from Yale's Robert M. Leylan Fellowship (1989–90) and from Dartmouth's Burke Award (1990–93). I am grateful to both of these institutions. Finally, none of this would have been possible without the help of my wife, Kirsten Murphy—not only for the usual support, encouragement, and patience but also for considerable editorial and technical assistance.

Abbreviations of Aristotle's Works

An. Post. Posterior Analytics
An. Pr. Prior Analytics
Cael. De Caelo
DA De Anima
DI De Interpretatione
Eud. Eudemian Ethics
GA De Generatione Animalium
GC De Generatione et Corruptione
HA Historia Animalium
IA De Incessu Animalium
MA De Motu Animalium
Mem. De Memoria
Met. Metaphysics
Meteor. Meteorologica
MM Magna Moralia
NE Nicomachean Ethics
OY On Youth
PA De Partibus Animalium
Phys. Physics
Poet. Poetics
Pol. Politics
Prob. Problems
Rhet. Rhetoric
SE Sophistici Elenchi
Top. Topics

Prologue

The Moral Economy of Labor

> What is most desirable for each and every man is the
> highest he is capable of attaining.
> Aristotle, *Pol.* 1333a29

This book is about the dignity and the degradation of work. Why do some kinds of work promote human flourishing whereas other kinds of work diminish it? Our work turns out to have considerable power either to foster or to stunt the development of our moral values and our cognitive skills. Nor should this be surprising. After all, not only is work the most prominent activity in the lives of most adults, but at least in our society, most people derive their sense of personal identity and their sense of social status from their work. Although in some societies people ask strangers first about their families, in our society we ask, "What do you do?" Indeed, the question "What do you do?"—although it often expresses an invidious interest in social status—embodies the insight that our work both reflects and determines our character: we become what we do.

Unfortunately, many if not most people find themselves in jobs that do not advance their happiness and well-being; because of what they do they become less healthy, less happy, less productive, and in fact less intelligent than they could otherwise be. These myriad jobs offer so little opportunity for the exercise of either manual or mental skills that the very capacity for these skills atrophies. A detailed manpower survey by the New York State Department of Labor, for example, found that "approximately two-thirds of all the jobs in existence in that state involve such simple skills that they can be—and are—learned in a few days, weeks, or at most months of on-the-job training." By contrast, the traditional industrial crafts, not to mention the professions, require apprenticeships of four to seven years. The existing organization of work produces a far-reaching and disturbing squandering of human moral, intellectual, and economic potential. As one business consultant put it: "We may have created too many dumb jobs for the number of dumb people to fill them."[1] With so many jobs requiring so few skills it is perhaps not surprising that only one-quarter of American jobholders say that they are working at full potential.[2]

What moral norms ought to govern work if it is to promote human flourishing? And what norms of justice ought to govern access to such work? Moral and political debate about work is usually associated with concerns extrinsic to work itself—the wages of work, the availability of work, the hours of work, the conditions of work, the authority of managers over workers. Yet it is rather the intrinsic aspects of work that seem to have the most profound effects on human happiness and well-being. When asked to rank some twenty-five aspects (both extrinsic and intrinsic) of work, most people consistently rank the "interest" of work—an intrinsic quality—first.[3] What intrinsic aspects of work make it subjectively interesting to most workers? Most say that these aspects are the opportunity to learn new skills and the opportunity to exercise initiative and independent judgment in the performance of tasks. Moreover, it is these same intrinsic qualities, rather than the pay or conditions of work, that most profoundly affect the objective physical and mental health of workers.[4]

That moral and political debate has been strangely blind to the moral dimension of work is evident when we look to theories of justice. Ever since Aristotle, we have had theories of justice in the distribution of goods (distributive justice) and theories of justice in the exchange of goods (commutative justice), but very

1. On the New York State survey and for the Case Western Reserve University consultant, see Harry Braverman, *Labor and Monopoly Capital* (New York: Monthly Review Press, 1974), 433n and 35.

2. According to a 1982 survey by Daniel Yankelovich and John Immerwahr, "many job holders are holding back from their jobs, and quality suffers accordingly. . . . Fewer than one out of four job holders (23%) say that they are currently working at their full potential. Nearly half of all job holders (44%) say that they do not put much effort into their jobs over and above what is required to hold on to a job. The overwhelming majority (75%) say that they could be significantly more effective on their jobs than they are now." Yankelovich and Immerwahr, *Putting the Work Ethic to Work*, cited in Robert E. Lane, *The Market Experience* (Cambridge: Cambridge University Press, 1991), 239–40.

3. For a discussion of this major survey, see *Work in America*, Report of a Special Task Force to the Secretary of Health, Education, and Welfare (Cambridge: MIT Press, 1973), 13.

4. Arthur Kornhauser's classic study, *Mental Health of the Industrial Worker: A Detroit Study* (New York: John Wiley, 1965), concludes: "By far the most influential attribute [of the comparatively high or low average mental health of occupational groups] is the opportunity the work offers—or fails to offer—for use of the worker's abilities" (263). For further empirical evidence that those who enjoy the intrinsic satisfactions of challenging work also enjoy superior physical and mental health, see Lane, *Market Experience*, 397.

little in the way of a theory of justice in the production of goods.[5] In our time, liberal capitalism and Soviet communism have represented two very different conceptions of distributive and commutative justice; defenders of both systems have emphasized the contrasting patterns of property rights, income distribution, and the role of exchange. In other words, the issue between capitalism and communism has always been the justice (and efficiency) of two rival systems of exchange and distribution. What has never been at issue is the justice of the organization of production: the communist division of labor in production mirrors the capitalist. East and West employed Frederick Taylor's "scientific management" to dissolve complex labor processes into simple and repetitive tasks. The detailed fragmentation of skilled labor into monotonous routines that once symbolized the horrors of capitalism became the basis of Soviet industry from Vladimir Lenin through Leonid Brezhnev. Indeed, Taylorism was more pervasive in Soviet Russia than it ever was in the United States.[6]

Those who saw the struggle between communism and capitalism as the struggle between good and evil had studiously to avoid discussion of the character of work because in both economic systems the worker is often treated as a mere instrument, a "factor of production" rather than as the subject of his or her work. The striking similarity in the organization of work in such different economies leads apologists for both systems to emphasize distribution and exchange rather than the dignity of work. For example, one leading Marxist theoretician, John Roemer, says that if we were to focus on the labor process we would be forced to the bizarre conclusion that socialist countries exploit workers just as much as do capitalist countries![7] When Charlie Chaplin satirized the mindless monotony

5. Adina Schwartz points out that the degradation of work is alluded to in only one paragraph of John Rawls's *Theory of Justice* (Cambridge: Harvard University Press, 1971), 529; whereas Robert Nozick, in *Anarchy, State, and Utopia* (New York: Basic Books, 1974, 246–50), concludes that what people do at work is a matter of individual preference, not political justice. See Schwartz, "Meaningful Work," *Ethics* 92 (July 1982): 635n.

6. Lenin was so enamored of Taylorism that Stalin once defined "the essence of Leninism" as "the combination of Russian revolutionary sweep with American efficiency." For the bizarre story of the seventy-year love affair between Bolshevism and Taylorism, see Mark Beissinger, *Scientific Management, Socialist Discipline, and Soviet Power* (Cambridge: Harvard University Press, 1988).

7. "If, for instance, one observes that the labor process appears much the same in existing socialism as it does in capitalism, then one might conclude that existing socialist countries are not essentially different from capitalist countries, insofar as the exploitation of workers is concerned" (John E. Roemer, "Exploitation, Class, and Property Relations," in *After Marx*, ed. Terence Ball and James Farr [Cambridge: Cambridge University Press, 1984], 198). To avoid this scandal, Roemer distinguishes exploitation as a property relation from mere alienation at work.

of the assembly line in *Modern Times* (1936), he was denounced in the United States as an enemy of capitalism and in Russia as an enemy of socialism—and in a sense he was guilty on both counts.

The exclusive focus on distribution and exchange in modern theories of justice has impoverished our moral theory and practice because distribution and exchange concern chiefly what people have rather than what they do. Of course, in the face of widespread material deprivation, what people have or do not have can be of considerable moral urgency, if only because a certain minimal having is a precondition for doing. But decades of research in social psychology and occupational health consistently show that personal happiness and well-being are produced more by what people do than by what they possess: above a certain minimum income, differences in the enjoyment of work are more important than differences in income for overall happiness.[8] If our real concern is for human happiness and welfare, then we should be more concerned about the distribution of challenging work than about the distribution of income.

What about leisure? Some theorists claim that for public policy to support meaningful work would merely reflect an arbitrary preference for one kind of human flourishing over other kinds. They argue that there is no reason why leisure could not become the primary sphere for the realization of human potential. Why not simply let people trade off empty work for meaningful leisure or let people in dull jobs compensate with exciting leisure?[9] But evidence from a variety of sources suggests that work is the key to leisure. As one leading researcher puts it: "Men whose jobs require intellectual flexibility, for example, come not only to exercise their intellectual powers on the job but also to engage in intellectually demanding leisure-time activities." People seem to apply the habits developed at work to their leisure: mindless work tends to lead to mindless leisure whereas challenging work leads to challenging leisure.[10] So for public policy to emphasize the moral priority of mean-

8. After surveying a great deal of the literature, Robert Lane concludes: "What we have found in this discussion of work is that working activities are the best agents of well-being and the best sources of cognitive development, a sense of personal control, and self-esteem in economic life, better than a higher standard of living, and, I believe, better than what is offered by leisure" (*Market Experience*, 335).

9. "But implementing the right to meaningful work elevates one particular category of good, intrinsic job satisfaction, and arbitrarily privileges that good and those who favor it over other equally desirable goods and equally wise fans of other goods" (Richard J. Arneson, "Meaningful Work and Market Socialism," *Ethics* 97 [April 1987]: 525).

10. On the psychological relation of work to leisure, see Melvin Kohn and Carmi Schooler, *Work and Personality* (Norwood: Ablex Publishing, 1983), 81 and 239–40.

ingful work is not an arbitrary preference but is grounded in the structure of the human personality.

In light of what we know about the sources of human happiness and well-being, the debate between capitalism and communism over the ownership of capital seems misguided: what workers value most is challenging work, not owning the means of production—although, as we shall see, worker ownership of the means of production may be a precondition for the design of challenging jobs. What matters most is not ownership of the means of production but their use in the labor process: does a productive technology augment the skill of the worker (like a power tool) or does it degrade the skill of the worker (like an assembly line)? In their research on the effects of work on personality, Melvin Kohn and Carmi Schooler rightly insist that "the central [moral] fact of occupational life today is not ownership of the means of production, nor is it status, income, or interpersonal relationships on the job. Instead, it is the opportunity to use initiative, thought and independent judgment in one's work—to direct one's own occupational activities."[11]

Although Aristotle's explicit theories of justice concern distribution and exchange, one can find in Aristotle's theory of human flourishing (*eudaimonia*) and in his theory of production (*poiēsis*) the fundamental norms for a theory of justice in production. The ultimate aim of all human activity, according to Aristotle, is to realize fully our capacities in complex activities—that is, to flourish. By human flourishing, Aristotle means both the subjective experience of happiness and the objective exercise of moral, physical, and intellectual excellence.[12] Indeed, social psychologists have come to see the wisdom of measuring both the subjective and the objective dimensions of occupational flourishing. Subjective job satisfaction, for example, is not a reliable indicator of human flourishing because job satisfaction is very sensitive to expectations; it is common, for example, for workers to have their jobs upgraded and have their satisfaction decline because of higher expectations; similarly, workers in very degraded jobs can report high satisfaction because of their very low expectations. For these reasons, researchers have taken an interest in such objective measures of flourishing as physical and mental health as well as performance on cognitive tests. Of course, like Aristotle, these social scientists

11. Kohn and Schooler, *Work and Personality*, 81.

12. John Cooper argues for "human flourishing" as a translation of *eudaimonia* in *Reason and Human Good in Aristotle* (Cambridge: Harvard University Press, 1975), 89–90.

assume that in the long run there is a close relation between subjective happiness and objective well-being—even though the two may diverge in the short run.[13]

According to Aristotle, both subjective pleasure and objective excellence arise from the exercise of complex skills. As John Rawls describes this Aristotelian principle: "Other things equal, human beings enjoy the exercise of their realized capacities (their innate or trained abilities), and this enjoyment increases the more the capacity is realized, or the greater the complexity."[14] Pleasure arises, says Aristotle, "when we are exercising some faculty" (*NE* 1153a9); and Aristotle repeatedly insists that virtue or excellence is a habitual activity, not a mere passive faculty.[15] As one scholar puts it: "Here virtue, as conceived by Aristotle, resembles the virtuosity of the accomplished games player or craftsman."[16] In Aristotle's view, then, human flourishing, meaning both subjective happiness and objective well-being, is the product of doing rather than having, of the exercise of skills rather than passive consumption. The reason we are willing to undergo the stress of practice and learning is that we anticipate the rewards of mastering complex new skills.

Both Aristotle and Rawls argue that this principle of human flourishing is rooted in the natural structure of the human personality. What evidence is there for this claim? Rawls suggests that "natural selection must have favored creatures of whom this principle is true." Perhaps the Aristotelian principle is rooted in what biologists call the "exploratory drive," that is, the propensity

13. For a critique of the exclusive emphasis on job satisfaction, see Kohn and Schooler, *Work and Personality*, 303–4. Amartya Sen reports that both subjective and objective measures of human flourishing are required even to measure public health: in India, in those districts where objective mortality is falling due to better health care, subjective morbidity is rising due to higher awareness of health problems; conversely, in those districts with low subjective morbidity there may be very high objective mortality. See Sen, *Commodities and Capabilities* (Amsterdam: North-Holland, 1985).

14. Rawls, *Theory of Justice*, 426. Rawls goes on to qualify this principle: "It formulates a tendency and not an invariable pattern of choice, and like all tendencies it may be overridden. Countervailing inclinations can inhibit the development of realized capacity and the preference for more complex activities" (429). And, of course, each individual will have a unique level of desirable complexity: "Thus it would appear that how much we learn and how far we educate our innate capacities depends upon how great these capacities are and how difficult is the effort of realizing them" (428).

15. All citations of Aristotle, unless otherwise noted, are from the Revised Oxford Translation, *The Complete Works of Aristotle*, ed. Jonathan Barnes (Princeton: Princeton University Press, 1984).

16. W. F. R. Hardie, *Aristotle's Ethical Theory* (Oxford: Clarendon Press, 1980), 104.

exhibited in play and other activities to experiment with the environment in order to gain a greater mastery of it.[17] The enjoyment of active mastery of the environment rather than passive consumption may have contributed to the survival of our ancestors. There is more direct evidence for our principle in the research of social psychologists. For example, many studies show that jobs requiring the exercise of complex skills promote not only subjective satisfaction but also the objective well-being of workers; conversely, monotonous and repetitive work undermines not only subjective satisfaction but also the mental and physical health of workers.[18]

Perhaps the most telling evidence in favor of our principle comes from a major longitudinal study of the relation of job complexity to cognitive complexity. By testing the intellectual capacities of a group of men in 1964 and in 1974 and by measuring the substantive complexity of their jobs, Kohn and Schooler found that the cognitive capacities of men with complex jobs developed through work whereas the cognitive capacities of men with simple and repetitive jobs deteriorated.[19] Adam Smith's observation that a worker "whose whole life is spent performing a few simple operations . . . generally becomes as stupid and ignorant as it is possible for a human creature to become" has been empirically verified. These findings have profound and disturbing implications. Workers in mindless jobs not only undermine their capacity for the enjoyment of complex activities at work but also their capacity for the enjoyment of complex activities during leisure. Since workers are not generally aware of the risk to their intelligence from mindless jobs, there are grounds here for protecting them from stultifying work. We now attempt to protect workers from harm to their physical capacities; why should we not protect them from harm to their mental capacities?

Even if we grant that the exercise of complex skills is necessary for human flourishing, we need to specify precisely what kinds of work afford the exer-

17. On the "exploratory drive," see Bernard Campbell, *Human Evolution* (New York: Aldine Publishing, 1985), 54–57.

18. On the relation of job satisfaction to the exercise of complex skills, see Victor Vroom, *Work and Motivation* (New York: John Wiley, 1964), 141–45. On the relation of physical and mental health to the exercise of complex skills, see Arthur Kornhauser, *Mental Health of the Industrial Worker* (New York: John Wiley, 1965), 97–105; and Lane, *Market Experience*, pp. 396–97.

19. "Hence, doing substantively complex work tends to increase one's respect for one's own capacities, one's valuation of self-direction, one's intellectuality (even in leisure-time pursuits), and one's sense that the problems one encounters are manageable" (Kohn and Schooler, *Work and Personality*, 304).

cise of these skills. Is mental work superior to manual work? Is a variety of tasks superior to a single complex task? Aristotle tells us that work is properly the unity of conception and execution, of *noēsis* and *poiēsis* (*Met.* 1032b15). What gives skilled work its dignity, according to Aristotle, is that a worker first constructs in thought what he then embodies in matter; conversely, what makes unskilled work sordid is that one man executes the thought of another: "It is the mark of a free man not to live at another's beck and call" (*Rhet.* 1367a32). Aristotle is right: all skill is developed through the dialectic of conception and execution. By learning the general principles of a craft, a skilled worker is able to solve problems that arise in its execution; and by solving these particular problems in execution, he deepens his conceptual knowledge of the general principles. Through this dialectic of conception and execution we become autonomous subjects, rather than mere instruments, of labor.

Yet it is perfectly possible, as Aristotle admits, to dissolve the unity of conception and execution so that what is conceived by one person is executed by another. The age-old relations of slave owner to slave, of adult to child, or of master to apprentice have always to some extent reflected this dissolution. But the Industrial Revolution, by reducing the proportion of independent farmers and artisans and by increasing the proportion of wage laborers and managers, seems to have created a more pervasive divorce between conception and execution. The dissolution of skill into mere dexterity reached its logical conclusion in the "scientific management" of Frederick Taylor. He insisted that "all of the planning which under the old system was done by the workman, as a result of his personal experience, must of necessity under the new system be done by the management."[20] Taylor's emphasis on moving all thought and initiative from the shop floor to the planning department—his use of job descriptions to specify what is to be done, how it is to be done, and how long is allowed for doing it—have become central tenets of management science. Indeed, what chiefly characterizes work in contemporary industrial and post-industrial society is precisely this divorce of conception from execution in the division of labor. Engineers and managers decide not only what is to be done but how it is to be done; line workers, secretaries, and bureaucratic functionaries execute tasks designed by their superiors.[21]

20. Frederick Taylor, *The Principles of Scientific Management* [1911] (New York: W. W. Norton, 1967), p. 38.

21. Harry Braverman's "deskilling hypothesis," that is, his argument that over the course of the past century the skill requirements of most jobs have declined—that dignified labor has

The first thing to be noted about this tendency is that it is quite general. We find it on the assembly line, in the typing pool, behind the automated loom, at the fast-food grill, on the word processor—wherever we find people at work producing goods or providing services, both in private firms and in public bureaucracies. Second, although the separation of conception from execution can be carried quite far, it is never complete. Since workers are not mere instruments of managerial designs but persons with their own ideas about work, they resist the efforts of managers to reduce their jobs to the execution of simple routines. Moreover, the separation is limited not just by the resistance of workers but by the very nature of work. Work of necessity requires some degree of unity of conception and execution: the effective design of a task requires some idea of how it would be executed just as the effective execution of a task requires some understanding of why it was designed.

In short, the divorce of conception from execution in the detailed division of labor undermines our capacity for the realization of complex skills and is therefore a profound obstacle to human flourishing. The Aristotelian view that work is properly the unity of conception and execution reveals how misguided are most attacks on the division of labor. Ever since the young Karl Marx attacked occupational specialization, many have seen the division of labor as an obstacle to human flourishing. But specialization is not itself the moral concern here: scientific, medical, legal, and craft specialization do not dissolve the integrity of conception and execution. On the contrary, the pride of craftsmanship stemming from the mastery of complex skills is the product of occupational specialization. Specialization is of moral concern only when it fragments work into monotonous routines that stifle the human capacity for thought, imagination, and skill. And attacks on the separation of mental from manual labor neglect the fact that white-collar mental work is equally subject to the divorce of conception and execution. The separation of mental from manual labor is only a special instance of this tendency.

If we are to gauge the feasibility of promoting human flourishing by insisting on the integrity of conception and execution in the design of jobs, we must

---

been steadily degraded by the divorce of conception from execution—is quite controversial. For a survey of the controversy, see William Form, "Resolving Ideological Issues on the Division of Labor," in *Sociological Theory and Research*, ed. Hubert M. Blalock (New York: Free Press, 1980), 140–55. My concern is the moral and political challenge posed by the existing degradation of work, not with the historical question of whether work is more or less degraded than in the past.

first attempt to understand how their divorce came to be accepted, in theory and in practice, as a technical requisite of modern economic life. Is it not paradoxical that American capitalism and Soviet communism adopted the same principles of job design and the same division of labor in production? If Taylorism is a capitalist strategy for class domination, as some Marxists insist, or a strategy to exploit mass markets for standardized goods, as some liberal economists insist, then how do we account for communist Taylorism?[22] Both Marxists and liberals may be partly right, but there must be, in addition, something more fundamental at work here. To make sense of this paradox will take us all the way back to Aristotle by way of classical political economy. For the paradox of capitalist and communist economic practice was prefigured in the paradox of bourgeois and proletarian economic theory in Adam Smith and Karl Marx. Smith and Marx diverged radically on the question of the necessity of markets and private property in a productive economy, but they converged on the question of the necessity of a detailed division of labor. The enthusiasm of both capitalist and communist managers for Taylorism makes sense only in light of the profound belief, shared by both Smith and Marx, that an increasingly productive modern industry necessarily requires an increasingly fragmented division of labor.

The classical political economists credited the division of labor with the enormous growth in the productivity of labor; at the same time, however, they blamed it for destroying the integrity of craftsmanship by deskilling the craftsman. Discussion of the degradation of labor as a moral evil was a pervasive theme in classical political economy, a theme most eloquently voiced by John Ruskin:

> We have much studied and perfected, of late, the great civilised invention of the division of labour; only we give it a false name. It is not, truly speaking, the labour that is divided; but the men:—divided into mere segments of men—broken into small fragments and crumbs of life; so that all the little piece of intelligence that is left in a man is not enough to make a pin, or a nail, but exhausts itself in making the point of a pin, or the head of a nail. . . . And the great cry that rises

22. For a Marxist view of Taylorism as class exploitation, see Ernest Mandel, *Marxist Economic Theory*, trans. Brian Pearce (New York: Monthly Review Press, 1968), 138. Economists Michael Piore and Charles Sabel interpret Taylorism as a response to competition to meet the demands of mass markets for standardized goods; see Sabel, *Work and Politics* (Cambridge: Cambridge University Press, 1984), 236n.

from all our manufacturing cities, louder than the furnace blast, is all in very deed for this,—that we manufacture everything there except men.[23]

As we shall see, both Smith and Marx implicitly appealed to the Aristotelian principle in their criticism of the separation of conception from execution in the industrial division of labor; nonetheless, they viewed the modern economy as a Faustian bargain whereby the wealth of nations necessitates the impoverishment of individuals. The classical political economists saw no way out of this conundrum: they accepted the evils of the increasing degradation of labor as an inescapable cost of economic progress. Nor is this Faustian bargain merely a historical artifact; there is a great deal of contemporary evidence that the division of labor and automation continue to reduce the skill requirements of many jobs, as can be seen with the automatic price-scanners in supermarkets. The moral question raised by classical political economy is, then, as pressing as ever: does productive efficiency require the divorce of conception from execution—meaning the removal of productive skill from workers? I will attempt to show that the argument that it does rests upon a theoretically mistaken and morally impoverished view of labor. As we shall see, empirical evidence from experiments with alternative forms of production suggests that there is a variety of equally efficient ways to organize production. Still, to address this question adequately requires us to consider such fundamental philosophical questions as: What is efficiency? What is labor? What moral criteria should govern the division of labor? Is the division of labor natural or conventional? All of these questions will take us back to Aristotle.

At the center of this book, both literally and figuratively, is a critique and reconstruction of Aristotle's philosophy of practical reason and of nature. My approach to Aristotle has three components: First, I make use of the scholastic insight that Aristotle's explicit logic (*logica docens*) is often at odds with his implicit logic (*logica utens*). After distinguishing Aristotle's explicit from his implicit doctrines, I will use his implicit doctrines to criticize his explicit doctrines. Second, to help interpret Aristotle and to delimit the Aristotelian tradition, I rely heavily on two Thomist commentators—namely, St. Thomas Aquinas, since he is the supreme interpreter of Aristotle, and John of St. Thomas, since he is the supreme interpreter of Thomas Aquinas. I thus pro-

23. John Ruskin, *The Stones of Venice*, vol. 2 (London: Smith, Elder, 1853), 6:165.

pose to continue the work of rescuing John of St. Thomas (John Poinsot) from obscurity—work begun by Jacques Maritain and Yves Simon and notably advanced in our day by John Deely. Third, in order to make Aristotle speak to contemporary political economy, I have taken the liberty of revising his doctrines in the light of modern philosophical, natural, and social sciences.

I will use my reconstruction of Aristotle's doctrines of practical reason and of nature to criticize classical political economy as well as to criticize Aristotle. In what sense, then, is my approach Aristotelian? I will attempt to show that some of Aristotle's explicit doctrines articulate the fundamental presuppositions of classical political economy. For example, Aristotle explicitly excludes moral reason from the realm of production; he argues that production is governed solely by technical reason. Similarly, Aristotle explicitly argues that many kinds of the division of labor are natural and not conventional. This twofold reduction of the division of labor to efficiency and to nature is what generates the conundrum of classical political economy: for if the existing division of labor is uniquely efficient, then we *ought* not subject it to social transformation; moreover, if the existing division of labor is natural, then we *cannot* subject it to social transformation. These two modes of explanation serve to remove the division of labor from the realm of moral and political deliberation because, as Aristotle said, we can deliberate only about those things that could be different.

Still, if Aristotle is a part of the problem then he is also the basis for a solution: my reconstruction of his implicit views of practical reason and of nature will offer us a way out of this moral conundrum. For Aristotle implicitly argues that production belongs to the realm of moral deliberation just as he implicitly argues that the division of labor is shaped by custom and by reason. I propose, then, to use Aristotle's implicit theory of practical reason and of nature to criticize his explicit reduction of the division of labor to technical efficiency and to nature. Since this reduction is at the center of classical political economy, my critique of Aristotle is at the same time a critique of classical political economy.

In short, classical political economy is characterized by a twofold reduction of labor to efficiency and to nature; labor is described both as the instrumental manipulation of objects and as man's metabolism with nature. What do these two reductions have to do with each other? It turns out that they are united in Aristotle's doctrine of the economy of nature—a doctrine that is pervasive in classical political economy. Although the Sophists had contrasted nature to art (*technē*), Aristotle's natural teleology is based on an elaborate analogy between the design of artifacts and the design of organisms. Aristotle insists that natural organisms be understood as if they were the products of efficient workmanship: nature economizes in her productions just like a good workman. Therefore, in the context of Aristotle's economy of nature, it makes perfect sense to argue that if labor is natural then it must be efficient and, conversely, that if labor is efficient then it must be natural.

My revised Aristotelian theory of practical reason and of nature will serve as the basis for a sustained conversation about some of the philosophical questions raised by theories of labor ranging over time from Antiphon to Hannah Arendt and ranging across disciplines from anthropology to metaphysics to zoology. What does it mean to describe the division of labor as efficient? Does it mean that there is some scientifically objective method for determining how many tasks one person can perform well? Can the efficiency of the existing pattern of the division of labor in the factory and the office be experimentally measured? What is the relation of technical efficiency to moral norms? Similarly, what does it mean to describe the division of labor as natural? Do people's social roles reflect their innate aptitudes? Are some forms of the division of labor natural because they are universal? What is the relation of nature to social conventions? Are some conventions natural?

The basis for our transhistorical conversation is the seemingly universal agreement that production has no politics. Ever since Aristotle explicitly excluded moral reason from the realm of production, we find in intellectual history little more than variations on this theme. J. S. Mill, for example, acknowledges the moral dimension of economic distribution but insists that production is governed by the immutable (and efficient) laws of nature. Marx attacks Mill's dichotomy of production and distribution, but then goes on to reproduce it in his distinction between the forces of production (which include the division of labor) and the relations of production (which concern the distribution of property rights). Jürgen Habermas in turn attacks Marx for reducing social action to the instrumentality of labor; but then he goes on to set labor in opposition to social interaction.

From Aristotle to Habermas, we find agreement that labor is the realm of technical and natural necessity whereas action is the realm of moral freedom and justice. Hannah Arendt, Hans-Georg Gadamer, and Jürgen Habermas have all invoked Aristotle's distinction between moral and technical reason to challenge the growing colonization of social action by productive technique. They interpret the ever-increasing bureaucratic and technological rationalization of social and political life as the reduction of action to production, of moral freedom to technical necessity. What they never question is the assumption that productive labor is governed solely by instrumental rationality.[24] Arendt and Habermas criticize the assumption that politics is subject to the same technical calculus as is production; they seek above all to protect the free action of the *zōon politikon* from the treadmill of *homo faber*. But is production itself subject to such a technical calculus? Is there an optimal solution to the question of how productive labor is divided? I will suggest that there is a politics of production, that *homo faber* is actually a political animal.

All of this brings us back to the paradox of Taylorism in the former Soviet Union: where we thought that capitalism is the antithesis of communism, we find upon closer inspection a profound and unsettling similarity in the division of labor. The unity of productive practice in capitalism and in communism is prefigured in the unity of the theory of production in Adam Smith and Karl Marx. The universality of Taylorism creates the impression that the increasing fragmentation and degradation of labor is an inescapable cost of economic progress. With the fall of the Berlin Wall, a radical political and economic transformation of the formerly communist societies in Europe has begun. The creation of capitalist economies in Russia and in Eastern Europe will require the restructuring of the entire political economy—except in the case of the division of labor in production. In many cases, factory commissars are simply becoming capitalist bosses with little or no change in the hierarchical relations of production. If Taylorism can survive first communist and then capitalist revolutions, what hope is there for reform?

And assuming that reform is possible, what role, if any, could our critique of political economy play? The detailed division of labor is in part a strategy for the domination of labor; as such, it is equally compatible with the interests of capitalist and communist managers. Are ideas any match for vested interests? John Maynard Keynes thought so: "I am sure that the power of vested interests is vastly exaggerated compared with the gradual encroachment of

24. As Thomas McCarthy describes Habermas's distinction between labor and interaction: "Under the category 'work,' Habermas thematizes questions concerning the technical mastery of the natural and social environment. Under the category of 'interaction,' he thematizes questions concerning social relations among communicating individuals (that is, moral relations)" (*The Critical Theory of Jürgen Habermas* [Cambridge: MIT Press, 1981], 30).

ideas." It is superficial, though, to set ideas and interests in opposition: economic, social, and political interests always embody some set of ideas. How interests are defined, how they are pursued—even what counts as an interest—depends upon some set of ideas. Philosophy cannot defeat vested interests, but philosophy may help to redefine what constitutes our interests. This Aristotelian critique of political economy aims to show that alternative patterns of the social division of labor are not only required by our moral interests in human welfare but are fully compatible with our economic interests in efficient production.

Part One

An Aristotelian Theory of the Division of Labor

Both the dignity and the degradation of labor are products of the division of labor. The dignity inherent in the mastery of a complex trade or profession is just as much the product of social specialization as the degradation inherent in the repetitive monotony of data entry or of an assembly line. Indeed, society itself is, in a sense, the product of the division of labor: by specializing our labor, we all become dependent on each other. The division of labor unites those it divides: the rule "we distinguish in order to unite" applies to human work as much as to philosophical method. The romantic impulse to abolish the division of labor—an impulse found in Jean-Jacques Rousseau and the young Marx—reflects a poor grasp of the social dimension of human labor. The question is not whether but how labor ought to be divided.

But before we can consider how labor ought to be divided, we must first have some notion of how labor is in fact divided. The universality of Taylorism reveals a poverty of moral imagination about the division of labor in production that is striking in comparison to the wealth of social experimentation in the realm of taxation, regulation, property rights, and welfare benefits. I believe that the poverty of moral imagination about how labor ought to be divided reflects a poverty of understanding about how labor is in fact divided. An inadequate prescription often reflects an inadequate diagnosis. Just as any viable scheme to reform the distribution of income should be based on an understanding of the forces that generate the existing distribution, so any viable scheme for the reform of the division of labor should be based on an understanding of the forces that generate the existing division of labor.

The poverty of moral imagination about the division of labor is especially striking in those thinkers, like Adam Smith and Karl Marx, who are notable precisely for the power of their moral imagination in other contexts. But once these thinkers had reductively explained the division of labor in terms of technical efficiency and human nature, they left no room for moral and social freedom. I propose to make room for the exercise of moral freedom by offering the elements of a nonreductionist theory of the division of labor. My purpose is not to set forth a systematic theory of the division of labor in all its sociological, economic, anthropological, and political complexity. Instead, I will develop two sets of fundamental philosophical distinctions that pave the way for a systematic theory of the division of labor. This Aristotelian conceptual framework will help us to explain the existing patterns of the division of labor in a way that creates an opening for efforts to experiment with alternative patterns.

Chapter 1

The Social and the Technical Division of Labor

The Reduction of the Social Division to the Technical Division of Labor

We begin with Adam Smith's famous description of the division of labor in a pin factory: "One man draws out the wire, another straightens it, a third cuts it, a fourth points it, a fifth grinds it at the top for receiving the head . . ."[1] Virtually every social scientist from Smith's day to our own accepts this as a simple and unambiguous description of the division of labor. Indeed, despite two centuries of theory and practice concerning the division of labor in production, it has been shown only quite recently that Smith is actually describing two very different operations. The first is the analysis and separation of a process into distinct steps; the second is the assignment of these steps to distinct workers.[2] What is misleading about Smith's description is his assumption that there must be a one-to-one correspondence between the division of work and the division of workers.

There is no doubt that the analysis and separation of a productive process into its constitutive parts greatly enhances the efficiency of labor. A single worker, however, can often realize this efficiency: he would draw wire for, say, a thousand pins, then straighten them all, cut them all, point them all, grind them all, etc. This division of labor is known as batch production. Since each step in a productive process requires setup and cleanup, batch production greatly reduces the time spent moving from one operation to another. Workers have always organized their tasks to realize the efficiency of the batch

---

1. Adam Smith, *The Wealth of Nations* [1776], ed. R. H. Campbell, A. S. Skinner, and W. B. Todd (Oxford: Oxford University Press, 1979), 1:1.15.

2. Harry Braverman presents the most systematic exposition of this distinction in his *Labor and Monopoly Capital* (New York: Monthly Review Press, 1974), 75; see also Steven A. Marglin, "What Do Bosses Do?" [1974], in *The Division of Labour*, ed. André Gorz (Brighton: Harvester Press, 1976), 18.

division of labor: a farmer, for example, plows a whole field, then harrows it, then drills it; he would never plow, harrow, and drill one furrow at a time.

There are, of course, constraints upon the number of tasks that can be efficiently performed by a single worker; at some point, the division of tasks requires the division of workers. Just as no one worker in an office or factory can perform every productive task, so no one person in society can perform every social role. There are two fundamental reasons for specialization. The first is the limit of time: no one has the time to develop all of his or her abilities to the fullest; the second is the limit of talent: no one can do all things better than can others. As John Rawls says: "One basic characteristic of human beings is that no one person can do everything that he might do; nor *a fortiori* can he do everything that any other person can do."[3] A considerable degree of specialization is indispensable to the functioning of large and complex societies. Nonetheless, there is considerable flexibility in the efficient distribution of specific tasks to specific persons. As we shall see, empirical experiments in the design of jobs show that not only does technical and economic efficiency not require a one-to-one correspondence between the division of work and the division of the workers, but that there is usually a wide range of equally efficient divisions of labor.

If the assignment of each task to a different worker cannot always be explained simply by efficiency, then how do we account for it? Several suggestions have been offered. According to Charles Babbage, low-wage, unskilled women and children can be used to perform one task where it would require a high-wage, skilled worker to perform all of the tasks in sequence. Thus, he says, the assignment of these tasks to different workers does not necessarily produce more pins, but more profits.[4] The detailed division of labor in production reflects, according to Babbage, not some timeless quest for efficiency, but the specifically capitalist logic of profit maximization. Harry Braverman argues that the Babbage principle is only a special case of a more general rule: the

3. John Rawls, *A Theory of Justice* (Cambridge: Harvard University Press, 1971), 523.

4. Charles Babbage, *On the Economy of Machinery and Manufactures* [1835] (New York: Augustus Kelley, 1963), 175. Of course, if Smith's division of labor leads to higher profits, then it could be seen as more economically efficient, even if not more technically efficient, than traditional methods. Many studies of job design, however, have shown that the detailed division of labor is not necessarily more profitable than other methods. Moreover, the division of labor is traditionally defended on the grounds that it produces more pins, not that it produces more profits. On the relation of technical to economic efficiency, see Robert Drago, "Capitalism and Efficiency," *Review of Radical Political Economics* 18 (1986): 72; and Philip Mirowski, *More Heat than Light* (Cambridge: Cambridge University Press, 1989), chap. 6.

capitalist's fundamental motivation for limiting each worker to a simple task is to gain control over the productive process. Skilled workers, because of their knowledge of productive processes, have the power to control the pace and methods of production. The detailed division of labor separates conception from execution, eliminates the skill and autonomy of the worker, and turns labor into a commodity manipulated by managers.[5]

Charles Sabel, in his critique of Braverman, notes that Smith's detailed division of labor is characteristic only of those firms that supply standardized goods to stable mass markets; firms that supply innovative and specialized goods to particular market niches make use of a much more flexible division of labor.[6] Sabel is right to point out that Smith's unskilled detail workers never replaced the highly skilled artisans who work in the small firms that provide specialized goods. But even in the case of mass production, Sabel's focus on the demand for standardized goods will not really explain the Smithian and later Taylorist division of labor because, as Sabel says, "performance standards can usually be met in several ways . . . the same goods can be produced using different technologies." If there are several ways to produce goods for mass markets efficiently, then why is the Taylorist way so pervasive?

These explanations all refer to the division of labor in a capitalist economy. But because the detailed division of labor is also pervasive in public bureaucracies and in communist economies, it cannot be explained simply as a specifically capitalist quest for profit or for class domination. The only theory sufficiently general in scope is Max Weber's theory of bureaucratic domination, whereby Taylorism is but a special case of the general rule of bureaucratic rationalization. Weber speaks of "the secretary, the engineer, or the worker in the office or plant, who is subject to a discipline no longer different in its nature from that of the civil service or the army."[7] Both a worker separated

5. Braverman, *Labor and Monopoly Capital*, 59–84. For a similar argument see Marglin, "What Do Bosses Do?"

6. Sabel thus attempts to explain the division of labor as a function of market structure: "the model explains why work clothes, white bread, and automobiles, for instance, are mass produced by assembly-line techniques in large factories, whereas fashionable ladies garments, fancy grades of pumpernickel and high-quality pastries, and trucks, buses, and agricultural and construction machinery are manufactured in small lots by much more skilled workers and craftsmen using general-purpose tools and methods that often approximate artisanal techniques." See *Work and Politics* (Cambridge: Cambridge University Press, 1984), 36–37.

7. Max Weber, *Economy and Society* [1925], ed. Guenther Roth and Claus Wittich (Berkeley: University of California Press, 1978), p. 944.

from the means of production and an official separated from the means of administration are reduced to executing the designs of their superiors. Weber believed that Taylorism and bureaucratic domination in general were uniquely efficient and inevitable; yet, as we shall see, both Taylorism and bureaucracy turn out to be a lot less efficient than Weber believed. Nonetheless, Weber's analysis suggests that just because this strategy for the control of production was invented and perfected by capitalists does not make it a specifically capitalist mode of domination; communists have found it well suited to their own mode of domination.[8]

None of these explanations does justice to the mix of technical and moral issues involved in the division of labor because none takes into account the fundamental ambiguity of the expression "the division of labor." This refers to two very different operations: first the labor is divided and then the laborers are divided. Therefore, any concrete division of labor requires two distinct explanations: an account of how the tasks are delineated and an account of how the workers are assigned to those tasks. The analysis of tasks I call the technical division of labor; the assignment of workers to those tasks I call the social division of labor. Since none of the classical political economists grasped the two senses of the division of labor, they all assumed that the social division of labor is explained by the same efficiency criteria that explain the technical division of labor. This reduction of a social phenomenon to a technical phenomenon is characteristic of political economy and has profound consequences for social theory and practice. The universality of Taylorism, I suggest, reflects in part the equally universal reduction of the social to the technical division of labor. Even in firms owned and managed by workers, we often find a detailed social division of labor—so deep-seated is the assumption that there must be a one-to-one correspondence between the social and technical division of labor.

Theories of the division of labor are often divided into efficiency theories and power theories. Is the existing division of labor the product of a quest for technical efficiency or of a quest by managers for power over workers? Actually, power and efficiency are both implicated in the complex historical processes that created our contemporary division of labor. Power over workers is what gave capitalist and communist managers the ability to divide the

---

8. "We must organise in Russia the study and teaching of the Taylor system and systematically try it out and adapt it to our own ends." See Vladimir Lenin, "The Immediate Tasks of the Soviet Government" [1918], in *The Lenin Anthology*, ed. Robert C. Tucker (New York: W. W. Norton, 1975), 449.

labor process efficiently into tasks simple enough for machines to perform them. Independent artisans probably would not have carried the technical division of their labor this far. The productive superiority of both capitalist and communist industry over traditional craftsmanship may well be due to this capacity for dividing labor technically into such simple components. Unfortunately, this quest for efficiency not only divided the labor but also the laborers; the detailed technical division of labor became an equally detailed social division of labor. Efficiency requires only that the work be analyzed into its fundamental elements, not that the workers be restricted to the performance of a few such elements. Once the labor had been technically analyzed it could then be synthesized efficiently in a variety of ways—from restricting each worker to a single task to enabling each worker to perform several tasks in sequence. How the technical division of labor became translated into a social division of labor depended in large measure on the power relations of the industry. Capitalism involved, then, both the quest for efficiency and the quest for power over workers; sometimes power enhanced efficiency, sometimes it was superfluous, sometimes it even diminished efficiency.

I argue that this distinction between the social and the technical division of labor is logically fundamental: any concrete account of the division of tasks, of occupations, of castes, presupposes the distinction between the division of functions and the division of persons. The specialization of legal, political, military, educational, and religious functions does not logically entail the social monopoly of these functions by specialists. It is well known that lay people can perform many of these functions for themselves perfectly well. How these functions have been historically appropriated by specialists is a fundamental question for the theory of division of labor.[9] Just as the technical division of tasks in the factory does not account for the detailed social division of workers, so the technical division of functions in society does not account for the social division of professionals and the laity.

Nonetheless, most theorists continue to treat Marx's distinction between the division of labor within a firm and the general division of labor in society as logically fundamental. It is important to note that Marx described the general division of labor as "social" and the division of labor in a firm as "technical." How then does this distinction differ from my distinction between the social and the technical division of labor? As I have shown, any concrete

9. See Ivan Illich, *Toward a History of Needs* (New York: Bantam Books, 1977).

instance of the division of labor—whether within a firm or in society as a whole—presupposes my distinction between the division of tasks and the division of persons. In other words, the distinction between the division of labor in society and in the firm presupposes but is not presupposed by the distinction between the technical division of tasks and the social division of persons.[10]

The argument that efficiency requires the social division of labor to correspond to the technical is already found in Plato: "The result, then, is that more things are produced, and better and more easily when one man performs one task according to his nature, at the right moment, and at leisure from other occupations" (*Republic* 370C). Plato concludes from this observation that the major social functions of production, warfare, and politics must be socially divided into castes. He has assumed, in other words, that because it is advisable to divide the tasks of making, fighting, and ruling, we must limit people to only one task. This emphasis on specialization is a radical attack on Athenian democracy, a democracy characterized precisely by the fact that most citizens participated in all three social tasks. Plato often defends his caste hierarchy on the basis of efficiency, but it is clear that his caste system is motivated less by a concern for technical efficiency than by a commitment to a hierarchy of status and power: if a carpenter were to do a shoemaker's trade, he argues, no great harm would be done; but if a carpenter were to become a guardian, disaster would befall the city (*Republic* 421A, 434A). What makes Plato's proposal for a philosopher-king so paradoxical is the notion that one person perform two tasks. From the beginning, then, the division of labor has been inseparable from the question of who shall rule—whether in the factory or in the city.

Aristotle follows Plato by noting: "For one business is better done by one man" (*Pol.* 1273b9, 1299a40). Aristotle, however, does not simply assume that the social division of labor must correspond to the technical; rather, he often treats this as a political question. "Shall every man be at once farmer, artisan, councillor, judge, or shall we suppose the several occupations just mentioned assigned to different persons? or, thirdly, shall some employments be assigned to individuals and others common to all?" (*Pol.* 1328b25). Aristotle observes

10. For examples of the view that Marx's distinction is logically fundamental see Braverman, *Labor and Monopoly Capital*, 70; Marglin, "What Do Bosses Do?" 16; Dietrich Rueschemeyer, *Power and the Division of Labor* (Stanford: Stanford University Press, 1986), 10; Louis Putterman, "Overview," in *The Economic Nature of the Firm*, ed. Louis Putterman (Cambridge: Cambridge University Press, 1986), 5.

here that in democratic regimes all citizens participate in politics, production, and warfare, whereas in oligarchic regimes each class is restricted to one function. Indeed, the republican ideal of the civic order is precisely one in which every citizen participates in economic, political, and military functions. Both ancient and modern advocates of this republican ideal have viewed the increasing social division of labor as a threat to liberty and democracy.

The great metahistorical theme of classical political economy is the inevitability of the increasing social division of labor. Smith, J. S. Mill, and Marx argue that the growing social division of labor accounts for the technical superiority of capitalist production over all previous modes of production. In a competitive world, they agree, the efficient detail labor of Smith's pin factory is bound to prevail.[11] What makes this story of economic progress less than happy is that Smith, Mill, and Marx all believe that the increasing social division of labor causes the moral and intellectual degradation of workers.[12] Yet because they reduce the social to the technical division of labor, none of these writers can see a way to reverse the growing specialization of workers. Smith and Mill hope that education will somehow compensate for degradingly narrow work; Marx despairs of humanizing work and hopes that automation will liberate man from the need to work. Thus history is a tragic drama: the material liberation of humanity requires its spiritual subjugation. The inexorably growing division of labor is a Promethean tale of how the destruction of the individual leads to the prosperity of the species.

Although the theory of the division of labor was at the heart of classical political economy, both neoclassical and neo-Marxian economics have relegated it to the science of engineering—which follows, given the assumption that the division of labor is simply a function of technical efficiency. Abandoned by its parents, the economists, the question of the division of labor was

11. For the classical political economists there seemed to be no limit to the increasing fragmentation of tasks in production: "It is found that the productive power of labour is increased by carrying the separation further and further; by breaking down more and more every process of industry into parts, so that each labourer shall confine himself to an ever smaller number of simple operations" (J. S. Mill, *Principles of Political Economy* [1871], ed. Sir William Ashley [New York: Augustus Kelley, 1976], 122).

12. Adam Smith says that since the worker "has no occasion to exert his understanding" he "generally becomes as stupid and ignorant as it is possible for a human creature to become" (*Wealth of Nations*, 5:1.782). J. S. Mill sees the industrial workers leading lives "of drudgery and imprisonment" (*Principles of Political Economy*, 751). Karl Marx describes the detail worker as "a crippled monstrosity" in *Capital*, vol. 1 [1867] (New York: International Publishers, 1967), 4:14.340.

soon taken up by sociologists. Unfortunately, the sociologists followed the example of political economists in conflating the distinction between the social and the technical division of labor. Indeed, most of the subsequent sociological investigation of the division of labor is but a series of variations on Smith's theme.

Alexis de Tocqueville, for example, echoes Smith's argument about the efficiency of limiting each worker to one task: "It is acknowledged that when a workman is engaged every day upon the same details, the whole commodity is produced with greater ease, speed, and economy." Tocqueville also follows Smith in asserting that the increasing social division of labor is inexorable and that it has tragic consequences for workers: "Thus at the very time at which the science of manufactures lowers the class of workmen, it raises the class of masters."[13]

Herbert Spencer is virtually unique among sociologists because of his implicit grasp of the distinction between the technical and the social division of labor. "The necessity of dividing any total work into parts, is, indeed, illustrated in the actions of a single person." Few social theorists have noticed the fact that the activity of even one person embodies a division of labor.[14] Unaware of the significance of this distinction, however, Spencer goes on to blur it by saying that the transition from "this individual [i.e., technical] division of labor to social division of labor is obvious." What makes it so obvious is Spencer's assumption that each task "is performed by a different person."[15]

Emile Durkheim also simply repeats Smith's arguments about the efficiency of the social division of labor. Moreover, he agrees with the economists that this greater efficiency accounts for the inevitable progression of the social division of labor: "It is general knowledge . . . that the law of division of labor applies to organisms as to societies; it can even be said that the more specialized the functions of the organism, the greater its development." Durkheim insists that in general the division of labor enhances social solidarity; but he saw the growing industrial division of labor as a threat to soli-

13. Alexis de Tocqueville, *Democracy in America*, vol. 2 [1840], ed. Phillips Bradley (New York: Alfred Knopf, 1945), 168–69.

14. Economist Richard Nelson observes, e.g., "Crusoe never had to face the issue of determining division of labor" (Nelson, "Assessing Private Enterprise," *Bell Journal of Economics* 12 [Spring 1981]: 67).

15. Herbert Spencer, *Principles of Sociology* [1896], ed. Stanislav Andreski (Hamden, Conn.: Archon Books, 1969), 644–45.

darity: "At the same time specialization becomes greater, revolts become more frequent." Indeed, Durkheim describes the degradation of workers as eloquently as does Smith and Marx.

> He is no longer anything but an inert piece of machinery, only an external force set going which always moves in the same direction and in the same way. Surely, no matter how one may represent the moral ideal, one cannot remain indifferent to such debasement of human nature.[16]

Blind to the distinction between the social and technical division of labor, Durkheim can see no alternative way to organize production. He therefore recommends increased governmental direction of the economy as a way of reducing the "pathological" effects of specialization on the worker.

Max Weber shares this general view that the increasingly specialized social division of labor is efficient, rational, and inevitable. "The specialization of functions, on the other hand, is crucial to the modern development of the organization of labor." He refers to Taylorism as the most recent example of the triumph of efficiency and rationality in modern life. Weber's inability to distinguish the social and the technical division of labor is evident in his theory of bureaucracy: he assumes that because bureaucratic tasks can be minutely divided, bureaucratic officials must be similarly specialized.[17] Speaking of such an official, Weber says, "In the great majority of cases he is only a small cog in a ceaselessly moving mechanism which prescribes to him an essentially fixed route of march."[18] The modern social division of labor—whether in a factory or a bureaucracy—emodies for Weber the objective necessity of formal rationality. Weber's reduction of the social division of labor to technical rationality leads him to the same historical pessimism as the classical political economists. The modern social order "is now bound to the technical and economic conditions of machine production which to-day determine the lives of all individuals who are born into this mechanism, not

16. Emile Durkheim, *The Division of Labor in Society* [1893], trans. George Simpson (New York: Free Press, 1964), pp. 393, 41, 355, 371.

17. Recent studies of bureaucracy reject Weber's claim that increasing specialization is always rational and efficient. "Weber perceives bureaucracy as an adaptive device for using specialized skills, and he is not exceptionally attentive to the character of the human organism" (J. G. March and H. A. Simon, "The Dysfunctions of Bureaucracy," in *Organization Theory*, ed. D. S. Pugh [Harmondsworth: Penguin Books, 1971], 30). In other words, Weber conflates the technical division of tasks with the social division of officials.

18. Weber, *Economy and Society*, pp. 119, 150, 998.

only those directly concerned with economic acquisition, with irresistible force."[19]

The Discovery of the Social and the Technical Division of Labor

Why did it take so long to discover the distinction between the social and technical division of labor? Durkheim wondered "why the theory of division of labor has made such little progress since Adam Smith."[20] Indeed, this remains worth pondering. Durkheim suggested that too much attention had been paid to Adam Smith and too little attention to empirical facts. There is merit in this suggestion, for our distinction was discovered by writers who either had had extensive experience on the shop floor or had read empirical studies of job design. Of course, there have been many observers of factory production who have not grasped this distinction. So empiricism seems to be a necessary but not sufficient condition for this insight.

The distinction between the social and the technical division of labor was not discovered by just any empirical observation but specifically through observation of factory production. This makes sense since the factory has long been the locus of deliberate experimentation with both divisions of labor, leading observers to reflect on the distinction between the two. These studies questioned the assumption that there must be a one-to-one correspondence between the two divisions. As George Homans observes:

> From Adam Smith to F .W. Taylor, the uncritical assumption was apt to be that the further the division was carried, the greater were the savings effected, that the further a job like shoemaking was broken down into its component specialties, and each assigned to a workman who did nothing else, the less would be the cost of making the shoe. Now we have begun to understand that the division of labor, like any other process, has its point of diminishing returns.[21]

19. Max Weber, *The Protestant Ethic and the Spirit of Capitalism* [1905], trans. Talcott Parsons (New York: Charles Scribner's Sons, 1958), 181.

20. Durkheim cites Schmoller's comment that Adam Smith's followers "had a dearth of worthy ideas [and] were obstinately attached to his examples and his remarks." See *Division of Labor in Society*, 46. Smith's discussion of pin-making has indeed cast a spell over two centuries of social theory, creating a nearly universal belief that the division of labor always entails the division of the laborers.

21. G. C. Homans, cited in Georges Friedmann, *The Anatomy of Work* (New York: Free Press,

By experimenting with alternative patterns of the division of labor, industrial psychologists discovered the importance of worker morale to productive efficiency. The classical political economists, by contrast, never understood that the division of labor could reach the point of diminishing returns. Although they were aware of the evil effects of excessive division of labor on the character of workers, our economists did not see that such moral degradation, by eroding the morale of workers, might undermine productivity. By discovering the importance of morale, the industrial psychologists unwittingly discovered the moral dimension of the division of labor. If workers find the division of labor to be morally degrading, then bad morale may reduce efficiency.

The contemporary study of the industrial division of labor began with the observation of the effects of Taylorism on productivity. The introduction of Taylorism provoked a range of responses among workers from violence and sabotage to strikes and slowdowns. Managers first responded to the discontent of workers by using industrial psychology and sociology in an effort to condition them to accept their fragmented tasks.[22] As a consequence there is often a considerable disparity between a firm's job design policy, which attempts to diminish the role of the worker, and its personnel policy, which attempts to convince the worker of his importance.[23] When workers could not be habituated to accept their monotonous tasks, managers launched experiments in

1961), 30. Peter Drucker criticizes Taylor for conflating the social and technical divisions of labor: "The first of these blind spots [of Taylorism] is the belief that because we must analyze work into its simplest constituent motions we must also organize it as a series of individual motions, each if possible carried out by an individual worker. This is false logic. It confuses a principle of analysis with a principle of action" (*The Practice of Management* [New York: Harper and Brothers, 1954], 282).

22. "Why have behavioral scientists not been more successful in their attempts to remedy motivational problems in organizations and improve the quality of work life of employees? One reason is that psychologists (like managers and labor leaders) have traditionally assumed that the *work itself was inviolate*—the role of psychologists is simply to help select, train, and motivate people within the confines of jobs as they have been designed by others" (J. R. Hackman and J. L. Suttle, *Improving Life at Work* [Santa Monica: Goodyear Publishing, 1977], 101).

23. Management "designs jobs based entirely on the principles of specialization, repetitiveness, low skill content and minimum impact of the worker on the production process. Management then frequently spends large sums of money and prodigious efforts on many programs that attempt to: a) counter-act the effects of job design; b) provide satisfactions, necessarily outside the job, which the job cannot provide; and c) build up the satisfaction and importance of the individual which the job has diminished" (Louis E. Davis, "Current Job Design Criteria," in *Design of Jobs*, ed. Louis E. Davis and James Taylor [Harmondsworth: Penguin Books, 1972], 81).

"job enlargement," rotating workers from one repetitive task to another.[24] Many workers found that such rotation eliminated the one thing that made repetitive work tolerable—the capacity to think about other things. Dissatisfaction with the effects of job enlargement in turn led to schemes for "job enrichment" in which workers were given more responsibility for the conception and execution of entire projects.[25] That job enrichment usually leads to greater satisfaction than job enlargement suggests that what workers want is not a greater diversity of unskilled tasks but a greater complexity of tasks— not a variety of executions but a unity of conception and execution.

These experiments in job design led researchers to appreciate the significance of the distinction between the social and the technical division of labor. Indeed, a leading school of job design is known as the "sociotechnical" school. Sociotechnical theory rests on the premise that production is the joint product of a social as well as a technical system.[26] The technical system is the analysis of a process into discrete tasks; the social system is the synthesis of these processes by workers. Frederick Taylor claimed that the analysis of productive operations into a few simple motions to train the dexterity of workers is no different from the analysis of surgery into a few simple motions to train the dexterity of surgeons. As Peter Drucker points out, however, each worker is restricted to one operation whereas a surgeon synthesizes the various operations himself. So the technical process of analysis tells us little about the social process of synthesis.[27]

24. On job enlargement studies, see Friedmann, *Anatomy of Work*, chaps. 3 and 4. On the failure of job enlargement, see Louis E. Davis, "Job Satisfaction Research: The Post-Industrial View," in *Design of Jobs*, 160; J. R. Hackman and M. Lee, *Redesigning Work: A Strategy for Change* (Scarsdale: Work in America Institute, 1979), 4.

25. "The tasks involved in providing nursing care to hospitalized patients, for example, might be combined so that each nurse would have responsibility for many aspects of the care and treatment of a given set of patients. This would contrast with a design for nursing work in which each nurse is responsible for only one or two tasks for a larger number of patients" (J. R. Hackman, *Work Redesign* [Reading, Mass.: Addison-Wesley, 1980], 136).

26. Louis E. Davis and E. L. Trist, "Improving the Quality of Work Life: Sociotechnical Case Studies," in *Work and the Quality of Life*, ed. James O'Toole (Cambridge: MIT Press, 1974), 247. The same point is put more simply by Hackman: "When all the outer layers are stripped away, many organizational problems come to rest at the interface between *people* and the *tasks* they do" (Hackman and Suttle, *Improving Life at Work*, 100).

27. Peter Drucker, *Management* (New York: Harper and Row, 1973), 199. Drucker illustrates this distinction with the example of surgery: "The work of the surgeon is based on the most minute breakdown of the job into individual motions. Young surgeons practice for months on end how to tie this or that knot in a confined space, how to change their hold on an instrument, or how

No adequate theory of technology is possible apart from our distinction between the social and the technical division of labor. Technology is just as much a social as a technical phenomenon. The design and deployment of productive technology is never simply determined by the technical division of labor; instead, technology translates the technical division of tasks into a social division of labor. There is no technical imperative that determines the design of technology: all productive technologies are designed for human use and therefore embody assumptions about the appropriate social division of labor. Technology is the interface between the technical division of tasks and the social division of workers; as such, it cannot be explained either by technical criteria or by social criteria alone.

First, for any series of tasks there is more than one technologically efficient way to integrate them; Ford introduced the assembly line to restrict each worker to a single task whereas Volvo introduced the assembly island to enable teams of workers to assemble entire vehicles. Second, even if we treat a technology as given, there are still several compatible social divisions of labor. Although assembly lines, for example, are designed to restrict each worker to one task, it is still often possible to rotate assembly-line workers from task to task.[28] There is freedom in the way technology synthesizes a group of tasks and there is freedom in the way technology translates tasks into jobs.

The relation between technology and the technical division of labor is a reciprocal one. The technical division of tasks into a series of simple motions makes possible the introduction of machinery; since machines are limited to simple motions, they cannot be employed until labor has been minutely divided.[29] For example, the technical division of labor known as batch production makes it feasible to introduce special jigs, templates, clamps, and presses—technologies that would not be feasible for individualized or custom work. Conversely, the introduction of new technology makes possible a new

---

to make stitches. . . . But the surgeon's job is of necessity integrated. . . . We have one man do the whole job" (*Practice of Management*, 294).

28. "The job design studies challenge the assumption that production technology is inviolate and its present organization and translation into jobs is the only one possible" (Louis E. Davis, cited in Gorz, ed., *Division of Labour*, 87).

29. Hegel was one of the first theorists to grasp this connection: "Further, the abstraction of one man's production from another's makes work more and more mechanical, until finally man is able to step aside and install machines in his place" (G. W. F. Hegel, *Philosophy of Right* [1821], trans. and ed. T. M. Knox [Oxford: Oxford University Press, 1967], par. 198).

technical division of labor: the combine unites reaping and threshing, the word processor integrates drafting and editing.

Similarly, the relation between technology and the social division of labor is a reciprocal one. Technologies are often designed with a particular social division of labor in mind. Typically, as with the assembly line, they are designed to effect a social division of labor between managers who plan and workers who simply execute.[30] David Noble tells the story of the development of automated machine tools: at every stage of their development, design choices were made to transfer control over the conception and execution of the tasks from the operator to the manager.[31] "That a substantial part of technological system design includes social design is neither understood nor appreciated. Frightful assumptions, supported by societal values, are made about men and groups and become built into machines and processes as requirements."[32] The design and deployment of our productive technology would be quite different if social norms required workers to be responsible for both the conception and execution of tasks.[33] Conversely, new technologies create the potential for new social divisions of labor. The personal computer, for example, by integrating the tasks of drafting, editing, and printing, can reduce the social division between a professional and a secretary. But if technology simply determined social relations, then the secretary would be an endangered species!

The importance of the distinction between the social and the technical division of labor was discovered through experimentation with the design of jobs

30. Peter Drucker observes: "What is today called automation is conceptually a logical extension of Taylor's scientific management." Since Taylor's explicit purpose was to remove all craft knowledge and skill from workmen, Drucker implicitly acknowledges that automated technology is designed to achieve the same goal. See Drucker, cited in David Noble, "Social Choice in Machine Design," in *Case Studies on the Labor Process*, ed. Andrew Zimbalist (New York: Monthly Review Press, 1979), 32.

31. See David Noble, *Forces of Production* (New York: Alfred Knopf, 1984). Indeed, according to its promoters, the chief virtue of the automated machine tool is that "it separates the intellectual work from the work of execution" (Braverman, *Labor and Monopoly Capital*, 205). Sabel, in his critique of Braverman and Noble, points out that managers who employ automated machine tools have not "been very successful at separating the conception from the execution of machining tasks, assuming that was their intention" (*Work and Politics*, 66).

32. Louis E. Davis, "The Design of Jobs," in *Design of Jobs*, 423.

33. Thus in the United States, the programming of automated machine tools is usually done by engineers; in Norway, by contrast, workers are responsible for all aspects of planning and programming. See David Noble, "Social Choice in Machine Design," in *Case Studies on the Labor Process*, ed. Andrew Zimbalist (New York: Monthly Review Press, 1979) p. 47.

in particular firms. However, these studies contribute to our understanding of the division of labor not just in the firm but in society as a whole: for if the social division of labor cannot be explained by the technical division of tasks (or by technology), then the social monopoly of medical, legal, educational, and religious functions by professionals cannot be explained as a technical requisite of modern society. Nurses in Europe, for example, perform many of the functions monopolized by doctors in America; businessmen in Japan perform many of the functions monopolized by lawyers in America. The existing pattern of social specialization and hierarchy in modern society is not a "technological imperative."[34] The firm is a miniature society; this reduction in scale makes social relations more perspicuous to the mind. The firm thus provides a unique locus for reflection on the general nature of the division of labor. All of which inevitably brings us back to Adam Smith: "The effects of the division of labour, in the general business of society, will be more easily understood, by considering in what manner it operates in some particular manufactures."[35]

The Distinction between Moral and Instrumental Reason

To say that the social division of labor cannot be reduced to the technical is to say that there is an irreducible moral dimension to production. It is often claimed, however, that production lacks a moral dimension. We should examine the two fundamental grounds for this belief. The first is the claim that production and technique are coextensive: material production is taken to be essentially instrumental and instrumentalism is taken to be essentially productive. The second is the claim that even if technique could be extended to social and political conduct, the presence of technique in any human activity would be incompatible with moral reason because technique lies in the realm of necessity whereas morality lies in the realm of freedom.

The claim that material production and technique are coextensive has had a strangely powerful hold on European thought. Despite the obvious and pervasive role of technique in all aspects of human conduct, the notion per-

---

34. Daniel Bell refers to the hierarchical relations of production as a "technological imperative." See *Work and Its Discontents* (Boston: Beacon Press, 1956), 9. H. A. Simon also describes the social relations of modern bureaucracy as a technical requisite: "Hierarchy is the adaptive form for finite intelligence to assume in the face of complexity." Simon, "Decision Making and Organizational Design," in *Organization Theory*, 204.

35. Smith, *Wealth of Nations*, 1:1.14.

sists that technique is found only in production. Aristotle, for example, explicitly restricts technical reason (*technē*) to the realm of production (*NE* 1140a9 and *MM* 1197a12). Aquinas follows Aristotle by asserting that technique concerns only things to be made, not things to be done.[36] Yves Simon concurs: "A technique is a rational discipline designed to assure the mastery of man over physical nature through the application of scientifically determined laws."[37] Indeed, we still associate instrumentalism (technics, technician, technology) almost exclusively with material production, even though we know that there are techniques of politics, warfare, and sports.

Even when technique is acknowledged in other realms of life, it is assumed to be by analogy with production. Plato's discussion of the role of technique in politics, for example, is always by analogy with craft production: "the argument from the arts." Aquinas acknowledges the existence of technique in the "liberal arts" but says that these activities are called "arts" only "by a kind of comparison" to the mechanical arts.[38] Where Plato approves of the extension of craft technique into politics, Hannah Arendt fears it: "Man, in so far as he is *homo faber,* instrumentalizes, and his instrumentalization implies a degradation of all things into means, their loss of intrinsic and independent value."[39] Why is instrumentalism so bound up with production? Perhaps the reason is simply historical: technique may have first achieved prominence in the productive arts.

Nonetheless, some theorists have attempted to abstract the notion of technique from the realm of production. John Poinsot (John of St. Thomas) was the first writer to extend the notion of art to any realm of instrumental calculation. He argues that technique is simply a methodical ordering of matter, whether the matter be thought ordered by the art of logic or actions ordered by the art of conduct.[40]

36. Thomas Aquinas, *Summa Theologiae*, 61 vols., ed. Thomas Gilby (Cambridge: Blackfriars, 1964), 1–2, Q. 57, art. 4.

37. Yves Simon, "Pursuit of Happiness and Lust for Power in Technological Society," in *Philosophy and Technology*, ed. Carl Mitcham and Robert Mackey (New York: Free Press, 1972), 173. Jacques Ellul also assumes that technique and material production are coextensive: "The technical world is the world of material things; it is put together out of material things and with respect to them" (Ellul, "Technological Order," in *Philosophy and Technology*, 90).

38. Aquinas, *Summa Theologiae*, 1–2, Q. 57, art. 3.

39. Hannah Arendt, *The Human Condition* (Chicago: University of Chicago Press, 1958), 156. Ellul expresses the same fear: "When Technique displays any interest in man, it does so by converting him into a material object" (Ellul, "The Technological Order," 90).

40. John Poinsot (John of St. Thomas), *The Material Logic of John of St. Thomas* [1632], ed. and trans. by Yves Simon, John Glanville, and G. Donald Hollenhurst (Chicago: University of Chicago Press, 1955), p. 46.

Similarly, Max Weber sees that ends-means instrumentalism is indifferent to the field of application: "There are techniques of every conceivable type of action, techniques of prayer, of asceticism, of thought and research, of memorizing, of education, of exercising political or hierocratic domination, of administration, of making love, of making war, of musical performances, of sculpture and painting, of arriving at legal decisions."[41] Despite these dissenting views, there has been nearly universal resistance to the notion that there is technique in moral and political action.

Yet even if one restricts technique to the realm of production, this alone does not exclude the possibility that production has a moral dimension in addition to a technical one. To exclude moral considerations from the realm of technique, one must show that moral reason and technical reason are in principle mutually exclusive. Aristotle argues, in fact, that technical and moral reason are mutually exclusive because *technē* is the realm of hypothetical necessity while *phronēsis* is the realm of contingent choice. In the realm of *technē*, once an end is posited, the means follow by necessity; there is, in short, only one right way to make something (*Phys.* 200a10). Aristotle compares the necessity relating ends and means in *technē* with the necessity relating premises and conclusions in mathematics (200a15, 24). Art, says Aristotle, does not deliberate; for we deliberate only about those things that are subject to contingent moral choice (*Phys.* 199b28, *NE* 1112a31). *Phronēsis* is wisdom in moral deliberation about contingent choice: thus while *technē* has the precision of scientific knowledge, *phronēsis* does not (*NE* 1142a23).

John Poinsot follows Aristotle in defining technique as the realm of necessity and moral reason as the realm of contingent choice.[42] Immanuel Kant agrees that moral and technical reason are mutually exclusive: "It is true that in us morally practical reason is essentially different in its principles from technically practical reason."[43] Insofar as the will is guided by technical considerations, says Kant, then it is outside of the domain of moral reason. Because political economy is the art of increasing the wealth of a nation, Kant

41. Weber, *Economy and Society*, 65.

42. "Art is one of the intellectual virtues; now no intellectual virtue is conversant with contingent truth, all deal with truths that are necessary and exclusive of error"; "Prudence exercises direction by an estimate of the pros and the cons, not by art, for it has no certain and determinate rules; it uses rules of good judgment, prudential rules, issued in relation to the circumstances as they arise" (Poinsot, *Material Logic of John of St. Thomas*, 16 and 13).

43. Immanuel Kant, *Critique of Judgment* [1790], trans. J. H. Bernard (New York: Hafner Press, 1951), par. 88.

denies that political economy involves moral reason; similarly, because rhetoric is the art of persuasion, Kant denies that rhetoric involves moral reason.[44] For Kant, any use of technique is subject to the causal determinism of natural law; as such, the employment of technique is not subject to moral precepts.[45] Thus from Aristotle's doctrine of hypothetical necessity, to Kant's doctrine of technically practical reason, to Taylor's doctrine that in any productive process there is "one best way," technique continues to be sharply opposed to freedom. Jacques Ellul, for example, says, "Technique is the contrary of freedom, an operation of determinism and necessity."[46]

If we are to insist that productive labor, like any human activity, has both a moral and a technical dimension, then we must reject the claim that technical and moral reason are mutually exclusive. We need a theory of moral reason that includes technical reason as a special case because moral reason always determines the legitimate role of technique in human affairs. Thus, the morally unsanctioned use of instrumental reason in human affairs is denigrated as "cunning" or "deviousness." How, then, should we define technical and moral reason? Technical reason is usually defined as the selection of the optimal means to a given end.[47] But to choose among means to a given end presupposes that the means are separable from the end; otherwise, different means would lead to different ends, and we could not compare means.

It is logically preferable to define technique in terms of the separability of ends and means. Technical reason concerns those activities in which the ends of conduct can be characterized apart from the means: the choice of which road I take is separable from the goal of getting home. Moral reason, by contrast,

44. Speaking of "housekeeping, farming, statesmanship," Kant says: "For all these contain only rules of skill (and are consequently only technically practical) for bringing about an effect that is possible according to the natural concepts of causes and effects, which, since they belong to theoretical philosophy, are subject to those precepts as mere corollaries from it (viz. natural science) and can therefore claim no place in a special philosophy called practical." Kant also excludes political persuasion and rhetoric from the moral domain: "Skill in exercising an influence over men and their wills" is part of "theoretical philosophy" (*Critique of Judgment*, introduction, 8–9).

45. According to Ernst Cassirer's account of the Kantian position, "statecraft and political economy" are not practical sciences because they are motivated by "natural causality" rather than "by freedom." See *Kant's Life and Thought* [1918], trans. James Haden (New Haven: Yale University Press, 1981), 295.

46. Ellul, "Technological Order," 91.

47. "The presence of a 'technical question' always means that there is some doubt over the choice of the most rational means to an end" (Weber, *Economy and Society*, 65).

concerns those activities in which the ends of conduct cannot be characterized apart from the means: the choice of coercion or persuasion is inseparable from the goal of eliciting someone's cooperation because the choice of means will profoundly shape the character of the end. This is why ethics is so concerned with the rectitude of means. In the realm of moral conduct, the target is not only constantly moving but is moving because of my efforts to hit it.

In order to show that technique is but a special case of moral reason, we must show that ends and means can only be provisionally separated. The relation of moral reason to technical reason is analogous to the relation of strategy to tactics. Tactics are a part of strategy, a special case of strategy: tactics concern those highly structured situations where there are several means to an unambiguous end; strategy concerns tactics plus those situations—like the "Pyrrhic victory"—in which ends and means are inseparable. It is strategy that determines the proper role for tactics, just as moral reason determines the proper role of technique.

The general rule of the inseparability of means from ends has been demonstrated in a variety of contexts. John Dewey's theory of the "ends-means continuum" presupposes that ends and means are never truly separable: "For what is deliberation except weighing of various alternative desires (and hence end-values) in terms of the conditions that are the means of their execution, and which, as means, determine the consequences actually arrived at?"[48] Dewey uses his end-means continuum, however, to argue that all human conduct is instrumental: since means can be instrumentally evaluated, and since ends are evaluated in terms of means, therefore ends can also be instrumentally evaluated.[49] Brian Fay, by contrast, uses the ends-means continuum to show that there is no role for instrumental reason in social and political conduct. Fay points out that if we are seeking the most efficient means to a given end, we must still define efficiency in terms of some social value: "Efficient in terms of what—monetary cost? human labor? suffering? the consumption of natural

48. John Dewey, *Theory of Valuation* (Chicago: University of Chicago Press, 1939), 25.

49. "For it cannot be denied that propositions having evidential warrant and experimental test are possible in the case of evaluation of things as means. Hence it follows that, if these propositions enter into the formation of the interests and desires which are valuations of ends, the latter are thereby constituted the subject matter of authentic empirical affirmations and denials" (Dewey, *Theory of Valuation*, 30). Dewey's analysis here suffers from a striking inconsistency: means can only be experimentally compared and evaluated when they are separable from ends; and yet such separability is precisely what his ends-means continuum excludes.

fuels? time? or what?"[50] Thus, since instrumental evaluations make use of moral criteria, there are no truly instrumental decisions. Dewey collapses ends into means while Fay collapses means into ends. Dewey's instrumentalism undermines his ends-means continuum, for we can instrumentally compare different means to the same end only if means and ends are separable. But since ends and means are only provisionally separable, instrumentalism is only provisionally viable. Fay, by contrast, is right to claim that there is no purely instrumental conduct, but he fails to acknowledge the important, albeit provisional, role of instrumental logic in all realms of human conduct.

The inseparability of ends and means can also be illustrated by the common phenomenon whereby means become ends.[51] The habitual use of certain means to attain an end often induces us to treat those means as an end. The love of money is an example of how habitual use of a means can turn it into an end. C. L. Stevenson describes how parents often teach children the qualities of honesty and politeness as a means to social approval: "Initially, this recommends the qualities as a means to egoistic ends; but with habituation it may be a factor which makes them ultimately valued for themselves."[52] One major criticism of the social division of labor in modern bureaucracy stems from this phenomenon: "Adherence to the rules, originally conceived as a means, becomes transformed into an end-in-itself; there occurs the familiar process of *displacement of goals* whereby an instrumental value becomes a terminal value."[53] Just as a bureaucrat unintentionally sabotages efficiency by treating rules as the goal of his or her activity, so the factory worker inten-

50. Brian Fay, *Social Theory and Political Practice* (London: George Allan and Unwin, 1975), 50. Fay must assume that there is no common metric to rank these various social goods.

51. Hans Vaihinger calls this "The Law of the Preponderance of the Means over the End" (*The Philosophy of 'As If'* [1911] [London: Routledge and Kegan Paul, 1935], xlvi). C. L. Stevenson distinguishes two versions of this phenomenon: Allport's Principle, "X, first sought as a means to Y, may later become an end"; and Wundt's Principle, "X, first sought as a means to Y, often promotes, unexpectedly, some further end, Z; and thereafter X may be sought as a means to Z no less than to Y" (*Ethics and Language* [New Haven: Yale University Press, 1944], 195–96.

52. "In somewhat the same way, a musician who first desires technique only as a means to artistic expression may later value it in part for its own sake. If he does not, he is unlikely to develop enough technique to forward his artistic aims" (Stevenson, *Ethics and Language*, pp. 194–95). In short, although technique requires the provisional separation of means from ends, technique benefits from the inseparability of means from ends.

53. R. K. Merton, *Social Theory and Social Structure* (Glencoe: Free Press, 1957), 199. Merton cites Lasswell's remark that "the human animal distinguishes himself by his infinite capacity for making ends of his means." On "displacement of goals" in modern bureaucracy, see J. G. March and H. A. Simon, "Dysfunctions of Bureaucracy," 32.

tionally sabotages efficiency by work-to-rule. The instrumental separation of means from ends is at best provisional; ends change in the course of the instrumental use of means.

Not all of the consequences of the displacement of goals are negative. C. L. Stevenson argues that this principle is fundamental to the success of a liberal polity. If the challenge of liberal politics is to enable people with divergent values to live together, then agreement on the procedural means necessary for allowing the pursuit of diverse goals could over time lead to agreement on ends. "An effort to establish commonly accepted means, even to divergent ends, can be a step that is necessary—not logically, of course, but practically—to establishing commonly accepted ends."[54] In other words, considerable moral consensus can be achieved even among individuals with divergent moral and political goals if we establish agreement on procedural means— which over time become valued as ends.

The relation of instrumental to moral reason is analogous to the relation of partial to general equilibrium analysis in economic theory. In partial equilibrium analysis we examine the effects of changes in demand for a particular commodity on the price and output of that commodity. To isolate the effects of such a change, we must control for the possible influences of all other variables. Thus partial equilibrium analysis must invoke the *ceteris paribus* principle: each market must be treated as if it were independent and self-contained; yet it has long been known that markets are not self-contained. General equilibrium analysis presupposes that the supply and demand for any commodity are intricately determined by the supply and demand for all commodities in the economy. Every market shapes, and is shaped, by every other market: general equilibrium analysis must invoke the *mutatis mutandis* principle. Of course, in order to make possible a finite analysis of any particular market we must invoke the *ceteris paribus* principle. Similarly, in order to make possible any form of instrumental or strategic conduct, we must treat our end as if it were separable from our means. Yet we know from a more general ontological perspective that ends and means are never separable: every step I take toward a goal has myriad effects on the future social configuration of which my goal is a part.

Ultimately, any theory of the relation of moral to technical reason goes to the heart of the question of what it is to be a human being. Ever since

54. Stevenson, *Ethics and Language*, 193. Even Hobbesian egoists who agree to establish peace purely as a means to selfish ends may come to value peace as an end. Stevenson points out that agreement about ends is not indispensable to all ethical agreement.

Benjamin Franklin defined man as a toolmaking animal—a definition Marx cites approvingly—most anthropologists have generally accepted this *homo faber* view of human nature: the epochs of human history were marked by the materials of tools, such as stone, iron, and bronze; and the enormous growth of the human neocortex was attributed to the need for ever-greater productive skills. Recently, however, the anthropology of *homo faber* has fallen into disrepute for a variety of reasons. To begin with, it is now clear that other animals both use and make tools; so at a minimum we may say that toolmaking is not distinctively human.[55]

Anthropologists are coming to the view that both in the evolution of the human species and in the development of each person, social skills are prior to technical skills. The fossil record shows that rapid expansion of human brain size is not correlated with any known developments in technology. Instead, what does seem to be correlated with the evolution of the neocortex is the development of social structures. What seems to have driven the growth of the neocortex is the need to learn complex social sign systems; human intelligence seems to have evolved because of the importance of social cooperation for survival.[56] Which is to say that human intelligence coevolved with language, since language is not only the most complex human activity but also the most important medium of social cooperation. And language, unlike toolmaking, seems to be a distinctively human achievement. Anthropology is returning to Aristotle's view that humans are the most social of animals because they alone have the power of speech (*Pol.* 1253a8).

Similarly, where developmental psychologists once emphasized the technical problem-solving nature of human intelligence, they now emphasize the social function of intelligence. Social cooperation makes astonishing demands on human intelligence: we must learn to interpret and to use complex nonverbal and then verbal sign systems; and we must learn how to predict the behavior of others and the consequences of our own behavior. Indeed, technical intelligence may be only an accidental by-product of social intelligence: our skills may have evolved to meet the demands of social cooperation but fortuitously enable us to manipulate tools and objects.[57] The communication framework that an infant establishes with his or her mother

55. See B. B. Beck, *Animal Tool Behavior* (New York: Garland Press, 1980).

56. For a discussion of the role of social cooperation in the evolution of the brain, see Roger Masters, *The Nature of Politics* (New Haven: Yale University Press, 1989), 22–26.

57. For the view that human intelligence evolved for social rather than technical skills, see

is not only the infant's most complex activity but it seems to lay the basis for the child's later technical mastery of objects. In other words, the technical skill involved in the manipulation of objects presupposes the prior social skill involved in eliciting the cooperation of other persons.[58] Phylogeny and ontogeny have converged to suggest the evolutionary and developmental priority of moral to technical reason.

If human intelligence did in fact evolve to meet the demands of social cooperation, then, as N. K. Humphrey suggests, one would expect to find a predisposition among humans to treat technical problems as if they were social. Thus the universal tendency of primitive peoples to bargain with nature, whether through prayer, magic, or ritual; agriculture and the domestication of animals are forms of productive technique based on social models of mutual give-and-take. "Thus many of mankind's most prized technological discoveries, from agriculture to chemistry, may have had their origin not in the deliberate application of practical [i.e., technical] intelligence but in the fortunate misapplication of social intelligence."[59] Not every application of social intelligence to technology, however, is so fortunate. Aristotle's comparison of machinery to a slave, for example, reveals a profound tendency to use technology to replace rather than to augment the skill of a worker. Aristotle says that if the shuttle would itself weave and the lyre itself play, then masters would not need slaves (*Pol.* 1253b37). Thus the social separation of conception from execution in slavery becomes the model for the technological separation of conception from execution in automation. Indeed, the design and deployment of automated technology often presupposes the master-slave relationship; the word *robot*, for example, means "indentured servant" in German. Some forms of technology, however, such as personal computers and power tools, augment skill rather than eliminate it—they are companions rather than slaves.

N. K. Humphrey, "The Social Function of Intellect," in *Growing Points in Ethology*, ed. P. P. G. Bateson and R. A. Hinde (Cambridge: Cambridge University Press, 1976), 314–15.

58. C. Trevarthen concludes "that human intelligence develops from the start as an interpersonal process, and that the maturation of consciousness and the ability to act with voluntary control in the physical world is a product rather than an ingredient of this process." See Judy Dunn, "How Far Do Early Differences in Mother-Child Relations Affect Later Development?" in *Growing Points in Ethology*, 481–82.

59. N. K. Humphrey, "Social Function of Intellect," 314.

The Moral and Technical Dimensions of the Division of Labor

What is the role of moral and instrumental reason in the constitution of the division of labor? Put simply, the technical division of labor is governed chiefly by instrumental reason whereas the social division of labor is governed chiefly by moral reason. Technology, as the interface between the social and technical divisions of labor, is the joint product of moral and technical reason. Since any concrete instance of production necessarily unites the social and technical divisions of labor, it is more precise to say that the division of labor has both a moral and a technical dimension. Instrumental reason concerns the efficient choice of means to a pre-given and separate end. The craftsman, for example, can choose several ways to divide his tasks in order to make a product. The nature of the product is relatively independent of his choice of means. Moral reason, by contrast, concerns those activities in which ends and means cannot be readily separated: moral reason chooses whole courses of action—ends and means. The employer's choice to limit each worker to one task is no mere means to efficient production: this social division has profound effects on the skill of workers, the dignity of labor, and the social relations within the firm. Ends and means are inseparable in the case of the social division of labor. Since technology constrains possible social divisions of labor, its design reflects moral as well as technical criteria.[60]

Instrumental conduct is effective only when there is a predictable relation between ends and means; moral reason is required both to determine the legitimate role of technical reason and to cope with the myriad situations when the relation is unpredictable. The relation is predictable only when the course of action can be relatively isolated from external contingencies. Specifically, there are two dimensions to the necessary isolation of instrumental conduct: the ends-means relation must be isolated from the external causal network; and the ends-means relation must be isolated from external semiotic networks.

Experimental design in the natural sciences attempts to establish a predictable ends-means relation between relevant variables by isolating a system through controls on intervening causal variables. All forms of instrumental

60. "When little employee discretion is required or allowed by the technology, work procedures are necessarily standardized and structured to a considerable extent. Under such circumstances, jobs are usually segmented and routinized; they contain little variety, autonomy, identity, or significance for the people who perform them" (Hackman and Lee, *Redesigning Work*, 7).

conduct reflect an attempt to isolate themselves from intervening causes in order to attain a predictable relation between ends and means. Strategic action in sports, for example, is possible only because the game has been relatively isolated from the contingencies of the social world: the rules governing legitimate behavior in the game—and even the uniforms—serve to place controls on behavior and isolate the system. Indeed, because most complex productive processes have been reduced to a few elementary motions, the technical division of labor is well suited to experimental treatment by workers and industrial engineers. The modern computer is the best example of the technical division of labor taken to its logical conclusion. A computer can process complex problems only by breaking them down to the simplest binary components and then reassembling these components.

Instrumental conduct must also be relatively isolated from the semiotic networks of communication. Because our actions must proceed through a linguistic network of interpretation, they often miss their goal. One reason why economic activity is so risky and economic prediction so unreliable is that economic action proceeds through the semiotic network of the price system. Both language and the price system are notoriously subject to the vagaries of interpretation. Linguistic action is perfectly instrumental only if I can control the interpretation of my words; but this experimental control of meaning is possible only in formal logic.[61] Economic action is perfectly instrumental only if I can control the interpretation of prices; but because economic actors tend either to exaggerate or to underestimate the significance of price changes, this is possible only if an actor has perfect information.

Although industrial engineering has had a long history of successful experimental inquiry into the technical division of labor, the social division of labor has long proven intractable to scientific procedure. In response to the conflict provoked by the introduction of Taylorism, armies of industrial psychologists and sociologists have conducted thousands of experiments attempting to establish a scientific basis for designing an efficient social division of labor. The upshot of a hundred years of experimentation is that there is no consistent

61. The requirement that instrumental action be isolated from semiotic networks helps to account for Aristotle's attempt to locate *technē* exclusively in the realm of fabrication (*poiēsis*). The craftsman who is mute while he manipulates his materials seems to be isolated from any semiotic network. Aristotle overlooks, however, the fact that the craftsman's end is to satisfy some socially and linguistically defined need; his ability to achieve this end is subject to the vagaries of interpretation.

relation between productivity and any particular social division of labor.[62] For example, it would seem to be a simple matter to determine the relation between the physical exertion required by a job and the fatigue of the worker; yet, except in extreme cases, there is not a clear relation between the two.[63] Whether physical exertion causes fatigue seems to depend on the morale of the worker: fatigue is as much a moral as a physiological condition. Nor is there a consistent relation between the performance of workers and the results of aptitude tests; indeed, performance on tests and performance on the job are often inversely related.[64] The difficulty of successful experimentation with the social division of labor is well illustrated by the fact that such experiments are plagued by the Heisenberg Effect. If workers are distrustful of management, then the scientific monitoring of work can cause a decline in productivity;[65] if workers trust the motives of management, then monitoring work can cause a rise in productivity (Elton Mayo's "Hawthorne Effect").[66] In either case, the experiment has been spoiled because of the impossibility of observing work without somehow influencing the morale of workers. Because the social division of labor cannot be isolated from myriad contingent moral, psychological, and social factors, its effects on productivity have proven quite unpredictable.[67]

62. "No methods for evaluating the effectiveness of job design can be said to exist" (Davis, "Current Job Design Criteria," 78). "In sum, it appears that despite the abundance of writing on the topic, there is little definite information about why work redesign is effective when it is, what goes wrong when it is not, and how the strategy can be altered to improve its general usefulness as an approach to personal and organizational change" (Hackman and Suttle, *Improving Life at Work*, 98).

63. See Frederick Taylor, *The Principles of Scientific Management* [1911] (New York: W. W. Norton, 1967), 55; and Georges Friedmann, *Industrial Society* (New York: Free Press, 1955), 77.

64. Thus Elton Mayo: "The belief that the behavior of an individual within the factory can be predicted before employment upon the basis of a laborious and minute examination by tests of his mechanical and other capacities is mainly, if not wholly mistaken" (cited in Braverman, *Labor and Monopoly Capital*, 144). Those with the greatest aptitude for a task are most easily bored in the performance of that task: "Using the very useful terms coined by German psychologists it may be said that *Übungsfähigkeit* (ability in performance) and *Übungsfestigkeit* (stability in performance) are in inverse ratio to one another" (Friedmann, *Industrial Society*, 137).

65. See Louis Putterman, "On Some Recent Explanations of Why Capital Hires Labor," in *The Economic Nature of the Firm*, ed. Louis Putterman (Cambridge: Cambridge University Press, 1986), 316.

66. See Elton Mayo, "Hawthorne and the Electric Company," in *Organization Theory*, ed. D. S. Pugh (Harmondsworth: Penguin Books, 1971), 216–17.

67. Hackman and Suttle list the factors that shape employee satisfaction and productivity: "1) individual differences among the employees who do the work; 2) the social and interpersonal context of the job; 3) the climate and managerial style of the organization as a whole; and 4) the technology of which the work is a part" (*Improving Life at Work*, 115).

This division of labor structures our social relations; as such it is indissolubly intertwined with our linguistic system. The assignment of people to particular tasks is always fraught with meaning, making it subject to the contingencies of interpretation.

Studies of the social division of labor bear out my fundamental claim that because instrumental conduct can be distinguished only provisionally from moral conduct, instrumental reason is subordinate to moral reason. Existing patterns of the social division of labor reflect not only the technical quest for efficiency but also specific moral norms about the nature of work. Because a worker's morale can be important to his or her productivity, the technical quest for efficiency cannot be separated from the moral quest for justice.

Job-design studies show that many different social divisions of labor are equally consistent with economic productivity. There is no reason to believe that the existing patterns of this division of labor are uniquely efficient.[68] Of course, even if a more humane division of labor were to reduce productivity it could still be defended on the grounds that meaningful work is more important to human well-being than more commodities.[69] If empirical evidence does not suggest that providing for greater job satisfaction will generally increase productivity, neither does it suggest that it will generally reduce productivity. What the evidence does strongly suggest is that designing jobs to unify conception and execution will directly improve the happiness and well-being of workers.

68. "Management designs jobs without systematic methods, without tested criteria, and without evaluating the effects of job designs on long-term productivity or costs. By adhering to the very narrow and limited criteria of minimizing immediate cost or maximizing immediate productivity, it designs jobs based entirely on the principles of specialization, repetitiveness, low skill content and minimum impact of the worker on the production process" (Davis, "Current Job Design Criteria," 81).

69. E. J. Mishan observed: "The potential increase in well-being that would come about as a result of providing work that is more creative, more communal, and generally more enjoyable might be worth more than the actual increase in well-being that is provided by yet more goods" (cited in Lane, *Market Experience*, 312).

Chapter 2

The Natural, Customary, and Stipulated
Division of Labor

Nature, Custom, and Stipulation

Nature, custom, and stipulation represent the three fundamental concepts of order: there is the natural order of physical, chemical, and biological processes; there is the customary order of habitual social practices; and there is the stipulated order of deliberate design. All forms of social explanation refer implicitly or explicitly to one or more of these categories. Thus, of a given institution we ask: is it natural, customary, or stipulated? Nature, custom, and stipulation have often been interpreted as mutually exclusive—as when we ask if something is natural or conventional—but I will suggest that these categories are mutually inclusive. In other words, every human institution has three dimensions: a natural, a customary, and a stipulated dimension. I will use the case of the social division of labor to illustrate these claims.

While this trichotomy can be found in a variety of historical guises, it makes its first full appearance in Aristotle: "There are three things which make men good and excellent; these are nature [*physis*], habit [*ethos*], and reason [*logos*]" (*Pol.* 1332a40). Just what is the meaning of this cryptic passage? Aristotle is saying that moral and intellectual self-realization has three dimensions: we start with our natural dispositions, we cultivate these dispositions into habits, and we reflect on our habits in order to stipulate new moral ideals for ourselves. In this model of moral development, our habits presuppose human nature but are not reduced to it, just as our stipulated rational ideals presuppose our habits but are not reduced to them.

Aristotle extended his model of individual moral development to the political development of the polis. Here social customs presuppose human nature, just as legal stipulation presupposes social customs. Over time, his nature, custom, and stipulation trichotomy was employed in the analysis of several other social institutions. For example, in his seventeenth-century treatise on semiotics, John Poinsot (John of St. Thomas) considers "whether the division of signs into natural [*naturale*], stipulated [*ad placitum*], and customary [*ex consuetudine*] is a sound division."[1] By natural signs he means those signs that relate to their objects independent of human activity: smoke is a sign of fire. By customary signs he means those signs that arise from the collective and nonreflective practices of human communities: napkins on a table are a sign that dinner is imminent. By stipulated signs he means those signs whose meaning is deliberately appointed by an individual, as when a new word is introduced. Although Poinsot does not refer to Aristotle in his discussion of the threefold division of signs, I argue that he is offering here an interpretation and extension of Aristotle's *physis*, *ethos*, and *logos*. [2]

F. A. Hayek also employs this trichotomy, at least implicitly, in his analysis of the three kinds of social order: "Yet much of what we call culture is just such a spontaneously grown order [custom], which arose neither altogether independently of human action [nature] nor by design [stipulation], but by a process that stands between these two possibilities, which were long considered as exclusive alternatives."[3] Hayek's distinction here between the spontaneous order of custom and the designed order of stipulation is drawn from Adam Ferguson: "Nations stumble upon establishments, which are indeed the result of human action, but not the execution of any human design."[4]

The nature, custom, and stipulation trichotomy differs from the more common nature-convention (*physis-nomos*) dichotomy in two important ways: first, the term *convention* collapses the distinction between the collective, habitual order of custom and the individually designed order of stipulation; second, Antiphon's nature and convention are mutually exclusive alternatives, whereas Aristotle's nature, custom, and stipulation are complementary and mutually inclusive. Many pre-Socratic philosophers defined nature as univer-

1. John Poinsot (John of St. Thomas), *Tractatus de Signis* [1632], ed. and trans. John Deely (Berkeley: University of California Press, 1985), 269.

2. For a critique and reconstruction of Poinsot's doctrine of signs, see James Bernard Murphy, "Nature, Custom, and Stipulation in the Semiotic of John Poinsot," *Semiotica* 83, 1/2 (1991): 33–68.

3. F. A. Hayek, "Kinds of Order in Society" [1964], in *The Politicization of Society*, ed. Kenneth Templeton, Jr. (Indianapolis: Liberty Press, 1979), 509.

4. Adam Ferguson, *An Essay on the History of Civil Society* (Edinburgh: A. Millar and T. Caddel, 1767), 187.

sal and unchanging whereas they defined convention as local and arbitrary; without a concept of custom, it was impossible to bridge the abyss between nature and convention.

The polarity between nature and convention has been a disaster for social thought. The natural became the necessary, the universal, the real; the conventional became the arbitrary, the local, the ephemeral. Only the natural is intelligible: to explain something we give an account of its "nature." The distinction between nature and convention became the distinction between the true and false, *ens reale* and *ens fictum*. But how satisfactory is a theory of social life that denigrates custom and stipulation as arbitrary, ephemeral, and illusory? No wonder European social thought is characterized by the recurrent effort to reduce custom and stipulation to nature — witness natural right, natural law, the state of nature, natural liberty, natural reason, natural prices and wages, and the natural level of unemployment. Yet from the standpoint of our nature, custom, and stipulation framework, it is misleading to describe a human institution as either natural or conventional: every human institution has a natural, a customary, and a stipulated dimension. Human language, for example, evolves due to natural physiology (ease of pronunciation), customary usage (the unconscious formation of grammatical analogies), and stipulation (the rules of grammarians and academies).

Conceptual clarity in social thought has long been obscured by the use of such terms as *convention, culture*, and *tradition*. The term *convention*, strictly speaking, means an explicitly stipulated agreement among individuals; as such, conventions have had a small role in the development of social institutions when compared to the enormous role of tacit customs.[5] To contrast the natural with the conventional, then, is to ignore the fundamental role of custom in social life; and if we stretch the meaning of convention to include custom, as is common, then convention becomes an empty concept.[6] Similarly,

5. Aristotle defines convention (*synthēkē*) as a legal contract in *Rhet.* 1376b1. In Latin, *conventio* refers to a compact or explicit agreement among parties: *conventio* is synonymous with *stipulatio*. What William Alston says of conventions in language is true of most social institutions: "We know very little about the mechanisms by which new words come into being and old words change their meaning, but what we do know about it indicates that conscious decision and deliberately adopted conventions have very little part to play" (cited in Bernard Rollin, *Natural and Conventional Meaning* [The Hague: Mouton, 1976], 61).

6. As Willard Quine says: "In dropping the attributes of deliberateness and explicitness from the notion of linguistic convention we risk depriving the latter of any explanatory force and reducing it to an idle label" (cited in Rollin, *Natural and Conventional Meaning*, 61).

the term *culture* is frequently opposed to *nature* and taken to mean both custom and stipulation. The term was first introduced to social science by E. B. Tylor in 1871; it has been used ever since to blur the crucial distinction between custom and stipulation.[7] Its profound ambiguity is evident in the expressions "he has no culture" or "he is uncultured." If culture includes custom, then these expressions are simply false: every human has customs. But if culture means deliberately stipulated knowledge, then some people are indeed without culture. Finally, the term *tradition*, meaning that which is handed down (*traditio*), obscures the distinction between the way in which customs are unconsciously imparted and the way in which knowledge is consciously taught. Most of what is written about tradition—about the character of our relation to tradition or about the rationality of tradition—is vitiated by this lack of clarity. For example, although our deliberate appropriation of literary traditions is no doubt subject to rational criteria, our unconscious assimilation of customs is not. In short, we may choose a stipulated tradition, but we do not choose our customary traditions any more than we choose our mother tongue.[8] Clear thinking in social science is impossible so long as the terms *convention*, *culture*, and *tradition* are not subordinated to the fundamental distinction between custom and stipulation.

What I intend to establish, in short, is the claim that nature, custom, and stipulation represent the three fundamental concepts of order in the sense that all other concepts of order can be shown to be derivative—as we saw with the concepts convention, culture, and tradition. But what role does order play in explanation? All forms of explanation, I suggest, presuppose a concept of order: "An order is a relation that orders the members of a class, i.e., a set of elements, in a certain way. When we know how a set of elements is ordered we have a basis for inference."[9] Nature, custom, and stipulation represent three bases for inference: one can infer B from A on the basis of the physical, chemical, or biological processes of nature; one can infer on the basis of the

7. "Culture, or civilization, taken in its wide ethnographic sense, is that complex whole which includes knowledge, belief, art, morals, law, custom, and any other capabilities and habits acquired by man as a member of society" (E. B. Tylor, *The Origins of Culture* [1871], ed. Paul Rodin [New York: Harper and Brothers, 1958], 1).

8. Thus Alasdair MacIntyre takes Burke to task for reducing tradition to custom, "'wisdom without reflection' . . . So that no place is left for reflection, rational theorizing as a work of and within tradition." See MacIntyre, *Whose Justice? Which Rationality?* (Notre Dame: University of Notre Dame Press, 1988), 353.

9. L. S. Stebbing, *A Modern Introduction to Logic* (London: Methuen, 1950), 228.

historical genealogy of custom; and one can infer on the basis of the intentional design of stipulation. Note that the order of custom is an order essentially dependent on time: we explain a custom by means of a historical narrative. By contrast, the order of stipulation is an order independent of time: we explain a designed order in terms of its purpose or function. Since any complex human practice involves both custom and stipulation, social explanation will need to refer to both history and function.

The Logic of Nature, Custom, and Stipulation: As Interdefinable

There is a profound tendency in European thought to treat nature, custom, and stipulation as a circle of interdefinability: that is, we tend to define each one of our concepts in terms of one or both of the other concepts.[10] In Aristotle and the Aristotelian tradition, nature, custom, and stipulation are not formally interdefined, but they are described through a circle of metaphors. For example, the order of nature is often described in terms of the order of legal stipulation: "the laws of physics"; whereas law is often described in terms of nature: "natural law" and "natural right." And custom is typically described both in terms of nature as "second nature" and in terms of stipulation as "unwritten law." Indeed, Aristotle's circle of interdefinability lives on in Pierre Bourdieu's recent description of custom (*habitus*) both as "immanent law" and as "history turned into nature."[11] What is the meaning of this circle of metaphors? Is this a vicious circle?

The use of these expressions to define nature, custom, and law is so ubiquitous that they have lost their metaphorical force. The notion of the "laws of physics," for example, has become such a cliché that it is now taken literally. These are dormant metaphors and we cannot interrogate them until they are awakened; and since a metaphor is a condensed analogy, we awaken it by making explicit the implicit analogy.[12] The metaphor "the laws of

10. "Cases are known where there is a set of concepts such that any member of the set may be defined in terms of one or more other members of the set, but no member can be defined otherwise. (Example: In logic, 'or' can be defined in terms of 'not' and 'and'; also, 'and' can be defined in terms of 'not' and 'or.')" (Rulon S. Wells, "Criteria for Semiosis," in *A Perfusion of Signs*, ed. Thomas A. Sebeok [Bloomington: Indiana University Press, 1977], 8).

11. For Bourdieu's theory of *habitus*, see his *Outline of a Theory of Practice*, trans. Richard Nice (Cambridge: Cambridge University Press, 1977), pp. 78–81.

12. On the logical structure of metaphor and analogy see C. Perelman and L. Olbrechts-Tyteca, *The New Rhetoric* (Notre Dame: University of Notre Dame Press, 1969), 370–410.

physics" is a condensed analogy of the form: human laws are to social order what physical laws are to natural order. The metaphor describing custom as unwritten law implies the analogy that custom is to law what the unwritten is to the written. We find in this way that these metaphorical descriptions of nature, custom, and law are merely abbreviations for rather elaborate analogies. The first step, then, in making sense of a metaphor is to unpack the implicit analogy.

If a metaphor is a condensed analogy then our circle of metaphors is actually a circle of analogies. Nature is analogous to custom, custom is analogous to law, and law is analogous to nature. What, then, is the meaning of this circle of analogies? An analogy is often described as a relation of resemblance, but analogy is more precisely described as a resemblance of relationship: $A:B :: C:D$.[13] Our circle of analogies reflects the Aristotelian insight that there are important logical similarities between natural, customary, and stipulated order. In response to Antiphon's influential claim that nature and convention are antithetical, Aristotle employs a variety of analogies to bridge the presumed chasm between the natural and the social. His favorite analogy compares rational teleology to natural teleology: just as the craftsman rationally orders his means to his end, so nature orders its means to its ends. Aristotle's insight that natural organs, like human artifacts, can be explained by their functions laid the basis for the fruitful scientific program of natural teleology. Similarly, Aristotle's metaphor of custom as "second nature" is an important corrective to the Sophistic view that customs are merely arbitrary; and the metaphor of custom as "unwritten law" rightly conveys the normative force of custom. The later Aristotelian-Thomistic doctrines of natural law and the laws of nature presuppose an analogy between the legal order and the natural order. Juristic natural law rightly emphasizes the universality of certain moral norms in human society; physical natural law rightly emphasizes the generality and necessity of many natural processes.

In this way, the frequent treatment of nature, custom, and stipulation as a circle of interdefinability has undoubtedly generated many fruitful analogies. The history of science shows that theoretical innovation is usually a matter of seeing analogical resemblance between different phenomena.[14] The dormant

13. See Perelman and Olbrechts-Tyteca, *New Rhetoric*, 372.

14. Pierre Duhem says: "The history of physics shows us that the search for analogies between two distinct categories of phenomena has perhaps been the surest and most fruitful method of all the procedures put into play in the construction of physical theories" (cited in

metaphor "electric current" abbreviates a complex analogy between electricity and hydrodynamics; and the metaphor "consuming inputs" abbreviates a complex analogy between production and consumption in neoclassical economics. Yet all analogies have implications that can distort theory if the analogies are not subjected to criticism. Niels Bohr, for example, conceived his theory of atomic structure by analogy to the solar system, but physicists soon dropped this analogy as misleading. Therefore, we must subject our circle of analogies to critical scrutiny: Are natural organs really designed for a specific function? Who does the designing? When were they designed? If customs are second nature, then why do they differ so much over time and place? Do customs differ from laws only by being unwritten? Were the laws of nature stipulated all at once or did they evolve over time like habits? Such critical scrutiny will, I suggest, lead us to the view that Aristotle's circle of analogies effaces some important distinctions. To say that custom is both "second nature" and "unwritten law" obscures the important insight that custom is precisely that kind of social order that is neither natural nor stipulated.

The Logic of Nature, Custom, and Stipulation: As a Progressive Hierarchy

A great deal of the history of social theory has consisted of the elaboration of this handful of Aristotelian metaphors. Nonetheless, as an account of nature, custom, and stipulation this circle of metaphors is radically defective. To begin with, metaphors are obscure in a way that analogies are not: because a metaphor fuses terms A and C but leaves terms B and D unexpressed, there are always several possible analogies implied by any one metaphor. A metaphor is not simply an abbreviated analogy; it is an abbreviation that may stand for many different analogies. Even if we know the context of the metaphor, the choice of the appropriate analogy is never unambiguous. For example, the metaphor "natural law" is an abbreviation for several different analogies between the natural order and the legal order. For Aristotle, natural law implies the analogy *natural law is to political law what the universal is to the local*; for Thomas Aquinas, natural law implies, in addition, the analogy *natural law is to biblical law what nature is to grace*; for Newton, it implies

---

Philip Mirowski, *More Heat than Light* (Cambridge: Cambridge University Press, 1989), 277–78.

the analogy *just as a monarch lays down laws for human beings, so God laid down laws for minerals, plants, and animals.* Moreover, in the fusion of a metaphor, the underlying analogy is not presented as a hypothesis for inspection but as a datum; indeed, the analogy functions as the concealed presupposition for grasping the metaphor. The rhetorical power of metaphor is precisely this ability of getting us to accept an implied analogy without knowing that we have.[15]

The capacity of a single metaphor to imply many different analogies helps to account for the paradox of identity and difference in intellectual history. Certain pervasive metaphors give continuity to intellectual history whereas their underlying analogies create radical differences. If we focus only on the continuity of metaphor, then we are forced to agree with Jorge Luis Borges's ironic dictum that "universal history is the history of different intonations given a handful of metaphors."[16] Nonetheless, as we saw in the case of "natural law," beneath the smooth continuity of metaphor lie the profound ruptures marking different underlying analogies. The pervasive use of our Aristotelian metaphors by various intellectual traditions does not mean that history is the eternal return of the same, nor does it mean that diverse traditions are essentially incommensurable.

In accordance with Aristotle's explicit logic of classification, I have thus far treated nature, custom, and stipulation as the three and only three species of the genus "order." But one shortcoming of this genus-species logic is that the genus "order" is more or less empty and does not add any information to the *differentiae* nature, custom, and stipulation. More important, the genus-species logic does not indicate the serial and hierarchical relations of the three: nature is prior to custom and custom is prior to stipulation.

Aristotle, however, offers an alternative logic of classification, which is most clearly illustrated by his analysis of the kinds of souls. Here, instead of defining the genus "soul" and the species of plant, animal, and human souls, Aristotle says that the plant soul is living (that is, nutritive and reproductive), the animal soul is living plus sensitive, and the human soul is living and sensitive plus rational (*DA* 414a29–415a13). I argue that nature, custom, and stipulation form such a hierarchy: "In every case the lower faculty can exist apart from the higher, but the higher presupposes those below

15. On the compatibility of several analogies with a single metaphor, see Perelman and Olbrechts-Tyteca, *New Rhetoric*, 400–1.

16. Jorge Luis Borges, cited in Mirowski, *More Heat than Light*, 1.

it."[17] Nature represents the physical, chemical, and biological processes of the created universe; nature can and did exist apart from human custom and stipulation. Human custom is rooted in the physiology of habit but transcends individual habit by becoming a collective system of normative behavior. Custom presupposes nature, but custom can exist without being the object of reflective stipulation by an individual mind: language can and did exist apart from grammarians. Stipulation is the synoptic order deliberately imposed upon the pre-reflective materials of custom; stipulation always presupposes custom: philosophy, law, engineering, and grammar never arise ex nihilo.

What does it mean to say that custom presupposes nature and that stipulation presupposes custom? First, our progressive hierarchy suggests that certain natural processes (like habit formation) are necessary but not sufficient causes for the emergence of social customs: for example, if human biology were not sexually bimorphic, then human customs defining gender would not arise. Second, custom is a necessary but not sufficient cause for the emergence of deliberate stipulation: reflective stipulation of a new definition for a term, for example, presupposes the existing customary definition. If nature were a sufficient condition for custom, then custom could be reduced to nature; if custom were a sufficient condition for stipulation, then stipulation could be reduced to custom. In Aristotle's terms, nature is potentially custom and custom is potentially stipulation; yet for potentiality to become actuality, other causal factors must be present. Our model of nature, custom, and stipulation thus creates the theoretical framework for testing empirical hypotheses about what biological conditions are necessary for the emergence of social customs and about what customary practices lead to the emergence of stipulation.

Our progressive hierarchy has a descending as well as an ascending moment. We have just seen the ascent from nature to custom to stipulation; now we shall briefly describe the descent from stipulation to custom to nature. Legal stipulation presupposes custom but is often intended to reform and even to negate custom: managers of factories and offices, for example, stipulate work rules intended to replace traditional customs and to create new customs. Stipulation, then, can create new customs that in turn will create the need over time for new stipulations. So we must consider the question: if customs are

17. R. D. Hicks, *Aristotle: De Anima* (Cambridge: Cambridge University Press, 1907), p. 335.

increasingly the product of legal stipulation, does it still make sense to argue that custom is logically prior to stipulation? The answer lies in the fact that although stipulation can influence the question of which customs will be formed, stipulation cannot alter the fundamental customary processes of habit and imitation whereby social practices are learned. The stipulations of grammarians have more influence on speech behavior now than they did in the past, but language remains a habitual social practice learned by imitation. Stipulation shapes human behavior chiefly by becoming customary. What has changed historically is not the role of custom so much as the source of customs.

Similarly, over time custom and stipulation have transformed nature: how, then, can nature be said to be logically prior to custom and stipulation if nature (at least this corner of nature called earth) is increasingly the product of human activity? Although we can transform pristine nature into a human environment, we cannot transform the basic processes or "laws" of nature. We transform pristine nature only by conforming to the processes of nature: if we destroy nature it will be through the laws of nature. Physical anthropology has revealed the far-reaching role of custom in the transformation of human nature from a small-brained protohuman *Australopithecus* into a large-brained, fully human *Homo sapiens*. Through the development of customs, "man determined, if unwittingly, the culminating stages of his own biological destiny. Quite literally, though quite inadvertently, he created himself."[18] Still, custom was able to shape human nature only because of natural selection; those individuals with greater social and technical skills had a selective advantage. With genetic engineering, we are now able for the first time to shape human nature through deliberate stipulation; whether we can predict the outcome of such manipulation is another question. The priority of natural order is evident: custom made use of natural selection; stipulation makes use of biochemical processes.

Traditionalists, like Edmund Burke and Michael Oakeshott, emphasize the ascent from custom to stipulation; they insist that rational stipulation ought not wander far from its moorings in custom. Rationalists, like Thomas Paine and Karl Marx, emphasize the descent from stipulation to custom: they insist on the power of reason to transform custom. Sociobiologists, like E. O. Wilson and Lionel Tiger, emphasize the role of nature in social life to the neglect of custom and stipulation. All of these perspectives are fatally one-sided. In

18. "Without men, no culture, certainly; but equally, and more significantly, without culture, no men" (Clifford Geertz, *The Interpretation of Cultures* [New York: Basic Books, 1973], 48–49).

short, viewing nature, custom, and stipulation as a progressive hierarchy with ascending and descending moments offers the most comprehensive and logically rigorous framework for social theory.

The Natural Division of Labor

From Plato to E. O. Wilson, we find a pervasive attempt to describe the division of labor solely in terms of nature. But such a reductive explanation cannot do justice to the role of custom and stipulation in the constitution of human labor and, indeed, of human nature. Labor is the unity of conception and execution, which for most of human history has meant the unity of the mind and the hand. Since the human brain and the human hand evolved in part through interaction with custom, there is no human nature and, a fortiori, no human labor apart from custom. We lack the appropriate instincts to divide and to coordinate social labor, so without customary norms we are lost.

I call "reductive naturalism" all attempts to reduce custom and stipulation to nature. There are two distinct species of reductive naturalism that should be carefully distinguished: something may be termed "natural" because it is causally determined by nature, or something may be termed "natural" because it is formally analogous to nature. The rhetoric of naturalism usually trades on the ambiguity of these two senses of "natural"—vitiating most of what has been written about the role of nature in social and political philosophy.

Plato, for example, says that the division of labor is natural because different individuals have different innate aptitudes; yet Plato also says that the division of labor is natural because the specialization of workers is analogous to the specialization of organs of the body: the metaphor of the body politic (*Republic* 370A, 462C). In the first case, the division of labor is causally determined by nature, and in the second, the division of labor is analogous to nature. Plato's elaborate analogy between the three parts of the soul and the three classes of the ideal city makes use of both senses of "natural." Each person is psychologically suited by nature to his social caste; and there is an analogy of proportionality between the hierarchy of classes and the hierarchy of the parts of the soul. The guardian rules by nature because his rational soul causes him to be fit to rule and because the dominance of reason in the ideal city is analogous to the dominance of reason in his soul.

According to Aristotle, the division of labor is natural in both senses. Within the household, roles are specialized according to biological differences in aptitude: "The freeman rules over the slave after another manner from that in which the male rules over the female, or the man over the child; although the parts of the soul are present in all of them, they are present in different degrees. For the slave has no deliberative faculty at all; the woman has, but it is without authority, and the child has, but it is immature" (*Pol.* 1260a7). Slavery is natural both because slaves have deficient minds and because the master-slave relation is analogous to the mind-body relation (1254a31).

Adam Smith also describes the division of labor as natural in both of these senses. In Smith's view, all scientific explanation has two parts: the first refers to the specific causal mechanisms involved—for example, the laws of motion; the second refers to the harmonious order that Providence creates out of these mechanisms. "Psychological and social science has to explain the operation of the mechanisms by which the Divine purpose is achieved. This argument makes it clear that Smith's references to the purposes of Nature, the 'guiding hand,' etc., were not substitutes for scientific explanations of social phenomena but an appendage to them."[19] The division of labor, says Smith, stems from the natural psychological propensity to truck, barter, and exchange. An invisible hand ensures that these individual propensities lead to an optimal division of labor. The division of labor—and the market economy as a whole—is natural both because it is rooted in causal psychological propensities and because the spontaneous order of the market is analogous to the spontaneous order of nature.[20] Smith, therefore, not only makes use of these two senses of "natural" but with his "invisible hand" provides a means of ensuring that causal determinism leads to a social order whose harmony is analogous to the harmony of the natural order.

In a fairly straightforward example of an argument from natural causal determinism, Karl Marx claims that the division of labor within a family "springs up naturally" and is a "purely physiological" division based on "differences of age and sex." But Marx goes on to describe the division of labor as natural in a very different sense: "Castes and guilds arise from the action of the same natural law that regulates the differentiation of plants and animals into species and varieties, except that, when a certain degree of development has been reached, the heredity of castes and the exclusiveness of guilds are

19. O. H. Taylor, *Economics and Liberalism* (Cambridge: Harvard University Press, 1955), 91.

20. See Adam Smith, *The Wealth of Nations* [1776], ed. R. H. Campbell, A. S. Skinner, and W. B. Todd (Oxford: Oxford University Press, 1979), 1:2.25, 4:2.456, and 4:5.530.

ordained as a law of society."[21] Marx is clearly developing an analogy between the speciation of organisms and the specialization of trades; yet he also means to suggest that this is more than an analogy. He does not specify what "natural law" is responsible for the social division of labor, but the language suggests that he is referring to Darwin's natural selection.[22] Since there is no evidence that the division of labor is caused by natural selection, Marx must trade on the ambiguity of the term *nature*: he suggests that if a social institution is analogous to nature, then it must be causally determined by nature. Of course, such analogies actually prove nothing about causal determination: analogies may serve as hypotheses for the empirical investigation of causation, but they do not constitute evidence of any causal relation.

Alfred Marshall then makes explicit Marx's implicit argument from analogy to causation: he asserts that the analogy between the social division of labor in a factory and the natural division of functions in an organism proves that the division of labor is causally determined by natural laws. Marshall writes of "the many profound analogies which have been discovered between social and especially industrial organization on the one side and the physical organization of the higher animals on the other." These analogies "have at last established their claim to illustrate a fundamental unity of action between the laws of nature in the physical and in the moral world."

> This central unity is set forth in the general rule, to which there are not very many exceptions, that the development of the organism, whether social or physical, involves an increasing subdivision of functions between its separate parts on the one hand, and on the other a more intimate connection between them.[23]

Finally, the complete collapse of the distinction between natural analogy and natural causation is found in the sociobiology of E. O. Wilson. He argues that there is a genetic explanation for the division of labor: "a single strong thread does indeed run from the conduct of termite colonies and turkey broth-

21. Karl Marx, *Capital*, vol. 1 [1867] (New York: International Publishers, 1967), 14.2. 321 and 14.4.332.

22. "My standpoint," wrote Marx, is that "from which the evolution of the economic formation of society is viewed as a process of natural history." See Lewis Feuer, "Marx and Engels as Sociobiologists," *Survey* 23 (1978): 111.

23. Alfred Marshall, *Principles of Economics* [1920] (Philadelphia: Porcupine Press, 1982), 200.

erhoods to the social behavior of man."[24] Is this "strong thread" a causal link between species or merely an analogy among species? And within causal theories, is Wilson saying that termites, turkeys, and humans inherit a genetic proclivity to the division of labor from a common ancestor, or simply that natural selection creates such a proclivity in diverse species because of a common functional need? If the human division of labor were the product of biological evolution, then we would expect to find resemblances in the division of labor among our close evolutionary relatives. However, the human division of labor strongly resembles the division of labor within certain insect societies; unfortunately, the evolutionary distance between humans and insects is so immense as to rule out any common ancestor or even any common functional needs. Conversely, the simple division of labor among primates has little in common with human division of labor even though we are closely related to primates. "My own guess is that the genetic bias is intense enough to cause a substantial division of labor even in the most free and most egalitarian of future societies."[25] What Wilson shows us, however, is merely an analogy between humans and other animals, not a "genetic bias."

If we are to avoid the reductionism inherent in both these types of naturalism, then we need a concept of nature that does not exclude custom and stipulation; indeed, we need a concept of nature that makes custom and stipulation possible. Such a concept of nature is implicit in Aristotle's doctrine that to become a morally good person we need nature, custom, and reason. What does Aristotle mean by nature in this trichotomy? He means that by nature we receive a set of potentialities that are made actual by habit and reason: "Neither by nature, then, nor contrary to nature do excellences arise in us: rather we are adapted by nature to receive them, and are made perfect by habit" (*NE* 1103a23). Nature provides the potentialities for us to become good or bad, depending on whether we form good or bad habits. Clifford Geertz rightly says that man is to be defined not by his innate capacities nor by his learned behavior "but rather by the link between them, by the way in which the first is transformed into the second, his generic potentialities focused into his specific performances."[26] In this view, nature does not determine human institutions;

24. E. O. Wilson, *Sociobiology* (Cambridge: Harvard University Press, 1975), 129.

25. E. O. Wilson, "Human Decency Is Animal," *New York Times Magazine*, Oct. 12, 1975. This comment is confused because Wilson neglects the fundamental fact that humans would find it efficient to specialize even if all persons had identical aptitudes.

26. Geertz, *Interpretation of Cultures*, 52.

nature simply provides the powers employed by custom and stipulation. In one sense, every human activity is natural because humans are a part of nature; in another sense, however, nothing humans do is natural because custom and stipulation have shaped even the most basic human behaviors such as eating, sleeping, and sex. This paradox vanishes as soon as we see that a social institution is at once natural, customary, and stipulated.

In place of this reductive naturalism we need what Ian Shapiro calls a "critical naturalism." Human beings, says Shapiro, are natural beings, but they are also emergent from nature.[27] Here Shapiro refers to the theory of emergence, which like my theory of social order is a nonreductionist account of complex phenomena. According to Lloyd Morgan (1894), "at various grades of organization, material configurations display new and unexpected phenomena." Just as the properties of water cannot be deduced from the properties of hydrogen and oxygen, so the properties of custom cannot be deduced from the properties of nature. The theory of emergent complexity is at the center of modern biology, which is another way of saying that modern biology is nonreductionist. Theory reductionism, says Ernst Mayr, is a fallacy because it confuses processes and concepts: "Such biological processes as meiosis, gastrulation, and predation are also chemical and physical processes, but they are only biological concepts and cannot be reduced to physico-chemical concepts." Customary and stipulated human behavior is also biological, chemical, and physical behavior, but custom and stipulation cannot be reduced to nature. Complex systems very often have a hierarchical structure, and the hierarchical structure of living systems shares some important features with our hierarchy, one being that higher levels can affect properties of components at lower levels. We observe this "downward causation" in social theory when stipulation shapes custom and when custom shapes nature. My theory of nature, like that of modern biology, is neither vitalist nor reductionist.[28]

The phenomena of emergent complexity is just as characteristic of human social and cultural life as it is of biological life. Michael Polanyi illustrates emergence with the example of a speech: "It includes five levels; namely the

---

27. For Shapiro's theory of "critical naturalism," see *Political Criticism* (Berkeley: University of California Press, 1990), 239–41. Shapiro draws on the theory of "critical naturalism" in Roy Bhaskar, *The Possibility of Naturalism* (New York: Humanities Press, 1979), 3–22, and *Scientific Realism and Human Emancipation* (London: Verso, 1986), 113–17.

28. On the theory of emergence and its importance for a nonreductionist biology, see Ernst Mayr, *The Growth of Biological Thought* (Cambridge: Harvard University Press, 1982), 59–67.

production 1) of voice, 2) of words, 3) of sentences, 4) of style, and 5) of literary composition. Each of these levels is subject to its own laws, as prescribed 1) by phonetics, 2) by lexicography, 3) by grammar, 4) by stylistics, and 5) by literary criticism." Polanyi points out that the operations of a higher level cannot be accounted for by the laws governing a lower level: grammar cannot be reduced to lexicography. Each level is subject to the control both of its own intrinsic laws and to the laws of the higher level: grammar is controlled both by its own rules and, in part, by the rules of stylistics. A lower level is open to determination by a higher level and also imposes restrictions on the higher level.[29] In the case of social life, nature creates potentialities that are actualized by custom but also imposes restrictions on the emergent customs; customs open possibilities for deliberate stipulations but also limit those possibilities. As Shapiro points out, understanding the ways in which the different levels interact may be just as important as understanding the laws governing each level.[30] To make sense of human labor, for example, it is not enough to study the physical anthropology of human evolution and the cultural anthropology of human history; one must also consider the role of human biology in shaping customs as well as the role of custom in shaping biological evolution. The theory of emergence reveals that there can be a fundamental unity of method between the natural and the social sciences.[31]

What precisely does "natural potentiality" mean? The plasticity of nature is a function of how we selectively use natural powers; the constraint of nature is a function of the limits of compossibility in our selection of a set of powers.

29. For Polanyi's theory of emergence, see *The Tacit Dimension* (London: Routledge and Kegan Paul, 1967), 35–49.

30. Shapiro points out the dangers of two kinds of reductionism: first, reducing the higher level of complexity to the lower (e.g., reducing social behavior to biological imperatives); second, reducing the lower level to the higher level, as in some versions of "emergent holism" (e.g., arguing that because custom and stipulation shape nature, nature ceases to play an independent causal role in human social life). Shapiro argues that "the assertion of the primacy of language in much contemporary philosophy and social theory commits just this [second] error." See *Political Criticism*, 240.

31. Roy Bhaskar carefully distinguishes a critical naturalism from both reductionism and scientism: "Naturalism may be defined as the thesis that there is (or can be) an essential unity of method between the natural and the social sciences. It must be immediately distinguished from two species of it: reductionism, which asserts that there is an actual identity of subject matter as well; and scientism, which denies that there are any significant differences in the methods appropriate to studying social and natural objects, whether or not they are actually (as in reductionism) identified" (*Possibility of Naturalism*, 3).

J. S. Mill defines the laws of nature as a set of such powers: "Though we cannot emancipate ourselves from the laws of nature as a whole, we can escape from any particular law of nature, if we are able to withdraw ourselves from the circumstances in which it acts. Though we can do nothing except through laws of nature, we can use one law to counter-act another."[32] All human activities are subject to natural causal laws, but to a considerable extent, custom and stipulation select which causal laws govern a particular activity. All forms of linguistic behavior, for example, make use of natural processes, but different forms of language select different natural laws: vocalization uses one process, writing another, sign language another, computer language still another.

Returning to the social division of labor, we are now in a position to see that nature's role is usually mediated by custom and stipulation. E. O. Wilson says that the sexual division of labor "appears to have a genetic origin." This is quite true, not in the sense that specific genes determine the sexual division of labor, but in the sense that it makes use of genetic differences between the sexes. Whether a person is male or female has a genetic origin; custom and stipulation divide tasks by sex; thus the sexual division of labor has a genetic origin—but only because custom selects sex as the basis of social function. Every division of labor selects among various natural differences among people: differences of sex, age, race, strength, or intelligence. As a general rule, traditional societies based the social division of labor on natural differences between social groups defined by sex, age, and clan; modern societies, by contrast, base the social division of labor increasingly on natural differences between individuals. This contrast could be interpreted as a transition from an emphasis on the qualitative differences between groups to an emphasis on the quantitative differences between individuals. Nature plays many roles in the division of labor, but custom and stipulation often determine which roles nature plays.

The Customary Division of Labor

Although the concepts of habit and custom were once central to social and political philosophy, they have been jettisoned from large parts of contempo-

32. J. S. Mill, "Nature," in *Three Essays on Religion* [1874] (New York: Greenwood Press, 1969), 7.

rary social science. The current *International Encyclopedia of the Social Sciences* (1968) no longer includes articles on habit and custom as it did in the previous edition (1930). Habit and custom were dropped from sociology during the transition from Max Weber to Talcott Parsons. Weber defined rational action as either the pursuit of explicit ultimate values or the deliberate selection of means to pursue explicit ends. For Weber, habitual or customary action is not only nonrational—it is not even meaningful. Parsons then proceeded to excise habit and custom from his typology of social action.[33] Recently, however, dissatisfaction with functionalist and Kantian modes of social theory has led to a renewed interest in tradition, interpretation, community, and history. Unfortunately, this general hermeneutic turn in social theory makes use of many vague concepts like tradition, community, convention, and culture instead of the more precise notions of habit, custom, and stipulation.

Similarly, whereas habit and custom once played a significant role in classical political economy, in the historical school of economics, and in American institutionalist economics, they have been abandoned for the most part by neoclassical economics. When habit or custom is treated by neoclassicism, the results are ludicrous: Ludwig von Mises, for example, argues that habits are always deliberately acquired and changed to conform with explicit criteria.[34] In short, habit and custom do not exist for neoclassicism.

The reasons for the excision of habit and custom go to the heart of the theoretical logic of much of modern social theory. We can only touch on the two basic grounds for the absence of habit and custom. The first stems from Kant's radical dichotomy between the causally determined realm of nature and the morally free realm of human action. Since Kant defines the moral realm as the locus of the free and deliberate stipulation of rules, habitual or customary action is thereby rendered incompatible with moral action. This explains why Kant banishes habit and custom from the realm of moral action.[35] Kant's

33. For the story of how habit was jettisoned from sociology, see Charles Camic, "The Matter of Habit," *American Journal of Sociology* 91 (March 1986). See Max Weber, *Economy and Society* [1925], ed. Guenther Roth and Claus Wittich (Berkeley: University of California Press, 1978), 24–25; and Talcott Parsons, *The Structure of Social Action* [1937] (New York: Free Press, 1949), 44–48 and 762–65.

34. Ludwig von Mises, *Human Action* [1949] (Chicago: Henry Regnery Co., 1966), 46–47. For a contemporary neoclassical argument that habits are optimizing strategies, see Richard Ault and Robert Ekelund, "Habits in Economic Analysis: Veblen and the Neoclassicals," *History of Political Economy* 20 (1988).

35. Nowhere is Kant's radical departure from Aristotelian philosophy more evident than in

dichotomy between nature and morality, between facts and values, is the basis of Wilhelm Dilthey's dichotomy between the natural sciences and the cultural sciences. Weber and Parsons accept this dichotomy: social science studies normative action whereas natural science studies factual regularities. Since they define social action in terms of the reflective choice of ends and means, habitual action is relegated to the sciences of nature. Clifford Geertz accepts Dilthey's dichotomy when he says that the analysis of culture should be "not an experimental science in search of law but an interpretative one in search of meaning."[36] The upshot is that any attempt to create a dichotomy between natural facts and moral values ultimately excludes habit and custom: for customary habit is precisely the indissoluble unity of factual regularity and normative value. Since habit is a bridge from nature to custom, the existence of habit is incompatible with the view that nature and custom are antithetical.

The second reason for the exclusion of habit and custom is that modern economics modeled itself on the mechanics of physical locomotion, where causal relations are independent of time. Neoclassical economics, by adopting the constrained maximization techniques of pre-entropic physics, presupposes that economic processes do not depend on time: market equilibrium is independent of any historical path and all transactions are reversible.[37] Economic coordination is a function of individual preferences that are given a priori and are independent of prior acts of choice. Economic equilibrium in neoclassical

---

his resolute opposition to habit and custom: "Customary habit [*assuetudo*], however, is a physical and inner compulsion to proceed farther in the very same way in which we have been traveling. Acquired habit deprives good actions of their moral value because it undermines mental freedom. . . . Generally, all acquired habits are objectionable." Habit, adds Kant, places us "in the same class as the beast." See Immanuel Kant, *Anthropology from a Pragmatic Point of View* [1800], trans. Victor Dowdell (Carbondale: Southern Illinois University Press, 1978), 35. "The more habits a man allows himself to form, the less free and independent he becomes; for it is the same with man as with all other animals; whatever he has been accustomed to early in life always retains a certain attraction for him in later-life. Children, therefore, must be prevented from forming any habits, nor should habits be fostered in them" (Kant, *Education* [1803], trans. Annette Churton [Ann Arbor: University of Michigan Press, 1960], 45).

36. Geertz, *Interpretation of Culture*, p. 5.

37. "The mathematics of pre-entropic physics was the pinnacle of the development of static mechanism, where all physical phenomena are portrayed as being perfectly reversible in time, and no system exhibits hysteresis. Nineteenth-century physical laws were thought, by definition, to possess no history" (Philip Mirowski, "Mathematical Formalism and Economic Explanation," in *The Reconstruction of Economic Theory*, ed. Philip Mirowski [Boston: Kluwer-Nijhoff, 1986], 189).

theory is not the product of a dynamic process of learning and adaptation, but is imposed by the timeless efforts of a hypothetical auctioneer.[38] By focusing on the preferences of individuals, the neoclassical theory of rational action makes it impossible to distinguish customary preferences from truly individual preferences; and by treating preferences as independent of prior acts of choice, neoclassicism neglects the role of habit in the formation of preferences. The extension of the neoclassical theory of rational choice to social and political theory renders any accommodation of habit and custom impossible.

I will argue that contrary to modern social theory, habit and custom are fundamental concepts for any adequate account of social institutions. Habits form a bridge from the simplest animal behavior to the most complex human semiotics of custom. Specifically, habits have three dimensions of importance to social theory: they are the foundation of all learned behavior; they are always general rules or concepts; and they are constituted by history. The area of the most substantial achievement and consensus in the study of habit concerns the basic substrate of habit known as "habituation"—now widely regarded as the first form of learning both in the evolution of organisms and in the development of individuals.[39] If a moderate stimulus to which an organism initially responds is repeated, the organism gradually ceases to respond. In other words, when an organism becomes habituated (or "accustomed") to its environment, it gradually ceases to respond to its environment. "It is perhaps the simplest form of learning—learning not to respond."[40] According to ethologist John Bonner, habituation is the first form of learning to have evolved: the ability of even the simplest organisms to learn to ignore mild disturbances through habituation, while avoiding those that are potentially dan-

---

38. Randall Bausor, in his analysis of Debreu's theory of general equilibrium, says: "The process of coordinating economic activity is explicitly removed to a timeless epoch *prior* to the operation of the economy: [prior] to production, trade, and consumption. No dynamic process of learning and adaptation, of ongoing organization and planning enters this picture of economic evolution." See "Time and Equilibrium," in Mirowski, *Reconstruction of Economic Theory*, 98.

39. According to William Estes: "Investigations ranging over the entire phylogenetic scale, and often using similar or even identical stimuli, demonstrate very similar properties for habituation from one-celled organisms to man. There is, however, no reason to think that the neural basis is the same in organisms at very different levels. Rather, functional properties appear to be those demanded by requirements of adaptation" (*Handbook of Learning and Cognitive Processes*, vol. 6, ed. William Estes [New York: John Wiley, 1978], 245–46).

40. R. F. Thompson, "Neural and Behavioral Mechanisms of Habituation and Sensitization," in *Habituation*, ed. Thomas Tighe and Robert Leaton (New York: John Wiley, 1976), 49.

gerous, is adaptive behavior in the evolutionary sense.[41] The human ability to become habituated to the most stressful environments has considerable adaptive and social significance: through the physiology of habituation, our social and natural environments become invisible to us.[42] Similarly, we become habituated to our own routine activities: it is of the essence of our habits and customs that they become invisible to us—every society depends upon foreigners to describe its customs.

Although habituation begins as a response to a particular stimulus, it becomes a general response to other related stimuli. Since learning is a process of generalizing our habits of thought from one area to other related domains, habituation seems to be a form of learning. According to C. S. Peirce, all habits are general rules of response. A habit is not a particular response to a particular stimulus; the habits of even the simplest mollusks are inductive generalizations. "Induction proceeds from Case and Result to Rule; it is the formula of the formation of a habit or general conception—a process which, psychologically as well as logically, depends on the repetition of instances or sensations."[43] There is thus a significant continuity between the habits of the simplest organisms and the most sophisticated of our inductive generalizations. Indeed, a concept has often been defined as a cognitive habit.[44] Of course, most organisms are not reflectively aware of their habitual concepts;

41. See John Tyler Bonner, *The Evolution of Culture in Animals* (Princeton: Princeton University Press, 1980), 113.

42. As Thomas Jefferson observed: "All experience hath shewn, that mankind are more disposed to suffer, while evils are sufferable, than to right themselves by abolishing the forms to which they are accustomed."

43. "For every habit has, or is, a general law" (C. S. Peirce, *The Collected Papers of Charles Sanders Peirce*, ed. Charles Hartshorne and Paul Weiss [Cambridge: Harvard University Press, 1960], 2.712 and 2.148). "Habituation of response to a given stimulus exhibits stimulus generalization to other stimuli" (Thomas Tighe and Robert Leaton, "Comparisons between Habituation Research at the Developmental and Animal-Neurophysiological Levels," in *Habituation*, 331).

44. Richard Robinson defines a concept as a habit of thinking in *Definition* (Oxford: Clarendon Press, 1950), 187–88. In a handbook of psychology we find this definition: "Concept: Any perceptual or representational habit, because all [habits] are more or less abstract or generalized or conceptual" (*Learning*, vol. 3, ed. Melvin Marx [London: Macmillan, 1970], 325). Learning is the transfer of habits from one situation to others: "The principal mechanism assumed to underlie the transfer of learning to new situations is stimulus generalization. This notion is represented in the theory by the assumption that, when a habit has been acquired relating a particular stimulus to a given response, the habit strength is automatically generalized to other stimuli which are similar to the given one" (William Estes, *Learning Theory and Mental Development* [New York: Academic Press, 1970], 99).

but then most human habits of thought—beliefs, concepts, and prejudices—are not conscious either.

Finally, to understand the fundamental role of history in the constitution of habit, we must first consider the role of time in physical processes in general. Classical mechanics, for example, concerns locomotion and position: physical equilibrium is defined independent of the historical path of the particle. Within a system of locomotion, time is in principle reversible: if a falling body strikes a perfectly elastic surface, it returns to equilibrium as if time were reversed. Historical time emerges in physics only with the phenomenon of hysteresis: any causal relation that is dependent upon prior history exhibits hysteresis. The behavior of a magnet, for example, depends upon its prior uses. Yet although the behavior of a magnet depends upon its history, the magnet's behavior is not habitual because it is neither general nor plastic, but specific and rigid. Moreover, a magnet can be demagnetized and remagnetized, so its behavior, though nonreversible, is not irrevocable. The Second Law of Thermodynamics (the Entropy Law) introduces a more profound dimension of time into physical processes: "The entropic degradation of the universe as conceived by classical thermodynamics is an irrevocable process: the free energy once transformed into latent energy can never be recuperated."[45] C. S. Peirce argues that the phenomenon of habit-taking illustrates the entropy law: first, because entropic processes are irrevocable; and second, because entropic processes are indeterminate and have the requisite plasticity for habit-taking.[46] William James also emphasizes the irrevocable nature of habits: "Nothing we ever do is, in strict scientific literalness, wiped out."[47] Habits and customs are constituted by a unique historical path. To explain a custom or habit we must tell how it was formed and modified in the course of time.

Ever since Pierre-Simon Laplace, the ideal of natural science has been to predict the future from knowledge of the present alone; but the phenomenon

45. "The first category of 'nonreversibility' consists of all processes which, though not reversible, can return to any previously attained phase. . . . Processes such as these are nonreversible but not irrevocable" (Nicholas Georgescu-Roegen, *The Entropy Law and the Economic Process* [Cambridge: Harvard University Press, 1971], 197).

46. On irreversible nature of entropy (what Peirce calls "non-conservative forces") and on the plasticity of entropy, see Peirce, *Collected Papers*, 7.471 and 6.23. "The thermodynamic principles, therefore, leave some substantial freedom to the actual path and the time schedule of an entropic process" (Georgescu-Roegen, *Entropy Law and the Economic Process*, 12).

47. William James, *Principles of Psychology* [1890] (Cambridge: Harvard University Press, 1981), 131.

of hysteresis shows that even in physics, knowledge of past history is necessary in order to predict future changes. Nevertheless, Paul Samuelson has said that to acknowledge hysteresis would be to take economics out of the realm of science and place it in the realm of history. The Laplacian ideal lives on in economics. Nonetheless, Jon Elster in his discussion of Nicholas Georgescu-Roegen's *Entropy Law and the Economic Process* shows that hysteresis plays an important role in the theory of capital, the interpretation of historical materialism, and the mathematical theory of social mobility. The sociological distinction between old money and new money, for example, shows that predicting behavior depends on knowing not only the amount of money but the history of that money.[48] Similarly, James Duesenberry demonstrates that one cannot predict current spending patterns on the basis of current income alone: "Past income has an influence on current consumption and saving." Although it may seem obvious that people attempt to maintain the standard of living to which they have become accustomed, this fact was regarded as a revelation in economic theory. Consumer behavior exhibits a truly habitual hysteresis, as opposed to a reversible magnetic hysteresis, because consumption patterns are not readily reversed: "The irreversibility of income consumption relations produces a sort of 'ratchet effect.'"[49] A rising standard of living threatens one's habits much less than does a falling standard of living.

We have thus far tended to use the terms *habit* and *custom* interchangeably. Yet to grasp the centrality of custom and habit to social theory, we must be careful to distinguish social custom from individual habit. Customs are social patterns of behavior with normative import; customs are rooted in individual habit, but they reside in collectivity. Customs cannot exist apart from habits, but idiosyncratic habits can exist apart from customs. "The mores [i.e., customs] come down to us from the past. Each individual is born into them as he is born into the atmosphere, and he does not reflect on them, or criticize them any more than a baby analyzes the atmosphere before he begins to breathe it. Each one is subjected to the influence of the mores, and formed by them,

48. See Jon Elster, "A Note on Hysteresis in the Social Sciences," *Synthese* 33 (1976): 371–72.

49. "The fundamental psychological postulate underlying our argument is that it is harder for a family to reduce its expenditures from a high level than for a family to refrain from making high expenditures in the first place" (James Duesenberry, *Income, Saving and the Theory of Consumer Behavior* [Cambridge: Harvard University Press, 1952], 85 and 114).

before he is capable of reasoning about them."[50] Customs embody an indissoluble unity of empirical fact and normative value; customs demand conformity simply by being customs.[51] Two aspects of this unity can be distinguished though not separated. First, customs are binding due to the force of habit: "It is the essence of routine to insist upon its own continuation."[52] Second, even trivial customs, like wearing socks, are experienced as binding because they signify membership in a community.

Many organisms have individual habits without having any social customs. From an evolutionary point of view the question emerges: what causes habits to become customs in certain species? The answer seems to lie in the proclivity to imitative behavior: in species where habits are learned through social imitation, we see the beginnings of custom. Aristotle had observed the innate propensity to imitation among humans: "Imitation is natural to man from childhood, one of his advantages over the lower animals being this, that he is the most imitative creature in the world, and learns at first by imitation" (*Poet.* 1448b6). After several decades of behaviorist research asserting that a child's proclivity to imitate must be learned, many developmental psychologists were astounded by Andrew Meltzoff and M. Moore's demonstration that newborn infants can imitate facial expressions.[53] Psychology and human ethology are returning to the Aristotelian view that imitation, like habit formation, is a key part of our biological inheritance. Adopting an evolutionary perspective, Jerome Bruner argues that since imitation is pervasive among the higher primates, it must have evolved along with man's communication skills as an adaptation to an existence increasingly dominated by

50. W. G. Sumner, *Folkways* (Boston: Ginn and Co., 1906), 76.

51. "The notion of right is in the folkways. It is not outside of them, of independent origin, and brought to them to test them. In the folkways, whatever is, is right" (Sumner, *Folkways*, 28). As John Dewey says: "Customs in any case constitute moral standards" (*Human Nature and Conduct* [1922] [New York: Modern Library, 1957], 70).

52. Dewey, *Human Nature and Conduct*, 71.

53. For a behaviorist argument that imitation is learned, see Neal Miller and John Dollard, *Social Learning and Imitation* (New Haven: Yale University Press, 1941). For the view that imitation is caused by an "innate releasing mechanism," see Irenaus Eibl-Eibesfeldt, *Human Ethology* (New York: Aldine de Gruyter, 1989), 55–56. Andrew Meltzoff and M. Moore, however, did not conclude that imitation is innate: "In brief, we hypothesize that the imitative responses observed are not innately organized and 'released,' but are accomplished through an active matching process and mediated by an abstract representational system." See Meltzoff and Moore, "Imitation of Facial and Manual Gestures by Human Neonates," *Science* 198 (October 1977): 78.

culture.[54] Since, as we have observed, man's physiology evolved in part due to the selective advantages of his culture, imitation is of great adaptive importance in a species whose prolonged immaturity makes possible much observation of the behavior of adults. The imitative behavior of children can be seen as a type of play that facilitates the transmission of cultural skills from one generation to the next.

When one considers the human species over time and place, it is clear that little of what we know is learned by deliberate instruction compared to what we learn by observation and imitation. Indeed, even in the context of formal instruction it has long been known that students learn in part by treating their teachers as role models. Among all primates, adults teach by example and children learn by imitation—or what is aptly called "aping." Scientific study at the Japanese Monkey Center has shown how proto-customs can emerge among primates. Groups of macaques (primates related to baboons) have been isolated on small islands to study the emergence of different customs. On one island, a young female macaque began to wash the sand off sweet potatoes before eating them; in addition, she discovered how to separate wheat from sand by throwing the mixture on the water and skimming off the wheat from the surface. These discoveries quickly spread by imitation, and they are now the established customs of this island colony.[55] Unfortunately, the study of these primate customs is termed *cultural primatology*; and the vagueness of the term *culture* has led leading biologists to both affirm and deny that animals have culture. Animals do have some customs but none of the products of reflective stipulation, such as law, poetry, speculation, or religion.[56] Thus animals both do and do not possess a culture.

Customs among human and other animals are usually thought to distinguish various subgroups within a single species. If a custom is adopted by an entire species, due to its ubiquitous diffusion (either by imitation or parallel discovery), does it cease to be a custom?[57] We often assume that what is uni-

54. Jerome Bruner, "Nature and Uses of Immaturity," *American Psychologist* 27 (August 1972).

55. For these and other examples of the evolution of custom, see Bonner, *Evolution of Culture in Animals*, 166–77.

56. Robert Hinde says "we can thus speak of the possession of a 'culture' as being a uniquely human attribute." What of primate customs? "But the existence of these traditions does not imply culture in the sense in which human societies have cultures." Precision is thus impossible with such terms as "tradition" and "culture." See Hinde, *Individuals, Relationships and Culture* (Cambridge: Cambridge University Press, 1987), 3–5.

57. Danilo Mainardi asks: "Can a tradition belong to an entire species, or at the other extreme, can it be shared by only two individuals?" See "Tradition and the Social Transmission

versal is natural and what is local is customary. But human biological nature varies across the subgroups of our species, as manifest, for example, in the rate of alcohol metabolism, the frequency of lactose intolerance, and the resistance to disease, whereas human customs like cooking and marriage seem to be universal. Indeed, the growing economic and ecological interdependence of the human community means that many customs are likely to become universal—beginning, perhaps, with the love of Coca-Cola.

Customs have two dimensions that are separable in thought but not in reality—the synchronic and the diachronic. At the synchronic level, there are in turn two primary features: customs reside in collectivity, and customs are sign systems. Individuals do not have customs; individuals participate in customs.[58] Although individual habits can, if imitated, create social customs, in general social customs create individual habits because we form our habits within the context of social customs. Nonetheless, in learning customs we modify and distort them by introducing subtle variations: our linguistic habits, for example, modify our customary language and lead to the dramatic transformations of languages over time.[59] Weber rightly terms custom "a collective way of acting [*Massenhandeln*]."[60] Indeed, what Ferdinand Saussure says of language is true of all customs: "It is a fund accumulated by the members of the community through the practice of speech, a grammatical system existing potentially in every brain, or more exactly in the brains of a group of individuals; for the language is never complete in any single individual, but exists perfectly only in the collectivity."[61]

All customs are signs that convey meaning to the community. Although Weber contends that many of the customs that constitute everyday life are devoid of meaning, every custom, no matter how trivial, is a sign of membership in a community.[62] Linguistic customs—like ritual greetings—convey

---

of Behavior in Animals," in *Sociobiology: Beyond Nature/Nurture?* ed. George Barlow and James Silverberg (Boulder: Westview, 1980), 242.

58. "The mores are social ritual in which we all participate unconsciously" (Sumner, *Folkways*, 62).

59. "In this educative process customs may be thought of as preceding habits, but if this were the whole story the weight of the past would repress all innovation, all readjustment, all development" (R. M. MacIver and Charles Page, *Society* [London: Macmillan, 1950], 196).

60. Weber, *Economy and Society*, 25.

61. Ferdinand Saussure, *Course in General Linguistics* [1916], trans. Roy Harris (La Salle, Ill.: Open Court, 1986), 13.

62. "Custom ever signifies community" (Ferdinand Toennies, *Custom* [1909], trans. A. F. Bornstein [New York: Free Press, 1961], 98).

no information but function to signify inclusion in a community. Indeed, knowing the local custom is like knowing the local language: without such knowledge, we would not know how to express affection, concern, anger, or gratitude. Customs are more than mere uniformities of habit; as Claude Lévi-Strauss has shown with the customs of naming plants and animals, they are organized into complex systems of meaning.

At the diachronic level customs are fundamentally constituted by history. The structure of our institutions, our behavior, our language, cannot be explained in terms of current function. Our institutions are the sediment of thousands of years of human practices; the sheer inertia of this historical inheritance resists adaptation to current functional needs.[63] The history of customs is analogous to the evolution of species. Organisms inherit a bodily architecture that constrains the possible future paths of development. According to S. J. Gould: "In many cases, evolutionary pathways reflect inherited patterns more than current environmental demands."[64] Humans, for example, suffer chronic backaches and hernias because our spinal vertebrae are the product of a long line of four-footed ancestors: we are not well designed for walking upright. "Evolution cannot achieve engineering perfection because it must work with inherited parts available from previous histories in different contexts."[65] Compare this view of natural evolution with Lévi-Strauss's view of the historical construction of myth: he calls the patchwork of myth a "bricolage," because the "bricoleur" uses whatever he has inherited.

> His universe of instruments is closed and the rules of the game are always to make do with "whatever is at hand," that is to say with a set of tools and materials which is always finite and is also heterogeneous because what it contains bears no relation to the current project, or indeed to any particular project, but is the contingent result of all the occasions there have been to renew or enrich the stock or to maintain it with the remains of previous constructions or destructions.[66]

63. This is not to deny that customs are subject to adaptive pressures: "The folkways are, therefore, 1) subject to a strain of improvement towards better adaptation of means to ends, as long as the [prior] adaptation is so imperfect that pain is produced. They are also 2) subject to a strain of consistency with each other, because they all answer their several purposes with less friction and antagonism when they cooperate and support each other" (Sumner, *Folkways*, 5).

64. S. J. Gould, *Hen's Teeth and Horse's Toes* (New York: W. W. Norton, 1983), 156.

65. S. J. Gould, *The Flamingo's Smile* (New York: W. W. Norton, 1985), 210.

66. Claude Lévi-Strauss, *The Savage Mind* (Chicago: University of Chicago Press, 1962), 17.

Like Gould, Lévi-Strauss contrasts the customary order of history with the stipulated order of the engineer.

That the structure of social institutions cannot be explained in terms of their current functions is most evident in cases where structure and function do not correspond: this lack of correspondence can be due either to inherited architectural constraints or to the presence of vestigial elements.[67] Indeed, Edward Tylor, the founder of modern anthropology, illustrates the distant historical origin of customs by offering examples of vestigial customs, which he terms "survivals." Tylor describes these survivals as "meaningless customs."[68] But here is where the analogy between biological and customary evolution misleads us: vestigial organs can indeed lose their function and become meaningless, but customs are never meaningless. Customs that have lost their original function can easily take on a new function: thus the useless buttons on clothes become fashionable. And customs, unlike organs, are always signs of membership in a community.

Even where structure is well adapted to function, we cannot assume that the structure is the product of its function. The feathers of birds seem ideally suited to flight; but feathers evolved for warmth not for flight. The principle of "preadaptation" in biology "asserts that a structure can change its function radically without altering its form as much."[69] Is the contemporary division of labor in production the product of the quest for efficiency or were customary patterns of the division of labor preadapted to contemporary efficiency? Social institutions like the division of labor are the product of a long historical inheritance; yet from Plato to E. O. Wilson, the division of labor is explained only in terms of its current efficiency. Studies of alternative job designs cast considerable doubt on the view that the prevailing social division of labor in the factory and the office is especially efficient; but even if one were to grant that the division of labor in a modern factory is uniquely efficient, we still have not shown that it can be explained by its efficiency. Only knowledge of the particular historical path of an institution can determine whether a structure is the product of inherited patterns or current utility. Perhaps the pervasive division of labor between those who plan and those who execute reflects the traditional relations between master and servants that are preadapted to contemporary economic life.

67. "The best illustrations of adaptation by evolution are the ones that strike our intuition as peculiar or bizarre" (S. J. Gould, *Ever Since Darwin* [New York: W. W. Norton, 1977], 91).

68. See Tylor, *Origins of Culture*, 16 and 94.

69. Gould, *Ever Since Darwin*, 108.

We are now in a position to illustrate the synchronic logic of custom in the case of the social division of labor. The one universally valid rule governing the division of labor is that every human society divides labor by sex. This rule is purely formal: it does not specify how tasks are divided; it states only that tasks are in fact divided. At the synchronic level, then, we can say two things about the customary division of labor: the first is that there tends to be a binary opposition such that tasks performed by men are forbidden to women, whereas tasks performed by women are forbidden to men; the second is that male tasks—no matter what the content—will be more highly valued than female tasks. As the structuralists have rightly emphasized, what is most important about customary patterns of behavior is the opposition of meaning: what is crucial, in other words, is the hierarchical division of tasks into male tasks and female tasks; how the tasks are divided is much less important. The division of even the most mundane human activities into male and female tasks endows them with the rich symbolic connotations associated with sexual difference. The Jibaros of Ecuador, for example, attribute to every plant either male or female sex; the male plants must be cultivated by men and the female by women.[70] It would be ludicrous to suggest that such a division of labor is determined by the natural differences between the sexes; rather, these aborigines have made use of sexual difference to create a binary system of meaning. Customary patterns of the division of labor convey symbolic meaning just as do art, religion, and poetry. Anthropologists have shown that even the most allegedly natural human tasks, such as cooking, eating, drinking, and bathing, are full of symbolic and speculative meaning. We tend to regard such elemental production and consumption as natural in contrast to the "higher" cultural activities. But this is an unfounded prejudice. Custom creates systems of metaphor, analogy, and allegory in every realm of human activity, and these customary patterns of meaning are not reducible to natural causes.[71]

All attempts to account for the sexual division of labor solely on the basis of innate natural capacities have failed because they neglect the symbolic meaning of customs. Bronislaw Malinowski, for example, commenting on

70. Richard Thurnwald, *Economics in Primitive Communities* (Oxford: Oxford University Press, 1932), 65.

71. Kinship terminologies, e.g., are not based on biological relations, but on metaphors of engendering and rearing; animals are taboo not because of gastronomic, but because of symbolic analogies; rituals of purification are not based on hygiene. See Mary Douglas and Baron Isherwood, *The World of Goods* (New York: Basic Books, 1979), 60–61.

the sexual division of labor among Australian aborigines, says "heavier work ought naturally to be performed by the man, [though] the contrary obtains"; therefore, he concludes, "compulsion is the chief basis of this division of labor."[72] Malinowski contrasts here what is natural with what is compulsory; however, if men are by nature stronger than women, then it is just as natural for men to compel women to do the heavy work as it is for men to do it themselves. Whether male strength is used to dominate women or to perform heavy labor is determined, then, by custom. Natural strength cannot be the basis for the sexual division of labor because some women are stronger than some men. If natural strength were the basis for the division of labor, then we would expect to see the heaviest work performed by the strongest men and the strongest women, whereas the lightest work would be performed by the weakest women and the weakest men; yet we never see this pattern: work is divided not by strength but by sex. Phyllis Kaberry correctly notes that the sexual division of labor among the aborigines has nothing to do with the strength requirements of tasks; rather "the men go out to hunt, the women to forage."[73] The contrast between hunting and foraging is full of symbolic meaning that has little to do with physiological requirements.

To make sense of these synchronic patterns of meaning, we must employ a diachronic analysis. To explain how specific tasks are sexually divided, for example, we must know the particular historical genealogy whereby each sex becomes symbolically linked to specific tasks. In some societies pottery is made by women whereas in others it is made by men. Melville Herskovits describes how the pattern of historical inheritance can produce either form of this customary division of labor. Men who hunted or kept herds became associated with large animals, just as women who foraged became associated with plants. When beasts of burden became attached to a plow, tilling the soil could become associated either with men (due to their links to animals) or with women (due to their links with plants). Next, when these beasts were used to pull a cart, the wheel became associated with the sex linked to tilling the soil. Finally, when pottery was turned on a wheel, it became associated with the sex linked to the wheel.[74]

72. Malinowski, cited in Melville Herskovits, *Economic Anthropology* (New York: Alfred Knopf, 1952), 128.

73. Phyllis Kaberry, cited in Herskovits, *Economic Anthropology*, 128.

74. Herskovits, *Economic Anthropology*, 129–30. A similar genealogy is described by Richard Thurnwald: "We have, therefore, two branches of progress from the hunter stage. The

This genealogy nicely illustrates the historical order of custom: there is a distinct causal pattern, but no rigid determinism. One could apply a similar analysis to show why women, for example, tend to enter some professions (medicine) or even learn some languages (French) rather than others—there is usually some customary association at work. The conventions of custom may be initially arbitrary, but over time they develop associations that are far from arbitrary. As Lévi-Strauss observes, there is no necessary relation between the color red and the concept of danger; but over time, red has become associated with danger. When traffic lights were introduced, the use of red for "stop" was not arbitrary, but the product of history: "The linguistic sign is arbitrary *a priori*, but ceases to be arbitrary *a posteriori*."[75] The customary division of labor makes use of natural differences between the sexes, but the order of custom certainly cannot be explained by these natural differences.

The Stipulated Division of Labor

Customs are rooted in habit: customary thought and practice are unreflective routines. How then does thought become reflective and practice become deliberate? The pragmatists insist that obstacles to routine create the occasion for reflection: if my key will not turn the bolt, I begin to reflect on the nature of locks.[76] Peirce argues that we reflect on our customary modes of thought— our prejudices—only when an anomaly disconfirms our tacit beliefs: "Thus, surprise is very efficient in breaking up associations of ideas."[77] Just as obstacles in habitual routines generate individual reflection, so conflicts over customary practices generate social reflection. Legal stipulation is the attempt to resolve conflict that arises within the realm of custom: "Custom begins to be

---

one, roughly speaking, leads from the hunting activity of the men to pastoral life, the other, from the collecting activity of the women to the tilling of the soil. Plough cultivation, where they meet, represents the fusion of these two main branches" (*Economics in Primitive Communities*, 7).

75. Claude Lévi-Strauss, *Structural Anthropology* (New York: Basic Books, 1963), 91. Aristotle makes the same point: he defines legal justice as "that which is originally indifferent, but when it has been laid down is not indifferent" (*NE* 1134b20).

76. "Reflection," says Dewey, is the "painful effort of disturbed habits to readjust themselves" (*Human Nature and Conduct*, 71). According to Martin Heidegger, it is only when the hammer breaks that one reflects on the nature of tools: "When its unusability is thus discovered, equipment becomes conspicuous" (*Being and Time* [1927], trans. John Macquarrie and Edward Robinson [New York: Harper and Row, 1962], par. 16).

77. Peirce, *Collected Papers*, 5.478.

law when it is brought into dispute and some means is provided for declaring or recognizing its obligatory character."[78] In the same way, the conflict between capitalists and workers brought customary work routines into contention; managers stipulated ever-new divisions of labor in the attempt to reduce industrial conflict.[79]

The transition from custom to stipulation has two related features: the habitual becomes the object of reflection; and the social system of custom becomes reduced to a synoptic perspective. A stipulated order is designed by an individual author or by a collective body acting as an individual.[80] The process of reflection or deliberation is always a conversation: either the internal conversation of thought (*in foro interno*) or the external conversation of politics (*in foro externo*).[81] But the product of reflection always aspires to the synoptic perspective of an individual author. The linguist stipulates a grammar both by reflecting on the habitual use of language and by reducing the social system of language to a synoptic perspective. The grammarian, the legislator, the philosopher, the engineer—all strive to impose a synoptic unity to the social system of custom.

The view that stipulation always presupposes custom, even as it modifies custom, avoids two common misunderstandings about the relation of custom to stipulation. The first misunderstanding is the pervasive traditional claim that social institutions may be attributed simply to the stipulation of an individual. In this way, the ancient Greeks ascribed virtually all social institutions— morals, constitutions, money, even language—to individual authors. Similarly, Cartesian method illustrates the reduction of philosophical reason to individual stipulation: we first set aside all habits of thought through systematic doubt and we then construct our knowledge from a strictly synoptic perspective.[82] Against

78. C. S. Lobingier, "Customary Law," *Encyclopedia of the Social Sciences* (New York: Macmillan, 1930).

79. On the role of industrial conflict in generating new forms of the division of labor, see Richard Edwards, *Contested Terrain* (New York: Basic Books, 1979).

80. Thus we speak of the "will of the Congress"; and legislation that is the product of collective debate is usually attributed to an individual author.

81. Thus for Aristotle, political wisdom is the highest form of moral wisdom (*NE* 1141b22).

82. As Descartes says: "There is very often less perfection in works composed of several portions, and carried out by the hands of various masters, than in those on which one individual alone has worked." See "Discourse on Method," in *Philosophical Works*, vol. 1, ed. E. S. Haldane and G. R. T. Ross (Cambridge: Cambridge University Press, 1931), 87. Karl Popper, however, seeks to show "the social character of reasonableness, as opposed to intellectual gifts, or

this view, Dewey insists that reflection expresses a conflict of custom and that the duty of reflection is to reorganize custom.[83]

The second common misunderstanding arose in response to the first: ever since the importance of custom was rediscovered in the eighteenth century, many theorists have asserted that language and other social institutions are the product of custom alone, that individual stipulation plays no role at all. Friedrich Carl von Savigny, for example, argues that legal stipulation could no more modify custom than a grammarian could modify language. Saussure shares this view: "No individual is able, even if he wished, to modify in any way a choice already established in the language. Nor can the linguistic community exercise its authority to change even a single word."[84] Modern structuralists often describe the individual mind as simply the unwitting vehicle for customary sign systems: customs have reasons unknown to individuals.[85] Within this all-powerful social system of custom, the individual is "decentered" or even "dissolved." Peirce anticipates this line of thought when he observes that it is more correct to say that we are in thought than to say that thoughts are in us.[86] Neither extreme position is plausible: in the realm of custom, we are vehicles for language and ritual; but in the realm of stipulation, we turn language and ritual into vehicles for our own synoptic projects.

From an epistemological point of view, the distinction between custom and stipulation is the distinction between what Gilbert Ryle calls "knowing how" and "knowing that" or "learning how" and "learning that." And just as custom is logically prior to stipulation, so knowing how is prior to knowing that. We learn how to do something through imitation and habit; we learn that something is the case by an explicit set of rules. Ryle shows that knowing how is logically prior to knowing that because the rules or principles governing an activity presuppose the exhibition of those rules in practice. "Rules, like birds,

---

cleverness. Reason, like language, can be said to be a product of social life" (*The Open Society and Its Enemies*, vol. 2 [Princeton: Princeton University Press, 1966], 225).

83. Dewey, *Human Nature and Conduct*, 73. According to Peirce, philosophy arises out of custom: "We cannot begin with complete doubt. We must begin with all the prejudices which we actually have when we enter upon the study of philosophy" (*Collected Papers*, 5.264).

84. Saussure, *Course in General Linguistics*, 71. Saussure is wrong on both counts: languages have been profoundly altered both by individual authors (like Chaucer, Dante, and Luther) and by public authorities (like the French and Prussian Academies).

85. See Lévi-Strauss, *Savage Mind*, 252.

86. Peirce, *Collected Papers*, 5.289n.

must live before they can be stuffed." Knowing how to do something exhibits the implicit knowledge of its principles, canons, and rules; but knowing the rules and principles certainly does not imply knowing how to do something. Only by knowing how to cook can one write a cookbook, just as only by knowing how to conduct experiments can one formulate hypotheses. The stipulation of rules, principles, and canons does not generate habitual practices; rather, habitual practices generate stipulated knowledge. What, then, is the use of stipulated rules and principles if they are not required for knowing how to do something? Ryle suggests that stipulated rules, though not necessary, may help the novice acquire the proper habits of action; too much attention to the rules of knowing that, however, actually becomes an impediment to knowing how—reflection interferes with the smooth operation of habit.[87]

Any theory of education must find the appropriate mix of customary learning and stipulated knowing. Although rationalist educators believe that we should cultivate reflective awareness of our activities, Alfred North Whitehead insists that it is much more efficient to operate from unthinking habit. "Civilization advances by extending the number of operations which we can perform without thinking about them." In this view, education consists of reducing deliberate operations to habitual ones. Aristotle, however, insists that reflective stipulation plays a crucial role in learning how to adjust, subdue, and redirect our habits; in the words of Peter Medawar: "Civilization also advances by bringing instinctive [i.e., habitual] activities within the domain of rational thought, by making them reasonable, proper and co-operative." Learning, says Medawar, is thus a twofold process: we learn to make deliberate thought habitual and we learn to make our habitual operations the subject of deliberate thought.[88]

The logic of stipulation is especially evident in the case of law. Law is the deliberate stipulation of an individual or of a legislature acting as an individual; as such, law stands in sharp contrast to the habitual and collective order of custom. Yet one often hears of "customary law." This expression usually refers to law stipulated by a judge, as opposed to law stipulated by the sover-

87. "In short the propositional acknowledgement of rules, reasons, or principles is not the parent of the intelligent application of them; it is a step-child of that application" (Gilbert Ryle, "Knowing How and Knowing That," *Proceedings of the Aristotelian Society* 46 [1945–46]: 9).

88. See Peter B. Medawar, "Does Ethology Throw Any Light on Human Behaviour?" in *Growing Points in Ethology*, ed. P. P. G. Bateson and R. A. Hinde (Cambridge: Cambridge University Press, 1976), pp. 500-1.

eign. The metaphor "customary law" implies an analogy between legal norms and customary norms that serves only to blur the distinction between the two. Legal officials stipulate laws in order to reinforce, reform, alter, or abolish customary norms; in every case, law presupposes custom. Legal stipulation has a double relation to custom: first, substantive law resolves conflicts that arise in the customs and practices of nonlegal institutions; second, procedural law resolves conflicts that arise in the customs of specifically legal institutions.[89]

Aristotle described custom both as "second nature" and as "unwritten law." We find the same metaphorical assimilation of custom to nature and to stipulation in the doctrines of natural law theorists and positivist legal theorists. The legal positivists Jeremy Bentham and John Austin, for example, argue that all social norms, including customs, are in principle sovereign commands: "For this purpose they invoked the idea of a 'tacit,' or 'indirect,' command resting on the principle that whatever the sovereign permits he commands."[90] This effort to incorporate custom into the realm of stipulation effaces all that is distinctive of custom. By contrast, advocates of natural law subsume custom into the order of nature. Natural law has long been invoked to account for the phenomenon of norms outside of stipulated law. These norms include the standards for judging the justice of positive law, the rules that govern behavior where there is no law (law between nations), and the reasons why people obey the law even when sanctions are improbable. The existence of such norms is undeniable; but why should we call them "natural"? *Custom* is a much more accurate description of the origin and character of such norms. Indeed, natural law (*ius naturale*) in Roman jurisprudence is derived from the law of nations (*ius gentium*); the law of nations was simply the codification of the customs of the various Italian tribes and other non-Roman peoples. The metaphor "natural law" implied an analogy between the universality of nature and the universality of certain customary norms—so what was common to the various Italian and foreign customs became defined as natural law.

The historical derivation of the *ius naturale* from the *ius gentium* reflects a deep confusion about the origin and character of social norms that are not explicitly stipulated. As Francisco Suárez points out, that a set of customs is universal does not make them natural—they could be diffused by imitation.

89. See Paul Bohannan, "The Differing Realms of the Law," in *The Ethnography of Law*, ed. Laura Nader (*American Anthropologist* 67, 1965).

90. H. L. A. Hart, "Legal Positivism," *Encyclopedia of Philosophy* (New York: Macmillan, 1967).

Here Aristotle's progressive hierarchy serves to sort out the competing claims made for natural law, customary law, and positive law. I suggest that we distinguish law as a species of social order from jurisprudence as the explanation of law. Thus law is essentially stipulated, but the jurisprudential explanation of law requires us to make use of our nature, custom, and stipulation trichotomy. Law, like any form of stipulation, presupposes natural order and customary order; but nature and custom cannot stipulate law—only a rational will can stipulate law. There is no such thing, in short, as a natural or a customary law; rather, nature and custom are categories belonging to the jurisprudential explanation of law.[91]

How, then, does the customary division of labor become the object of reflection? Adam Smith tells us that he discovered the importance of the division of labor in society by studying the division of labor within a firm.[92] Indeed, the capitalist factory led not just Smith but a host of managers and workers to reflect on the division of labor. The earliest factories were simply agglomerations of traditional crafts organized by a customary division of labor.[93] Gradually, managers began to break up customary modes of production and then reconstitute them on a new basis. At first managers assumed control over the acquisition of raw materials and the marketing of the product; then they assumed control over the productive process itself and stipulated both the technical and the social division of labor. Marx was the first economist to thematize the role of deliberate stipulation in the design of the division of labor within a factory. According to him, the assignment of workers to tasks in manufacturing follows "a fixed mathematical relation" that "has been experimentally established."[94] There is no doubt that the industrial conflict between owners and workers is a fundamental reason why customary modes of production became the object of deliberate stipulation: as we saw in chapter 1, managers found that highly detailed divisions of labor reduced the autonomy and power of workers.

The stipulated social division of labor in the modern factory or office is

---

91. For a more expansive effort to make sense of the conflicting claims made for natural law, customary law, and positive law, see James Bernard Murphy, "Nature, Custom, and Stipulation in Law and Jurisprudence," *Review of Metaphysics* 43 (June 1990).

92. Smith, *Wealth of Nations*, 1:1.14.

93. See Harry Braverman, *Labor and Monopoly Capital* (New York: Monthly Review Press), 59; and Steven A. Marglin, "What Do Bosses Do?" [1974]. In *The Division of Labour*, ed. André Gorz (Brighton: Harvester Press, 1976), 28.

94. Marx, *Capital*, 1:14.3.327.

based on the principle of the separation of conception from execution: managers plan and workers execute. According to the classical political economists, including Marx, this division of labor is solely the product of a rational quest for maximum profit. There is, thus, considerable agreement that the stipulated division of labor is simply a function of rational economic calculation. Yet it is easy to show that the capitalist division of labor is not only the product of profit maximization; this division of labor also reflects various historical customs. The contrast between Marx and Burke is instructive on this point. Marx sees a radical discontinuity between the rationally stipulated relations of capitalist production and the customary relations of feudal production: "The bourgeoisie, wherever it has got the upper hand, has put an end to all feudal, patriarchal, idyllic relations. It has pitilessly torn asunder the motley feudal ties that bound men to his 'natural superiors,' and has left remaining no other nexus between man and man than naked self-interest, than callous 'cash payment.'"[95] Burke, by contrast, sees considerable continuity between the feudal relations of master and servant and the capitalist relations of employer and employee.[96] This fact helps to explain the apparent paradox that Burke simultaneously champions traditional feudal hierarchy and the capitalist market economy. Burke insists that capitalism not only needs feudal hierarchy, but that capitalism is the best way to preserve hierarchy in a changing world.[97] Burke, in short, defends legislation promoting capitalist relations of production because he believes that they embody traditional customs of class dominance and subordination.

Burke's emphasis on the role of custom in the capitalist division of labor is well justified by the historical evidence. The separation of conception from execution in the modern firm is directly derived from customs governing the relation of master and servant. The traditional master, like the modern

95. Karl Marx and Friedrich Engels, "Manifesto of the Communist Party" [1848], in *Collected Works*, vol. 6 (New York: International Publishers, 1976), 486–87.

96. "No slave was ever so beneficial to the master as a freeman that deals with him on an equal footing by convention, formed on the rules and principles of contending interests and comprised advantages" (Edmund Burke, "Thoughts and Details on Scarcity" [1795], in *The Works of Edmund Burke*, vol. 4 [Boston: Charles Little and James Brown, 1839], 262).

97. See C. B. MacPherson, *Burke* (New York: Hill and Wang, 1980), 63. J. G. A. Pocock concurs with MacPherson on this point: "Burke declared that manners [which Pocock terms *consuetudines*] must precede commerce, rather than the other way round, and that modern European society need and must not sever its roots in a chivalric and ecclesiastical past" (*Virtue, Commerce, and History* [Cambridge: Cambridge University Press, 1985], 209–10).

employer, has the right to specify not only what shall be done but how it shall be done.[98] Similarly, the capitalist employer owns the produce of labor just as did the slave employer. James Mill noted the similarity between slave production and capitalist production: "The only difference is, in the mode of purchasing [labor]."[99] Many early factories were associated with prisons, orphanages, and workhouses, so that the division of factory labor assimilated customs derived from forced labor. The principles of unity of command and of the separation of line from staff functions in the modern firm derive from military practices.[100] Marx often remarks on the analogy between the factory regime and the army; but he usually fails to mention that there is a direct causal relation.[101] The capitalist division of labor turns out to embody many feudal customs, just as any form of stipulation presupposes customary norms.

Although the factory regime has antecedents in the deployment of slaves and the deployment of soldiers, the deliberately stipulated division of labor did not become general until the rise of modern industrial firms. According to Adam Smith, the division of labor is "more easily understood" if we see the firm as a microcosm of the society. The firm generates reflection in the same way that all miniaturization generates reflection: by making relations more perspicuous to the mind. Lévi-Strauss sees the miniature as the universal type of the work of art, because it reveals the structural relations obscured by size: "In other words, the intrinsic value of a small-scale model is that it compensates for the renunciation of sensible dimensions by the acquisition of intelligible dimensions."[102] Before the factory, the production of a complex product involved the cooperative efforts of many spatially dispersed tradesmen; it was only when their disparate efforts were concentrated within a factory that the logic of the customary division of labor became apparent. Perspicuity has

98. In *Black's Law Dictionary*: 5th ed. (St. Paul: West Publishing, 1979), under "employee" we read: "'Employee' is synonymous with 'servant.'" The standard work on employer-employee law is called *The Law of Master and Servant*, by Francis Batt (New York: Pitman Publishing, 1929).

99. "He [employer of wage-labor] is equally therefore the owner of the labour, with the manufacturer who operates with slaves" (James Mill, *Elements of Political Economy* [London: Baldwin, Cradock, and Joy, 1826], 21).

100. "It was unfortunate for society at large that a large power-organization like the army, rather than the more human and cooperative craft-guild, presided over the birth of the modern forms of the machine." See Lewis Mumford, *Technics and Civilization* (New York: Harcourt Brace, 1934), 89 and 96.

101. Marx, *Capital*, 1:13.314.

102. Lévi-Strauss, *Savage Mind*, 24.

long been known as an aid to comprehension and reflection: the development of writing makes language more perspicuous and leads to reflection on the grammatical structure of language; law existed before writing, but writing clearly aided the rise of legal stipulation out of custom; and the development of perspicuous notation was crucial to the development of formal logic. The firm, as a miniature version of social production, is where stipulation shapes the customary division of labor.

Part Two

A Critique and Reconstruction of Aristotle

Figuring out just what Aristotle thinks about a given topic can be frightfully difficult. Although his treatises are not dialogues, they are often even more dialectic than a Platonic dialogue. Aristotle's dialectic involves an articulation, an interrogation, and a revision of the commonly held opinions of his day (*endoxoi andres*). As Robert Filmer said: "He disputes subtilely to and fro of many points, and judiciously of many errors, but concludes nothing himself."[1] As a guide through this labyrinth, I have distinguished Aristotle's explicit doctrines (*logica docens*) from his implicit doctrines (*logica utens*). As evidence of his explicit doctrines I consider the frequency and baldness of his more dogmatic statements and definitions; his implicit doctrines I construct from disparate comments and suggestions he makes that are at odds with, or in opposition to, his more explicit "official" views. Instead of trying to reconcile these two currents, I use his less familiar implicit views to criticize his more familiar explicit views. I emphasize the counterpoint of these two Aristotelian melodies more than their harmonic resolution.

Aristotle's explicit doctrines articulate some of the fundamental presuppositions of classical political economy. As we saw in chapter 1, our economists attempt to explain the social division of labor solely as a function of technical efficiency; it seems never to have occurred to them that this division of labor could reflect moral norms. Such a reductive explanation presupposes Aristotle's doctrine that production is governed solely by technical reason, whereas action is governed solely by moral reason. Similarly, our economists attempt to explain the customary and stipulated aspects of the division of labor in terms of nature; it seems never to have occurred to them that the existing division of labor might reflect contingent customs rather than natural necessity. This reductive explanation in turn reflects Aristotle's reductive description of

1. Robert Filmer, *Patriarcha* 2.10.

custom as "second nature" and of customary norms as "natural law." Indeed, our economists believe that the division of labor is uniquely efficient precisely because it is natural; the unity of these two reductions stems from the Aristotelian notion that nature economizes, that nature acts with optimal efficiency.

Still, if Aristotle's explicit doctrines help generate the moral conundrum of political economy, then his implicit doctrines will help us escape it. For Aristotle shows us that technical reason always presupposes moral reason; there are, in other words, techniques of action just as there is justice in production. Similarly, Aristotle offers a profound alternative to his own reductive naturalism in his treatment of nature, custom, and stipulation as a progressive hierarchy—enabling us to make sense of the role of nature in the division of labor without reducing custom to nature. I will employ Aristotle's implicit doctrines to revise his explicit doctrines and to lay the foundation for an Aristotelian critique of classical political economy.

Chapter 3

Aristotle: Moral and Technical Reason

The Theoretical, the Practical, the Productive

According to Aristotle, not just production but all complex human activities are characterized by the unity of conception and execution. There are three and only three types of such human activity (*energeia*), says Aristotle (*NE* 1178b20): contemplation (*theōria*), action (*praxis*), and production (*poiēsis*). Each of these activities is governed by a distinct form of rational excellence (*aretē*): contemplation is governed by theoretical reason (*sophia*); action is governed by moral reason (*phronēsis*); and production is governed by technical reason (*technē*).[1] Far from setting thought and activity, conception and execution, in opposition, Aristotle tells us that there are three types of thought (*dianoia*)—each defined by its relation to a specific activity: theoretical thought speculates on something, practical thought does something, and productive thought makes something.[2] Our concern here is with Aristotle's twofold claim: first, that there is a universally valid metaphysical distinction between action and production; and second, that action is governed exclusively by moral reason whereas production is governed exclusively by technical reason.

Aristotle's claim that action and production are distinct and mutually exclusive has led to a vast and inconclusive literature exploring the question of just how action and production differ. I argue, first, that Aristotle's explicit attempt to distinguish action from production can best be explained as an implicit attempt to distinguish moral reason from technical reason. Aristotle's

---

1. *NE* 1140a1ff. This scheme is a commonplace in the literature. See L. H. G. Greenwood, *Aristotle: Nicomachean Ethics Book Six* (Cambridge: Cambridge University Press, 1909), 24–25; and David Charles, *Aristotle's Philosophy of Action* (Ithaca: Cornell University Press, 1984), 66n.

2. See *Top.* 145a15; *Met.* 1025b25, 1064a16; *NE* 1139a26.

criteria for defining the realm of action fail to distinguish it from the realm of production; yet his distinction between action and production does help to define the difference between moral and technical reason. Because Aristotle so closely linked moral reason to action and technical reason to production, it seems likely that his distinction between action and production will have considerable bearing on the distinction between moral and technical reason.[3] Second, I argue that contrary to Aristotle and most of his commentators, moral reason is not limited to action and technical reason is not limited to production. I will attempt to show that any human practice—whether in the realm of action or production—has both a moral and a technical dimension. Finally, I will suggest that the distinction between production and action is understood best as the historically contingent and evolving distinction between the economic and noneconomic realms of social life. From Aristotle to Hannah Arendt, however, we find a vast literature devoted to elucidating the allegedly universal metaphysical distinction between production and action.[4]

The Distinction between Action and Production

Aristotle's distinction between action and production in *Nicomachean Ethics* (1140a1–b30) involves three claims that are rarely distinguished. The first is that action and production correspond to different forms of teleology: that is, the means-end relation in action is different from the means-end relation in production. The second claim is that action and production form distinct and mutually exclusive classes of events. The third claim is that action is governed exclusively by moral reason whereas production is governed exclusively by technical reason. Each of these claims generates a host of conceptual and exegetical tangles.

Aristotle often says that every action is directed toward some end; just as the archer aims for the target, so our actions aim at the good (*NE* 1094a1, 23). But there are different kinds of ends: "For while making has an end other than itself, action cannot; for good action itself is its end" (1140b6). At first glance,

---

3. Yet the vast literature on the action-production distinction almost never refers to the concomitant *phronēsis-technē* distinction. As a survey of, and contribution to, this literature, see David Charles, "Aristotle: Ontology and Moral Reasoning," *Oxford Studies in Ancient Philosophy* 4 (1986).

4. Arendt's *The Human Condition* (Chicago: University of Chicago Press, 1958) is chiefly devoted to this distinction.

Aristotle seems to be saying that although all human conduct is teleological, the relation of means to end differs in action and in production. However, Aristotle's repeated insistence that good actions (*eupraxia*) are chosen "for their own sake" (*di' autas*) suggests that action is not teleological at all, that the archer does not aim for the target but simply enjoys archery. These passages have long posed a challenge to commentators.[5] How can actions both be directed toward ends and be ends in themselves? If actions are directed toward ends, how do they differ from productions directed toward ends? If actions can be ends in themselves, why cannot productions be ends in themselves? Many of Aristotle's contemporary commentators see "incoherences" and "contra-dictions" in these passages, leading to an interpretive impasse.[6]

Our Thomist commentators, as we shall see, argue that action and produc-tion correspond to two distinct notions of teleology: in the first, the end is immanent in the means; in the second, the end is transitive to (or apart from) the means. L. H. G. Greenwood translates this piece of Scholasticism into the distinction between a component means and an external means. This is a use-ful distinction, but it serves to distinguish moral from technical reason better than it serves to distinguish action from production. I follow the Thomist commentators by arguing that an explication and reconstruction of Aristotle's views on action and production should retain Aristotle's teleological frame-work of means and ends. Some recent commentators, however, suggest that in the case of moral action, Aristotle rejects an ends-means scheme in favor of the rule-case scheme of the practical syllogism.[7]

5. For the view that all actions are directed to some end, see *NE* 1094a15, 1112b32; *Pol.* 1331b26, 1333a10; *Met.* 996a26. For the view that good actions are their own ends, see *NE* 1176b5, 1105a32. For the view that production is directed to an end, see *MM* 1197a5 and *Phys.* 199a17.

6. See, e.g., René Gauthier and Jean Jolif, *L'Ethique à Nicomaque*, vol. 2 (Louvain: Publi-cations Universitaires, 1970), 203–4; J. L. Ackrill, "Aristotle on Action," in *Essays on Aris-totle's Ethics*, ed. Amelie Rorty (Berkeley: University of California Press, 1980), 100; T. H. Irwin, ed., *Nicomachean Ethics* (Indianapolis: Hackett, 1985), 342; W. D. Ross, *Aristotle* (Lon-don: Methuen, 1971), 188; Martha C. Nussbaum, *The Fragility of Goodness* (Cambridge: Cam-bridge University Press, 1986), 444n.

7. See D. J. Allan, "The Practical Syllogism," in *Autour d'Aristote* (Louvain: University of Louvain, 1955), 338; and Takatsura Ando, *Aristotle's Theory of Practical Cognition* (The Hague: Martinus Nijhoff, 1971), 243. I have distinguished *phronēsis* from *technē* within an ends-means scheme because Aristotle distinguishes *praxis* from *poiēsis* within an ends-means scheme. "It is also remarkable that in making the *praxis-poiēsis* distinction Aristotle does not after all break the teleological conceptual framework. He does not say, as we might perhaps expect him to do, that certain types of activities do not have a definite end which they strive to

Aristotle's second claim, that action and production are mutually exclusive classes of events, is a bold innovation. "Nor are they included one in the other; for neither is acting making nor is making acting" (*NE* 1140a5). Plato, following ordinary Greek usage, often uses terms for "activity" that can refer to either action or production, such as *prattein, ergon*, and *poiein*.[8] According to Jaakko Hintikka: "There were several verbs for doing and making in the Greek language, but none of them was entirely free from the ambiguity between making and doing."[9] Despite Aristotle's insistence on the distinction between action and production, he often adopts the same ambiguous terms as did Plato.

The claim that action and production form distinct genera leads to some real conceptual puzzles. Does Aristotle claim that action and production are separable in reality or only in thought?[10] In other words, are actions and productions separate and mutually exclusive events, or can the same event be described alternatively as an action and as a production? J. L. Ackrill insists that for Aristotle, actions and productions are not mutually exclusive and differ only by definition: "Commentators discussing this distinction often fail to face the real difficulty, that actions often or always *are* productions and productions often or always *are* actions." Since many of our moral actions take the form of productions—to repay a debt, for example, I mend a neighbor's fence—Ackrill argues that it is absurd to suppose that we can divide activity into distinct actions and productions. David Charles, however, takes issue with Ackrill: "Aristotle, it appears, held that *praxeis* and productions are distinct and exclusive sets of occurrence."[11]

I follow Charles's view that Aristotle holds actions and productions to be mutually exclusive—but for reasons different from his. First, I suggest that we remember that action and production form a trichotomy with contempla-

---

bring about. For a Greek, every rational activity *must* have a *telos*" (Jaakko Hintikka, "Remarks on *Praxis, Poiēsis*, and *Ergon* in Plato and Aristotle," *Annales Universitatis Turkuensis Sarja - Series B* [Osa-Tom, 1973], 54).

8. Plato plays on the ambiguity of these terms in *Charmides* 163A.

9. As examples, Hintikka mentions *poieō, prattō*, and *ergazomai*. See his "Remarks on *Praxis, Poiēsis*, and *Ergon* in Plato and Aristotle," 59.

10. As Aristotle puts it in another context: "Whether these are separated as the parts of the body or of anything divisible are, or are distinct by definition but by nature inseparable, like convex and concave in the circumference of a circle" (*NE* 1102a27).

11. Ackrill, "Aristotle on Action," 94; Charles, "Aristotle: Ontology and Moral Reasoning," 119.

tion: Aristotle says that if we take away action and production from life, all that is left is contemplation (*NE* 1178b20). This arithmetic language of subtraction makes sense if action, production, and contemplation are mutually exclusive classes of activities. Moreover, Ackrill's commonsense intuition that actions often take the form of productions founders on Aristotle's trichotomy: are we to suppose that contemplation often takes the form of production, or that actions often are contemplations? Second, action and production must be mutually exclusive because Aristotle insists that the instruments (*organa*) used in action are different in kind from the instruments used in production (*Pol.* 1254a6). A loom, says Aristotle, is an instrument of production, whereas a slave is an instrument of action. If, therefore, actions and productions make use of separate and distinct instruments, then one could not describe the same event as both an action and a production.

The way in which Aristotle defines the difference between action and production has profound and disturbing implications for the dignity of work. Actions, he says, are done for their own sake, whereas productions are done for an external end. If actions and productions are mutually exclusive, then Aristotle is saying that all activities must be pursued either for their intrinsic good or for an external good—but never for both. "Where there are ends apart from the actions, it is the nature of the products to be better than the activities" (*NE* 1094a5).[12] In other words, in production the product is inherently more worthwhile than the process, so there is no point in looking for happiness in the dignity of work. Happiness, says Aristotle, is to be found in action, for action is sought for its own sake; happiness is not to be found in activities directed at a product (1176b1). By Aristotle's account, if a worker enjoys producing then he is no longer engaged in production but in action. If production is wholly concerned with the product and has no bearing on the happiness of the producer, then we can see why Aristotle excluded moral reason from the realm of production.

In the transition from Kant to Hegel, we see a dramatically new evaluation of the moral psychology of work. As we saw in chapter 1, Kant follows Aristotle by arguing that work has a merely instrumental and not an intrinsic value; this helps to explain why Kant removes production from the realm of

12. As W. F. R. Hardie rightly objects: "But an activity which aims at producing a result may be an object either of aversion or of indifference or of a positive desire which may be less or greater than the desire for its product" (Hardie, "The Final Good in Aristotle's Ethics," in *Aristotle*, ed. J. M. E. Moravcsik [Notre Dame: University of Notre Dame Press, 1968], 309).

moral reason. Hegel, by contrast, fuses Aristotle's concepts of action and production by insisting that labor transforms the moral personality of the laborer: "By making something, the agent makes himself. Hegel writes, *'Die Arbeit bildet.'*"[13] Marx extends Hegel's fusion of action and production by using both terms interchangeably to describe a multiplicity of human activities from simple labor to revolutionary politics—wherever human activity transforms the world as it transforms the agent.[14]

Aristotle's third claim, that *technē* is limited to *poiēsis* just as *phronēsis* is limited to *praxis*, breaks sharply with Plato's use of these terms. "Wisdom [*phronēsis*], then, is concerned with doing [*praxis*] and things done [*prakta*], but art [*technē*] with making [*poiēsis*] and things made [*poiēta*]; for it is in things made rather than in things done that artistic contrivance [*technazein*] is displayed" (*MM* 1197a12; see *NE* 1140a15). By contrast, Plato uses *phronēsis* to refer to the intellectual wisdom guiding both action and production and *technē* to refer to the exercise of skill in both action and production.[15] Since the *phronēsis-technē* distinction is almost never discussed by commentators in conjunction with the *praxis-poiēsis* distinction, Aristotle's remarkable claim that *technē* is confined to production and *phronēsis* to action has been all but overlooked.[16] Yet is it really plausible that there is no moral dimension to production or that there are no techniques of action?

This counterintuitive claim has profound implications for Aristotle's understanding of the nature of politics and economics. Since politics is a form of action governed exclusively by moral reason, political action must be pursued

13. According to Kant: "In work the occupation is not pleasant in itself, but it is undertaken for the sake of the end in view" (*Education* [1803], trans. Annette Churton [Ann Arbor: University of Michigan Press, 1960], 68). For Hegel, see Guy Planty-Bonjour, "Hegel's Concept of Action as Unity of *Poiēsis* and *Praxis*," in *Hegel's Philosophy of Action*, ed. Lawrence Stepelevich and David Lamb (Atlantic Highlands, N.J.: Humanities Press, 1983), 22.

14. As Nicholas Lobkowicz says of Marx: "There is nowhere in his writings anything resembling a definition of *praxis*; in fact, considering how central this notion is to his thought, one time and again is astonished to see how relatively seldom Marx uses it." See *Theory and Practice* (Notre Dame: University of Notre Dame Press, 1967), 419.

15. Plato's broad use of *phronēsis* and *technē* reflected popular Greek usage. Aristotle observed, for example, that lawmakers were often popularly compared to craftsmen (*NE* 1141b28); indeed, Aristotle himself even occasionally describes statesmen as craftsmen (*NE* 1152b1, *Pol.* 1325b40).

16. E. M. Cope, however, rightly observes that if *technē* is restricted to *poiēsis*, then rhetoric must be a branch of production. Since Cope takes it to be obvious that rhetoric is a form of moral action, he denies that Aristotle is the author of the passages restricting technique to production! See *An Introduction to Aristotle's Rhetoric* (London: Macmillan, 1867), 16n and 18n.

for its own sake: instrumental or strategic action is banished from politics. Thus Aristotle tells us that what makes Pericles a great statesman is his knowledge of what is good—not his political skill (*NE* 1140b7). Although it is customary to describe a statesman as skilled in politics, for Aristotle this would be a contradiction in terms: politics is governed by moral not technical reason.[17] Politics makes use of the strategic and rhetorical arts but there is no political skill or art. Similarly, Aristotle says (*Pol.* 1253b1ff.) that economics (*oikonomia*) as a branch of moral reason is the science of managing the persons who compose the household; but economics as a branch of technique is the art of acquiring property (*chrēmatistikē*). As with politics, Aristotle must concede that economics makes use of various productive skills. The productive arts are a means to action.[18] Instead of simply saying that politics has both a moral and a technical aspect, Aristotle is forced to say that political action makes use of rhetorical production. And instead of simply saying that economics has a moral and technical aspect, Aristotle is forced to say that household action makes use of wealth production. As a way out of these conceptual tangles, I suggest that we interpret Aristotle's subordination of production to action as the subordination of technical to moral reason.

The Distinction between Process and Activity

Virtually every commentator uses the distinction between process (*kinēsis*) and activity (*energeia*) to explain the distinction between production and action. I will suggest, however, that the distinction between *kinēsis* and *energeia* throws more light on the distinction between *technē* and *phronēsis* than it does on the distinction between *poiēsis* and *praxis*.

The distinction between *kinēsis* and *energeia* can only be understood as subsequent to the distinction between potentiality and actuality. Aristotle refers to a person's aptitude or capacity as his "potential" (*dynamis*) and to the exercise of that potential in thought, action, and production as "actuality" or "activity" (*energeia*). Unfortunately, Aristotle uses the term *energeia* to mean

17. In this case, Aristotle could be misled by ordinary Greek usage. Since an artisan is a *technitēs* and a statesman is a *phronimos*, it makes sense to link *technē* with production and *phronēsis* with action.

18. "While *praxis* or doing is really different from *poiēsis* or making, there is [Aristotle holds] a certain relation between them—*poiēsis* is essentially a means to *praxis*" (Greenwood, *Aristotle*, 41).

both generic activity and a specific kind of activity. When opposed to mere potential (*dynamis*), then, *energeia* refers to the whole range of activities in thought, action, and production. When opposed to process (*kinēsis*), however, *energeia* refers only to the psychological activities of thought, happiness, and perception. In this specific sense, Aristotle distinguishes a process (*kinēsis*) that is directed to a goal but is incomplete (*ateles*) until it reaches its goal from an activity (*energeia*) that is its own goal and is complete (*teleios* or *entelecheia*).[19] A process, like dieting, ceases once it reaches its goal, whereas an activity, like seeing or thinking, embodies its goal and does not have a natural limit (*Met.* 1048b18).

Of these things, then, we must call the one set processes [*kinēseis*], and the other activities [*energeias*]. For every process is incomplete [*ateles*]—making thin, learning, walking, building; these are processes and incomplete processes. For it is not true that at the same time we are walking and have walked, or are building and have built, or are coming to be and have come to be—it is a different thing that is being moved and that has been moved, and that is moving and that has moved. But it is the same thing that at the same time has seen and is seeing, or is thinking and has thought. The latter sort of thing, then, I call an activity [*energeia*], and the former a process [*kinēsis*].[20]

It is thus understandable why the distinction between *kinēsis* and *energeia* is almost always used to explain the distinction between *poiēsis* and *praxis*.[21] After all, Aristotle says that action is its own end (*entelecheia*), whereas production is directed to a separate end and is incomplete (*ateles*). Aristotle even

19. On *dynamis* and *energeia*, see *Met.* 1017b1 and 1050a30; on *kinēsis* and *energeia*, see *Met.* 1048b18ff. Aristotle was the first philosopher to use *energeia* as a technical term: he tells us that it is derived from *ergon* (*Met.* 1050a22) and means "being at work" (*en-ergeia*). Aristotle seems to have coined *entelecheia* as a synonym for *energeia* (*Met.* 1047a30), since an activity, in contrast to a process, includes its end (*telos*).

20. *Met.* 1048b28. I have altered the Revised Oxford Translation to render *kinēsis* as process and *energeia* as activity.

21. For the view that these two sets of distinctions are the same, see Joseph Owens, *The Doctrine of Being in the Aristotelian Metaphysics* (Toronto: Pontifical Institute, 1978), 405; Gauthier and Jolif, *L'Ethique à Nicomaque*, vol. 2, 459; René Gauthier, *La morale d'Aristote* (Paris: Presses Universitaires de France, 1958), 33; H. H. Joachim, *The Nicomachean Ethics* (Oxford: Clarendon Press, 1951), 205. J. L. Ackrill says that the two sets of distinctions are "closely related." See "Aristotle's Distinction between *Energeia* and *Kinēsis*," in *New Essays on Plato and Aristotle*, ed. Renford Bambrough (London: Routledge and Kegan Paul, 1965), 121.

uses the term *praxis* to illustrate *energeia*; and he uses the term *poiēsis* to illustrate *kinēsis*. Still, there are good reasons to question whether these two sets of distinctions truly correspond.[22]

Perhaps the chief reason for the view that *praxis* and *energeia* coincide is the equivocity of the term *act*. The word, like the Latin *actus*, can refer both to the realization of a potency, such as an "act of thought," or to an instance of moral conduct, such as a good "act." Although both *energeia* and *praxis* are rendered in Latin as *actus*, Thomas Aquinas carefully distinguishes the two senses of *act*. Indeed, Aquinas sees a relation between the two senses: we perform good moral acts, he says, insofar as we realize our potentiality in actuality; moral excellence, in short, is self-realization. Thus God, who is pure act, is perfectly good.[23] Although Aristotle uses *energeia* chiefly to refer to an act of mind and *praxis* chiefly to refer to moral conduct, he does not distinguish *energeia* from *praxis* as clearly as Aquinas distinguishes the two senses of *act*. For example, Aristotle sometimes uses the term *praxis* to refer to an act of mind. How could he confuse moral conduct (*praxis*) with the actuality of mind (*energeia*)? I suspect it is because the term *energeia* is derived from the term *ergon*, and *ergon* can refer both to moral conduct and to the function of mind.[24] If *praxis* and *ergon* are interchangeable in some contexts, so might be *praxis* and *energeia*.

By using the terms *praxis* and *praktikos* to refer to psychological activity rather than to moral conduct, Aristotle confuses *praxis* and *energeia*: "Not that a life of action must necessarily have relation to others, as some persons think, nor are those ideas only to be regarded as practical which are pursued for the sake of practical results, but much more the thoughts and contemplations which are independent and complete in themselves" (*Pol.* 1325b15). Aristotle, who elsewhere so carefully distinguishes *praxis* from *theōria*, asserts

22. On *praxis* and *energeia*, see *Met.* 1048b21; *NE* 1098b15, 1099a2, 1176b7. On *poiēsis* and *kinēsis*, see *Met.* 1074a19; similarly, a *technē* is never an *energeia* (*NE* 1153a25). However, although Aristotle in some places calls *praxis* an *energeia* (*NE* 1098a13; *Pol.* 1325a32; *MM* 1197a10), in other places he calls *praxis* a *kinēsis* (*Met.* 996a27, 1048b18; *Eud.* 1220b27). Indeed, Charles writes: "In the *Physics*, the account of processes [*kinēseis*] is applied explicitly to actions: teaching, learning, walking, building, doctoring, jumping." See *Aristotle's Philosophy of Action*, p. 63.

23. Aquinas, *Summa Contra Gentiles*, trans. Anton Pegis (Notre Dame: University of Notre Dame Press, 1975), 1:16, 28, 36–37. In the *Summa Theologiae* (1–2, Q. 1, art. 1), Aquinas distinguishes the *actus humanus* as moral action from the *actus hominis* as nonmoral activity.

24. See F. E. Peters, *Greek Philosophical Terms* (New York: New York University Press, 1967), 61.

here that nothing is more practical than theory. What he means to say is that *theōria* is the supreme form of actuality (*energeia*), not the supreme form of action (*praxis*).

This use of the term p*raxis* to refer to *energeia* has led commentators to assume that moral conduct is *energeia* and that production is *kinēsis*. Yet where Aristotle develops the *energeia-kinēsis* distinction, he illustrates *energeia* exclusively by psychological examples: seeing, thinking, being happy (*NE* 1174a14, b8); and he illustrates *kinēsis* with examples from the realms of both action and production: dieting, learning, walking, and building.[25] If this is not, then, the distinction between action and production, what is being distinguished?[26] Yves Simon understands Aristotle to be drawing a distinction between those activities that exist by way of change from those activities that exist by way of rest. Manual work, he says, exists by way of change: the worker changes the material until the object is produced and then stops; reasoning also exists by way of change: we reason until we solve the problem and then stop. But some psychological operations also exist by way of rest, such as contemplation, joy, and love. These activities have no intrinsic terminus.[27] There is, then, some agreement that *energeia* refers primarily to certain psychological operations.

What this means is that we should not confuse an act of mind with a moral act. "To see or to contemplate is not to produce. Should it be said that it is to act?" John Poinsot rightly insists here on the distinction between the two senses of *act*: "Immanent action [for example, seeing or contemplating] does

25. This fact has led some commentators to describe action as a subset of *energeia* and production as a subset of *kinēsis*: see Ando, *Aristotle's Theory of Practical Cognition*, 149; Roger Sullivan, *Morality and the Good Life* (Memphis: Memphis State University Press, 1977), 60n; Charles, "Aristotle: Ontology and Moral Reasoning," 129n. Anthony Kenny takes *praxis* to be a subset of *energeia*, but takes *poiēsis* to be equivalent to *kinēsis*; Kenny's examples of such productive *kinēseis*, however, include "discover, learn, convince." Are these really productions? See Kenny, *Action, Emotion, and Will* (London: Routledge and Kegan Paul, 1963), 173n.

26. Ackrill points out that any activity can be described in such a way as to make it either a *kinēsis* or an *energeia*; still, Ackrill illustrates the *kinēsis* by production and the *energeia* by thought. See "Aristotle's Distinction between *Energeia* and *Kinēsis*," 122 and 132. W. F. R. Hardie goes further and denies that this is the distinction between action and production: "The distinction which he indicates is rather between activities, including productive activities, which have a definite terminus, the completion of a task, and activities which have not such definite or defined terminus, e.g. taking country walks, listening to music, or thinking philosophically" (*Aristotle's Ethical Theory* [Oxford: Oxford University Press, 1980], 309).

27. Yves Simon, *Work, Society, and Culture* (New York: Fordham University Press, 1971), 6–7.

not belong to the category of action directly."[28] Moral action properly understood is intentional or teleological in orientation: it is an activity of change, like reasoning or making, and not an activity of rest, like contemplation or joy. Love is an action when one seeks the beloved and when one expresses love; love is a state of rest, not an action, when one is simply in love. So when Aristotle says that a good action is its own end, he is referring to action in the sense of an act of mind; and when he says that action is directed to an end, he is referring to action in the sense of moral conduct.[29] Indeed, Aristotle even acknowledges in one place that contemplation is the only activity pursued for its own sake, whereas in moral action (*praxis*) there is always a separate goal (*NE* 1177b1).[30]

The distinction between *energeia* and *kinēsis*, then, has little bearing on the distinction between action and production; yet it does have some bearing on the distinction between *phronēsis* and *technē*. Moral reason concerns the general character of human activity in which means and ends are inseparable: in this sense, every means is an end since every means causally shapes its end. Technical reason concerns the particular realm of human activity in which means and ends are provisionally separated to allow for strategic and instrumental calculation: in this sense, means are directed to a separate end. Aristotle's *energeia* is an activity with an immanent end; like *phronēsis*, it is *entelecheia*. Aristotle's *kinēsis* is an activity directed toward a transitive end; like *technē*, it is *ateles*. Just as *energeia* is the general term for activity, of which *kinēsis* is a special case, so *phronēsis* is the general wisdom governing human activity, of which *technē* is a special case. For ultimately, ends and means cannot be separated; but the provisional separation of ends and means has made possible the

---

28. "*Hanc conclusionem saepe docuimus . . . quod 'actio immanens non est directe in praedicamento actionis'*" (John Poinsot [John of St. Thomas], *Cursus Philosophicus Thomisticus* [1632], ed. Beatus Reiser [Turin: Marietti, 1930], 3:346b14); also cited in Yves Simon, "An Essay on the Classification of Action and the Understanding of Act," *Revue de l'Université d'Ottawa* 41 (October 1971): 524. Thus Ando: "It would be a hasty conclusion to make seeing and thinking practice [*praxis*] because of their being called actuality [*energeia*]" (*Aristotle's Theory of Practical Cognition*, 148).

29. Aristotle's commentators have often assumed that Aristotle gives two contradictory accounts of moral conduct. See Gauthier and Jolif, *L'Ethique à Nicomaque*, 2:203–4; Ackrill, "Aristotle on Action," 100.

30. "So if among excellent actions political and military actions are distinguished by nobility and greatness, and these are unleisurely and aim at an end and are not desirable for their own sake, but the activity of intellect, which is contemplative, seems both to be superior in worth and to aim at no end beyond itself" (*NE* 1177b15).

comparison of alternative means in the development of techniques in human action and production.

The Distinction between the Immanent and the Transitive

Within the Thomist tradition, Aristotle's distinction between action and production is understood to correspond to two distinct forms of teleology: in the first, the end is immanent; in the second, the end is transitive. Within this same tradition, however, there are two very different views of this distinction. Thomas Aquinas distinguishes the immanent from the transitive with respect to the agent; John Poinsot distinguishes the immanent from the transitive with respect to the activity itself. Most contemporary accounts of the distinction between action and production follow either Thomas Aquinas or John Poinsot—typically without acknowledgment.

Aquinas's understanding of the distinction between the immanent and the transitive is based on Aristotle's distinction between those activities that remain in the agent and those activities that alter an external object. "Where, then, the result is something apart from the exercise, the actuality is in the thing that is being made, e.g. the act of building is in the thing that is being built . . . but when there is no product apart from the actuality, the actuality is in the agents, e.g. the act of seeing is in the seeing subject" (*Met.* 1050a30). Aquinas interprets this passage to mean that action is immanent to the agent, whereas production is transitive to the agent: "Producing [*facere*] and doing [*agere*] differ, as stated in the *Metaphysics*, in that producing is an action passing into external matter, thus to build, to saw, and the like; whereas doing is an activity abiding in an agent, thus to see, to will, and the like."[31] Although Aristotle at *Metaphysics* 1050a30 is discussing his distinction between *energeia* and *kinēsis*, Aquinas reads this passage as drawing a distinction between action and production. This interpretation of action as immanent to the agent and production as transitive remains central to the Aristotelian literature.[32]

31. *Summa Theologiae*, 1–2, Q. 57, art. 4. In his formal commentary on this passage by Aristotle, Aquinas introduces the distinction between the immanent and the transitive: "*Nam actio manens in ipso agente operatio dicitur, ut videre, intelligere, et velle. Sed factio est operatio transiens in exteriorem materiam ad aliquod formandum ex ea, sicut aedificare et secare*" (*In Decem Libros Ethicorum Aristotelis Ad Nicomachum Expositio*, ed. Angeli Pirotta [Turin: Marietti, 1934], 383).

32. See Gauthier and Jolif, *L'Ethique à Nicomaque*, 2:5; Jules Tricot, ed., *Aristote: Ethique à Nicomaque* (Paris: J. Vrin, 1983), 31n; Joseph Owens, *Aristotle: The Collected Papers of*

Aquinas's interpretation of the immanent and the transitive has severe shortcomings both as an interpretation of Aristotle and as a theory of action and production. Although Aristotle sometimes uses the terms *praxis* and *energeia* interchangeably, *energeia*, as we saw, refers primarily to psychological activity, and *praxis* refers primarily to moral conduct.[33] Moreover, Aristotle always defines justice, the highest form of action, as conduct directed toward others: "The best man is not he who exercises his excellence towards himself but he who exercises it towards another, for this is a difficult task" (*NE* 1130a6). Indeed, Aquinas considers the question: if action is the perfection of the agent, and justice concerns our relation to others, how is justice a form of action? He responds, naturally, with a distinction: "The other virtues are commended only for the good they do their possessor, justice, however, for the good it does to another."[34] But if justice is the supreme moral virtue, and justice is transitive, then how can moral action be immanent? Indeed, in a major recent defense of the view that action is immanent to the agent, David Charles acknowledges that distributive justice must be excluded from the category of action.[35]

The notion that action is the perfection of the agent and production the perfection of the product will not adequately distinguish action from production. It is true, of course, that actions shape the agent: our actions create and modify our habits and character; but production also shapes the habits and character of the producer.[36] Aristotle implicitly acknowledges that production shapes the producer in his many comments asserting that the mechanical arts make artisans incapable of moral excellence (*Pol.* 1319a25). At a more profound level, actions are not immanent to the agent because all moral actions are sign relations.[37] Language is the most fundamental form of action, and language, as a

Joseph Owens (Albany: SUNY Press, 1981), 27–28; Charles, *Aristotle's Philosophy of Action*, 66; and "Aristotle: Ontology and Moral Reasoning," 128.

33. Indeed, *praxis* can hardly be immanent to the agent, since Aristotle explicitly contrasts *praxis*, as external action, with *prohairesis*, as interior intention. See Gauthier and Jolif, *L'Ethique à Nicomaque*, 2:4.

34. *Summa Theologiae*, 1–2, Q. 58, art. 12.

35. Since action is immanent to the agent, says Charles, "bringing about maximal welfare will not be a *praxis* since its effects are generally located in others." See "Aristotle: Ontology and Moral Reasoning," 140n.

36. Even Aristotle admits in one place (*Met.* 1046b3) that the productive arts change not only external objects but also the artists themselves.

37. Of course, actions, like words, are more than signs: they have a causal efficacy in addition to their signifying efficacy.

sign system, requires three elements: a concept is conveyed through a sign to an interpreter. All action is social, because all action conveys meaning from one person to another.[38] Production is also based in a social sign system: any product is a sign of a socially defined need; for a product to function as a product it must be interpreted as satisfying some need.[39] Contrary to Aristotle, the *telos* of production is not a product (a technical relation) but a human need (a social relation).[40]

For these reasons, John Poinsot argues that Thomas Aquinas is wrong to characterize the immanent and the transitive with respect to the agent; rather, an action is immanent if the end of the action is within the activity, and an action is transitive if its end is external to the activity.[41] "The reason is that any action which consists in the production of an effect is transitive, whether its effect resides in an external subject or remains within the agent." On this view, even purely interior activities may be either immanent or transitive: reading a poem for sheer pleasure is an immanent activity, whereas reading the poem in order to memorize it is a transitive activity. Indeed, any activity aimed at perfecting the agent would be transitive: "What difference does it make to the essence of action that the patient in which the term inheres be the agent itself or a subject extraneous to the agent?" If we extend this analysis to the realm of moral action, Poinsot is saying that any activity, psychological or moral, can be engaged in for its own sake or for an external end. As Yves Simon puts it: "All difficult cases can be clarified by ascertaining the direction and the term of the teleological relation: if this relation reaches the product through the act, so that the act is a way to the product, this act is transitive, no matter how interior it may be in other respects; if the teleological relation terminates in the act itself, this act is immanent, no matter how important and noticeable its results may be."[42] Poinsot's

38. Private action, like a private language, is always parasitic on social action. We are good to ourselves only by analogy with being good to others, just as we talk to ourselves by analogy with talking to others.

39. Purely private productions are only products by analogy to social products: thus we find these private products (such as a Rube Goldberg device) to be humorous—not unlike the humorous aspect of a private action such as talking to oneself.

40. Aristotle insists, of course, that *politikē*, as the architectonic art, determines the use of commodities; but Aristotle never suggests that the origin and design of commodities is the product of socially determined human needs.

41. John Poinsot, as we noted above, objects to the use of the term *actus* to refer both to psychological actuality (*energeia*) and to moral conduct (*praxis*). According to Poinsot, Aristotle's *energeias*, such as seeing and contemplating, are immanent actions, as opposed to true or transitive actions. Any activity that aims at the production of an effect is a transitive action.

42. For citations and analysis of John Poinsot's theory of action, see Yves Simon, "An Essay

analysis here has the virtue that it enables us to see that any human action or production can be pursued for immanent or transitive reasons.

Aristotle seems to have Poinsot's notions of the immanent and the transitive in mind when he says that some actions are desirable in themselves whereas others are desirable for the sake of something else (*NE* 1176b1). Aristotle, however, is not content simply to observe that any activity can be pursued for immanent or for transitive reasons; he claims that certain classes of activities are pursued for their own sake, whereas others are pursued for external ends. Of activities pursued for their own sake, he lists sight, contemplation, understanding, and noble actions; of activities pursued for external ends, he often mentions production. Aristotle's view that production is never pursued for an immanent end and that action is only pursued for an immanent end is highly implausible; he resists the more plausible view that any activity, from thought to building, can be pursued for immanent or for transitive ends.

According to John Poinsot, whether an activity is immanent or transitive depends on the disposition of the will: an immanent activity is one in which the will is directed to a goal within the activity, whereas a transitive activity is one in which the will is directed to a goal outside of the activity. As Yves Simon puts it: "Immanent action cannot *consist in* a production, yet something may be produced by it."[43] In other words, there is no external and objective way to determine whether someone is, say, learning for the sake of knowledge or for the sake of high marks. High marks may be a by-product of the love of knowledge, but the love of knowledge does not consist in the production of high marks. Poinsot's emphasis on the disposition of the will is absent from Aristotle's account; perhaps this fact helps to explain why Aristotle insists on objective criteria to distinguish the immanent from the transitive. Action is immanent, in Aristotle's view, because it does not issue in a product, whereas production is transitive because it does. Alasdair MacIntyre's distinction, however, between the internal and external goods of a practice does depend upon the disposition of the will: one may play chess for its intrinsic pleasure or one may play chess to make money. "A virtue is an acquired human quality the possession and exercise of which tends to enable us to achieve those goods which are internal to practices and the lack of which prevents us from achiev-

on the Classification of Action and the Understanding of Act," *Revue de l'Université d'Ottawa* 41 (October 1971): 523–25.

43. Ibid., 524n.

ing any such goods."[44] That MacIntyre's distinction is equivalent to Poinsot's is evident when one considers that the internal good of playing chess does not *consist of* making money, though money may be made by it. MacIntyre's distinction, like Poinsot's, is not intended to distinguish action from production: any activity can be pursued for immanent or transitive ends.

The Distinction between Moral Reason and Technical Reason

I now propose to define moral reason (*phronēsis*) in such a way as to detach it from its identity with action; and I will define technical reason (*technē*) in such a way as to detach it from its identity with production. Only through such a process of analysis will we see that there is justice in production just as there are techniques of action.

There is a fundamental ambiguity in the term *technē*, an ambiguity reflected in the alternative translations of *technē* as "art" or "skill." *Technē* refers to the realm of craft production: the fundamental *technai* are the manual or industrial arts; but *technē* also refers to instrumental method: the technician (*technitēs*) is skillful in using means to achieve his or her ends. What is of interest here is the assumption embodied in the term *technē* that instrumental calculation belongs chiefly to the industrial arts. Such an assumption leads Hans-Georg Gadamer to define *technē* as "the knowledge of the craftsman who is able to make some specific thing."[45] Indeed, we still describe someone who is skillfully instrumental in the realm of action as "crafty"—as if cleverness were logically bound to carpentry.[46]

The ambiguity of *technē* is analogous to the ambiguity of "economy." As Karl Polanyi points out, "economy" can refer to a realm of human activity (the realm of material production and exchange) and to a mode of thought (the instrumental calculation of efficiency known as "economizing").[47] Since we can economize in any human endeavor, we must consider why economizing is assumed to be logically bound to production and exchange. Just as the two

44. Alasdair MacIntyre, *After Virtue* (Notre Dame: University of Notre Dame Press, 1984), 191.

45. Hans-Georg Gadamer, *Truth and Method* (New York: Crossroad, 1975), 281.

46. Thus Aristotle says: "For it is in things made [*poiēta*] rather then things done [*prakta*] that artistic contrivance [*technazein*] is displayed" (*MM* 1197a3ff.). Since the verb *technazein* means "cunning" or "crafty," Aristotle is arguing here that one can be crafty only in the industrial crafts.

47. Karl Polanyi, *Primitive, Archaic, and Modern Economies*, ed. George Dalton (Boston: Beacon Press, 1971), 140.

senses of "economy" are not logically but only historically bound, so the two senses of *technē* are not logically but historically bound. Perhaps the instrumental calculus of *technē* arose originally in connection with the industrial crafts (*technai*), but technical reason is equally at home in politics, war, and sport. Similarly, economizing arose originally in connection with the economy, but economizing is compatible with logic, science, and charity.

The first step, therefore, in the effort to detach *technē* from production is to define *technē* as technical reason. Even though ends and means are not ultimately separable, if one treats an end as separate and given, then one can compare the relative efficiency of different means. As Aristotle puts it: "Having set the end they consider how and by what means it is to be attained; and if it seems to be produced by several means they consider by which it is most easily and best produced" (*NE* 1112b15).[48] The ability of the technician to evaluate the relative efficiency of alternative means makes the realization of the end relatively predictable.[49] Establishing predictable causal relations between events is the method of experimental science. It is thus not surprising that both Plato and Aristotle define *technē* as a form of scientific knowledge (*epistēmē*).[50] "In all arts and sciences both the end and the means should be equally within our control" (*Pol.* 1331b36). Progress in science is possible because experimentally verified knowledge is cumulative. This is why Aristotle acknowledges progress in the development of the arts (*NE* 1098a22; *Pol.* 1268b33).

One of the more curious, and overlooked, aspects of Aristotle's theory of *technē* is his notion that technique is subject to hypothetical necessity. According to Aristotle, once an end is given, the means are of necessity; there is, in short, only one correct way to make something.[51] Aristotle has immense respect for the precision of the arts: he compares the necessity relating ends and

48. Compare R. G. Collingwood's definition of *technē*: "Craft always involves a distinction between means and ends, each clearly conceived as something distinct from the other but related to it" (*The Principles of Art* [Oxford: Clarendon Press, 1938], 15).

49. On the antithesis of *technē* and chance (*tuchē*) and the notion that *technē* overcomes *tuchē*, see Nussbaum, *Fragility of Goodness*, 89 and 442n.

50. *Met.* 981b7. "In fact, to judge from my own work and in the consensus of philologists, there is, at least through Plato's time, no systematic or general distinction between *epistēmē* and *technē*" (Nussbaum, *Fragility of Goodness*, 94). Aristotle uses *technē* and *epistēmē* as synonyms in several places: *An. Pr.* 46a22; *Met.* 981a3, b8, 1074b11; *Pol.* 1288b10; *Rhet.* 1392a26.

51. *Phys.* 200a10; *PA* 639b24. This is why Aristotle says that art does not deliberate; we deliberate only about things that could be different; technical procedures, however, are of necessity. See *Phys.* 199b28 and *NE* 1112a31.

means in production to the necessity relating premises and conclusions in mathematics.[52] Since the exemplar of necessity for Aristotle is the syllogism, when Aristotle talks about a practical syllogism, he must be referring to *technē* and not to *phronēsis*. For Aristotle insists that *phronēsis* is not a science (*epistēmē*); therefore, it cannot possibly have the necessity characteristic of the syllogism.

Is the practical syllogism actually a technical syllogism? Anthony Kenny suggests that the practical syllogism be renamed the technical syllogism because, he says, most of Aristotle's examples of practical syllogisms concern the arts.[53] But if we detach *technē* from production, we must say instead that these syllogisms are technical because they enable one to compare the efficacy of a variety of means to the same end. Martha Nussbaum explicitly defines the practical syllogism as moral, but she goes on to say that this syllogism enables us to make "a selection among various possible routes to the end"; however, since such a selection of different means to the same end is possible only for technical reason, she has implicitly defined the practical syllogism as a technical syllogism. In short, the practical syllogism is a technical syllogism, despite the fact that Nussbaum and many other commentators treat the practical syllogism as a central part of the doctrine of *phronēsis*.[54]

Aristotle seems to be of two minds concerning *technē*: in some places he describes art as a state (*hexis*) whereas in other places he describes it as a faculty (*dynamis*).[55] We begin with art as a *hexis*: "Art, then, as has been said, is a state

52. *Phys.* 200a15 and 24. The Greeks commonly included mathematics as one of the *technai*. Plato argues (*Republic* 522B) that the defining characteristic of any *technē* is that it involve numerical quantification. Nussbaum follows Plato in insisting that instrumental calculation requires numerical commensurability—see *Fragility of Goodness*, 108. In fact, however, all that is required for an instrumental calculus is ordinal, not cardinal, commensurability. See Joseph A. Schumpeter, *History of Economic Analysis* (New York: Oxford University Press, 1954), 1060–66.

53. See Anthony Kenny, *Aristotle's Theory of the Will* (New Haven: Yale University Press, 1979), 113.

54. See Martha Nussbaum, *Aristotle's De Motu Animalium* (Princeton: Princeton University Press, 1978), 165–220. Allan argues that there are two forms of practical syllogism: a means-end syllogism related to *technē* and a rule-case syllogism related to *phronēsis* (see "Practical Syllogism," 336). This view is widely accepted. See Ando, *Aristotle's Theory of Practical Cognition*, 242–43; Gauthier, *La morale d'Aristote*, 34; Kenny, *Aristotle's Theory of the Will*, 117; J. D. Monan, *Moral Knowledge and Its Methodology in Aristotle* (Oxford: Clarendon Press, 1968), 51. For a critique of Allan, see David Wiggins, "Deliberation and Practical Reason," in *Essays on Aristotle's Ethics*, ed. Amelie Rorty (Berkeley: University of California Press, 1980), 230.

55. Plato defined *technē* as a *dynamis* (see *Statesman* 303D). Aristotle concurs at *Met.*

concerned with making [*poiētikē hexis*], involving a true course of reasoning, and a lack of art [*atechnia*] on the contrary is a state concerned with making, involving a false course of reasoning" (*NE* 1140a20). In this sense, Aristotle defines *technē* as an intellectual excellence by which the soul possesses truth (*NE* 1139b15). *Technē* is a virtue (*aretē*) and *atechnia* is a vice. By this Aristotle does not mean that *technē* leads to the morally good; rather *technē* leads to the intellectually correct. *Technē* is an intellectual virtue, not a moral virtue (*NE* 1103a4). Whether the end be good or evil, *technē* will provide the most efficient means of obtaining it.

Yet since Aristotle claims that all virtues are oriented toward the good, *technē* does not seem to qualify as a virtue; *technē*, after all, can be put to evil use. Aristotle does not see that the term *good* is equivocal: *technē* means good reasoning that can lead to the morally bad. Aristotle wants to argue that even the intellectual virtues are oriented toward the morally good, but this view leads him into both affirming and denying that *technē* is a virtue. Aristotle resists the view that something can be intellectually good and morally bad. Thus he in some places describes art as a mere faculty (*dynamis*) that can be put to opposite uses: "The medical art can produce both disease and health" (*Met.* 1046b7).[56] Of course, if *technē* is a *dynamis*, then it cannot be a virtue, for all virtues are *hexeis* (*NE* 1103a9). We can now see why Aristotle in one place drops *technē* from his list of intellectual virtues (*NE* 1141a3).[57]

It is traditionally asserted that *technē* is an intellectual virtue. But is there such a thing as an intellectual virtue? If science and art can be used for good or evil then perhaps they are faculties and not virtues. Another way of putting this dilemma is to say that for *technē* to become a virtue, it must be subordinated to *phronēsis*. As Aquinas says: "Accordingly, just as science is always related to good . . . so is art; and it is for this reason that it is called a virtue. Yet it falls short of the notion of perfect virtue, because it does not ensure the good use of what it produces, for which something further is required,

---

1046b2. On Aristotle's equivocation concerning *technē*, see Ando, *Aristotle's Theory of Practical Cognition*, 188.

56. Indeed, Aristotle defines a faculty (*dynamis*) as that which can be put to opposite uses, whereas a *hexis* is that which has but one use (*NE* 1129a12).

57. There is no agreement among scholars as to why *technē* is dropped from the list of virtues. See Greenwood, *Aristotle*, 163.

although there cannot be a good use without a good art."[58] Not only does art need practical wisdom, but practical wisdom also needs art, as suggested by the phrase "there cannot be a good use without a good art." To be good, technical reason requires moral reason, but to effect the good, moral reason needs technical reason. Indeed, in comparison to *phronēsis*, *technē* is not a virtue at all. "Plainly, then, practical wisdom [*phronēsis*] is an excellence [*aretē*] and not an art" (*NE* 1140b25). What this highly elliptic passage suggests is that since *phronēsis* is not *technē*, and *phronēsis* is a virtue, therefore *technē* is not a virtue.[59] From the subordination of *technē* to *phronēsis*, we dialectically progress to the view that *phronēsis* subsumes *technē*. *Phronēsis* is the general wisdom of ends and means, of which the science of efficient means (*technē*) is but a special case. *Phronēsis* includes and perfects *technē*: "When you have art, you still need virtue to make a good human use of it; but if you have prudence [*phronēsis*], you do not need extra virtue to make good use of it, because prudence, being a moral as well as an intellectual virtue, supplies this good use of itself."[60]

A careful examination of Aristotle's implicit doctrines concerning moral and technical reason reveals further that *technē* is actually a special case of *phronēsis*. Whenever practical wisdom (*phronēsis*) is contrasted with theoretical wisdom (*sophia*), for example, *phronēsis* is taken to include *technē* (*NE* 1141a20–b22, 1142a11–30, 1143b14). Political science (*politikē*), which is the highest form of *phronēsis*, governs all of the arts (*technai*). *Phronēsis* as an actuality (*energeia*) includes and perfects *technē* as a capacity (*dynamis*) (*NE* 1153a25). *Phronēsis* concerns both the universal and the particular, whereas *technē* concerns only the universal (*NE* 1141b14, 1180b20; *Met.* 981a15). By seeing *technē* as a special case of *phronēsis*, we can solve the paradox noted by Nussbaum: Aristotle can attack the Platonic view that *phronēsis* is a *technē* and yet at the same time incorporate *technē* into practical reason.[61]

58. *Summa Theologiae*, 1–2, Q. 57, art. 3. Simon goes further and denies that the intellectual virtues are true virtues. See *Work, Society, and Culture*, 163.

59. See Gauthier and Jolif, *L'Ethique à Nicomaque*, 2:476.

60. Yves Simon, *The Definition of Moral Virtue* (New York: Fordham University Press, 1986), 98.

61. Nussbaum says both that "Aristotle has, then, attacked the *technē* conception of practical reason" and that "he can claim to have a *technē* of practical reason just in the sense and to the degree that Protagoras can also make this claim" (*Fragility of Goodness*, 309–10). She resolves this tension by suggesting that *phronēsis* is a *technē* "to a point"; I suggest that *technē* is a special case of *phronēsis*.

Unfortunately, Aristotle often describes moral deliberation on the model of technical deliberation.

> We deliberate not about ends but about what contributes to ends [*ta pros to telos*]. For a doctor does not deliberate whether he shall heal, nor an orator whether he shall convince, nor a statesman whether he shall produce law and order, nor does anyone else deliberate about his end. Having set the end they consider how and by what means it is to be attained; and if it seems to be produced by several means they consider by which it is most easily and best produced (*NE* 1112b11ff).

In this passage, Aristotle has clearly reduced moral to technical deliberation. According to Nussbaum, Aristotle is simply making "the reasonable point that if one is already at work at this sort of activity, one does not continue asking oneself, 'Shall I pursue the end?,' but rather deliberates about how to fulfill it." Yet one of the profound moral shortcomings of the medical profession is precisely this view that the doctor need not ask himself whether to heal a patient. There have always been many circumstances in which doctors have needed to deliberate about whether to withhold treatment—triage on the battlefield, for example, or consideration of the age and strength of the patient— circumstances made all the more common with modern life-support technology. Nussbaum's attempt to defend Aristotle's view here reveals a radically deficient notion of moral deliberation. Indeed, what is most characteristic of moral deliberation is not "how should I do something" but "should I do something."[62]

Similarly, Aristotle's comparison of moral deliberation with archery (*NE* 1094a22) tends to reduce *phronēsis* to *technē*: in archery the question of whether to hit the target never arises; moreover, in moral life, the target is constantly moving—partly because of our efforts to hit it. The analogy to archery seems to be responsible for the following analysis of moral deliberation: "Sometimes the right end is set before men, but in practice they fail to attain

---

62. Nussbaum, *Aristotle's De Motu Animalium*, 170n. In her defense of Aristotle, Nussbaum places a great deal of weight on the phrase *ta pros to telos*. She argues here and in *Fragility of Goodness* (297) that this phrase includes not just the instrumental means to the end but also the component means—i.e., deliberation about what constitutes the end. But this cannot possibly be true of *NE* 1112b11, since Aristotle explicitly contrasts *telos* with *ta pros to telos*; moreover, Aristotle says here that deliberation compares several means to the same end, which is possible only where means are instrumentally separable from their end—where, in short, the end is simply a given.

it; in other cases they are successful in all the contributory factors, but they propose to themselves a bad end" (*Pol.* 1331b31). What we have here is clearly technical, not moral, deliberation because Aristotle uses the method of concomitant variation to show that ends and means are separable. Alasdair MacIntyre claims that although *phronēsis* was pervasive in Athenian political life, the only contemporary context in which we find the exercise of Aristotelian *phronēsis* is in a sport like hockey. But since Aristotle himself uses the sport of archery as a model of moral deliberation, it is not surprising that MacIntyre can find *phronēsis* in hockey. What is troubling is the view, shared by Aristotle and MacIntyre, that the technical deliberation of an athlete can serve as a model for moral deliberation.[63]

Although Aristotle in some places reduces moral to technical deliberation, in other places he does distinguish *phronēsis* from *technē*. *Phronēsis*, unlike *technē*, is a moral virtue, a stable disposition (*hexis*) to seek the good as a *telos*. This disposition to seek good ends is not simply an addition to but is an ingredient in the ability to select the best means: "It is not possible to be good in the strict sense without practical wisdom, nor practically wise without moral excellence" (*NE* 1144b30). In this passage, Aristotle says first that the choice of a good end will depend on the goodness of the means required to attain it; if an end requires illicit means, it must be rejected. Second, Aristotle says that the goodness of the means depends on the goodness of the end; ends and means, after all, are relative to each other: until I attain a means, I treat it as an end, and when I attain an end, I treat it as a means to further ends. This analysis of what John Dewey calls the ends-means continuum is in sharp contrast to those passages where Aristotle separates ends from means. In technical deliberation, we can have the right end but the wrong means and the wrong end but the right means; in moral deliberation, however, we cannot seek the right end until we know the right means, and we cannot find the right means unless we propose the right end.

There is a close analogy between the *technē-phronēsis* relation and the *deinotēs-phronēsis* relation. Aristotle uses the term *cleverness* (*deinotēs*) to refer to instrumental reason in the realm of action, just as *technē* refers to

63. Here is MacIntyre's example of Aristotelian moral deliberation: "A hockey player in the closing seconds of a crucial game has an opportunity to pass to another member of his or her team better placed to score a needed goal. Necessarily, we may say, if he or she has perceived and judged the situation accurately, he or she must immediately pass" (*Whose Justice? Which Rationality?* [Notre Dame: University of Notre Dame Press, 1988], 140–41).

instrumental reason in the realm of production. The close relation between these two terms has been overlooked by Aristotle and most of his major commentators, perhaps because of the assumption that since production and action are radically distinct, so must be *technē* and *deinotēs*. Aristotle defines cleverness as the ability (*dynamis*) to calculate the means to any given end: "Now if the mark be noble, the cleverness is laudable, but if the mark be bad, the cleverness is mere villainy [*panourgia*]" (*NE* 1144a26). As Gadamer puts it, what makes the *deinos* so frightful is that he is *panourgos*, that is, capable of anything.[64] Like *technē*, cleverness is indifferent to the moral quality of the end; and again like *technē*, even when cleverness is laudable it is not a moral virtue. *Deinotēs* is a capacity (*dynamis*) that must be perfected by *phronēsis* in order to become a state (*hexis*) (*NE* 1144a29). Just as *phronēsis* includes *technē* as a special case, so *phronēsis* includes *deinotēs*. "Practical wisdom is not the faculty [of *deinotēs*], but it does not exist without this faculty" (*NE* 1144a28).[65] In Aristotle, *technē* and *deinotēs* can refer either to good instrumentality or to both good and bad instrumentality.[66]

In Attic Greek literature there is an important distinction between *technē* and *deinotēs*, a distinction that reveals the fact that technical reason always presupposes moral reason. *Technē* is the socially approved use of instrumental reason in the legitimate arts (*technai*); *deinotēs* is the socially suspect use of instrumental reason outside of the legitimate arts—what we call "cunning" or "deviousness." Why did the Greeks place such a profound emphasis on the distinction between *technē* and *deinotēs*? Because of their understanding that the separation of ends and means in a *technē* is only provisional, that ultimately all instrumental questions become moral questions. So it is that *phronēsis* alone can determine the legitimate role of technique in human conduct.

How does my view of the relation of technical to moral reason differ from the standard view that Aristotle's *phronēsis* includes deliberation about both external means and component means to our ends?[67] The standard view arose

64. Gadamer, *Truth and Method*, 289.

65. *Phronēsis* includes *deinotēs*, but *deinotēs* does not include *phronēsis*: "For cleverness and the clever man are not wisdom and the wise man; the wise man, however, is clever, hence cleverness cooperates in a way with wisdom" (*MM* 1197b19).

66. For *technē* as good, see *NE* 1140a20; as both good and bad, see *NE* 1140b21. For *deinotēs* as good, see *NE* 1144a27; as both good and bad, see *NE* 1152a10.

67. Greenwood, unlike Nussbaum, does not make the notion of a component end central to

in response to the claim that according to Aristotle, moral deliberation is restricted to the choice of external means. Although it is undeniable that Aristotelian moral deliberation is broader than the instrumental calculus of external means, the distinction between external and component means does not capture what is distinctive about moral deliberation. To begin with, deliberation about the optimal external means to an end belongs not to *phronēsis* but to *technē*; it is only when external means are no longer regarded as external that moral deliberation arises. Moreover, my analysis of the causal relations between means and ends shows that there are no purely external means to an end because ultimately different means lead to different ends. The static distinction between external and component means obscures the dynamic fact that external means are only provisionally separable from their ends, just as technical reason is only provisionally distinct from moral reason. And the notion of a component means—for example, L. H. G. Greenwood's notion that viewing beautiful pictures is a component means to happiness—is itself only a special case of the general rule that ends and means are inseparable. Since, for example, the agent shapes himself through his selection of means, every choice of means, no matter how seemingly "external," is inseparable from the end of happiness. In the final analysis, all means are components of their ends. Component means may be closer than external means to their end on the ends-means continuum, but both are merely examples of the many ways in which means and ends interact in moral life.

Action and Production in Classical Political Economy

Aristotle's attempts to distinguish action from production are not very successful. He offers these criteria for action: it is its own end; it is governed by moral reason; and it shapes the agent. But production can also be its own end; it is also governed by moral reason; and it also shapes the agent. Aristotle's insistence that production concerns only the product, not the producer, blinds him to the moral dimension of productive activity. Indeed, the

---

his treatment of *phronēsis*: he says that the only place where Aristotle appears to feel the distinction between external and component means is at *NE* 1144a3–6. See *Aristotle*, 47. For Nussbaum's discussion of Greenwood's distinction, see *Aristotle's De Motu Animalium*, 170n, and *Fragility of Goodness*, 297 and 375.

treatment of labor as a mere "factor of production" in modern economic theory and practice similarly ignores the important insight that production fashions producers as much as products.

When Aristotle says that making has an end other than itself whereas action is its own end, he suggests that production issues in a tangible object whereas action issues in an intangible goodness. As it happens, this corresponds closely with Adam Smith's distinction between productive labor, which issues in a vendible and tangible commodity, and unproductive labor, which "perishes in the very instant of its performance."[68] In the contemporary economy, however, it is clear that production includes intangible services as well as tangible objects: indeed, most production in America is the production of services.

Where Aristotle and Smith err is in the assumption that action and production are distinguished by universally valid physical (or metaphysical) criteria. Actually, the distinction between action and production is best understood as the distinction between the noneconomic and the economic spheres of society. Action and production are defined by historically evolving social norms governing the relation of the economy to other spheres of social life. Production includes any purposeful activity oriented toward economic exchange; action includes any purposeful activity not oriented toward exchange. Thus, depending upon the specific social circumstances, any activity can be either an action or a production. When I lecture my students, I am producing a service; when I lecture my family, I am not producing, but acting. When I make furniture in a factory, I am engaged in production; but when I make furniture for myself, I am engaged in action.[69]

There are hints of such a distinction between action and production in both Aristotle and Smith. In *Politics*, Aristotle asserts that a slave is an instrument of action and not an instrument of production. The reason, says Aristotle, is that a slave works for the household and not for exchange (1254a5). Similarly, when Adam Smith describes productive labor as issuing in a "vendible commodity," he clearly means to define production in terms of exchange. The reason why

68. Adam Smith, *The Wealth of Nations* [1776], ed. R. H. Campbell, A. S. Skinner, and W. B. Todd (Oxford: Oxford University Press, 1979), 2:3.130.

69. This is the same distinction made in the U.S. national income accounts. A house built for sale adds to gross national product (GNP); but if I build a house for myself, GNP is unchanged. If I keep house, GNP is not altered; but if I hire a housekeeper, GNP rises.

both Aristotle and Smith assume that production creates physical objects is that most exchangeable commodities in the past were physical objects.[70] What is surprising is that the metaphysical quest for an eternally valid distinction between action and production continues even in the age of the "information economy."

70. Dugald Stewart was the first economist to distinguish the vendibility from the durability of commodities: "Mr. Smith seems to have considered these two circumstances as coinciding; or, in other words, he seems to have considered the want of vendibility in the fruits of unproductive labour, as a consequence of their want of durability." See "Lectures on Political Economy" [1810], in *The Collected Works of Dugald Stewart*, vol. 8, ed. Sir William Hamilton (Edinburgh: Thomas Constable, 1855), 280.

Chapter 4

Aristotle: Nature, Custom, and Stipulation

Transcending the Nature-Convention Dichotomy

No set of concepts has been more influential in the history of social theory than the nature-convention dichotomy—dubbed by modern social science the "nature-nurture" debate. Aristotle himself often reverts to the Sophistic dichotomy, as when he asks whether slavery is natural or merely conventional or when he claims that money exists not by nature but by convention. Aquinas follows Aristotle by considering the relation of natural justice to legal justice and of natural law to positive law. J. S. Mill says in his *Principles of Political Economy* that whereas the laws of production are natural the laws of distribution are merely conventional. The foreground of social theory continues to be dominated by the Sophistic dichotomy of nature and convention. Indeed, one prominent contemporary theorist, G. A. Cohen, asserts: "The Sophists' distinction between nature and convention is the foundation of all social criticism."[1] But just because the nature-convention dichotomy is in fact the basis of most criticism does not mean that it ought to be. The pervasive influence of the nature-convention dichotomy is due to its simplicity (and, perhaps, simplemindedness), as well as to the absence of an alternative framework for social theory.

Although the Sophists made the most rhetorical use of this dichotomy, the opposition between *physis* and *nomos* was pervasive in Greek thought from the Milesians to Aristotle. The meaning of this dichotomy is derived not so much from the meaning of the individual terms *physis* and *nomos* as from the semantic field within which the dichotomy is embedded. Felix Heinimann's classic *Nomos und Physis* describes the historically prior semantic field as a

1. G. A. Cohen, *Karl Marx's Theory of History* (Princeton: Princeton University Press, 1978), 107.

set of antitheses onto which the *nomos-physis* distinction was mapped: word versus deed, appearance versus reality, opinion versus truth, arbitrary violence versus necessity.[2] Because of this prior semantic field, convention came to be identified with word, appearance, opinion, and arbitrary violence whereas nature came to be identified with deeds, reality, truth, and necessity. Democritus, for example, claims: "By convention [*nomō*], there is sweet and bitter, by convention, hot and cold, and by convention, there is color; but in reality [*eteē*] there are atoms and the void" (Diels-Kranz [DK] frag. B9).

Heinimann sees Antiphon as the bridge from the earlier Milesian natural science to the later Sophistic moral and political philosophy.[3] What makes Antiphon so seminal is that his work alone defines the entire semantic field within which the *nomos-physis* antithesis is embedded. Indeed, his discussion of nature and convention is titled "On Truth" (*peri alētheias*), revealing the dependence of the Sophistic *nomos-physis* antithesis on the prior *doxa-alētheia* antithesis. Antiphon argues that one should prefer nature to convention: "The reason is that the affairs of law [*ta tōn nomōn*] are arbitrary [*epitheta*] while the affairs of nature [*ta tēs physeōs*] are necessary [*anankaia*]; and the affairs of law are created by covenant and not by organic growth [*phynta*] while the affairs of nature are the reverse."[4] Since it had long been identified with reality and truth, nature became a weapon with which to attack convention, which had long been associated with mere appearance and opinion. But human society could not even exist if it simply negated human nature; and society could not persist if conventions were merely arbitrary and illusory.

Although the Sophists are famous for setting nature and convention in opposition, the greatest of all the Sophists had already begun to transcend this antithesis. Protagoras said: "Learning [*didaskalia*] requires both nature [*physis*] and practice [*askēsis*]."[5] As teachers of rhetoric, Protagoras and the

2. On the set of oppositions forming the semantic field of convention and nature (*logos* versus *ergon*, *onoma* versus *pragma*, *doxa* versus *alētheia*, *bia* versus *anankaia*) see Heinimann's *Nomos und Physis* [1945] (Darmstadt: Wissenschaftliche Buchgesellschaft, 1972), chap. 2.

3. Heinimann, *Nomos und Physis*, 133.

4. Antiphon in *Die Fragmente der Vorsokratiker*, ed. Hermann Diels and Walter Kranz (Berlin: Weidmannsche Verlagsbuchhandlung, 1954), frag. 44A (my translation).

5. Protagoras in Diels and Kranz, *Fragmente der Vorsokratiker*, frag. 3. Paul Shorey rightly argues that *didaskalia* must be rendered here by "learning" and not, as is usual, by "teaching." Shorey traces the history of Protagoras's trichotomy through Plato and all the way to Cicero's

other Sophists understood that a student cannot grasp organized knowledge unless he or she has both a natural aptitude and the proper study habits. Plato develops this Sophistic trichotomy in his own theory of education: "If you have an innate capacity [*physei*] for rhetoric, you will become a famous rhetorician, provided you also acquire knowledge [*epistēmē*] and practice [*meletē*], but if you lack any of these three you will be correspondingly unfinished" (*Phaedrus* 269D). That this fundamental and powerful insight into the logic of social life should originate in a reflection on education is characteristic of the Greek mind. For, as John Dewey was fond of pointing out, there is an important sense in which all of Greek philosophy is the philosophy of education.

There is no doubt that Aristotle is drawing on these views of the tripartite structure of education in the development of his *physis*, *ethos*, *logos* trichotomy. Indeed, the alternative version of this trichotomy in Aristotle's work reads: "Now some think that we are made good by nature [*physei*], others by habituation [*ethei*], others by teaching [*didakē*]" (*NE* 1179b20). Still, although Aristotle begins with a concern for education, his use of the term *logos*, instead of *didakē*, in the *Politics* version suggests that he is developing a more general conceptual rule, of which education is only a special case. Teaching, after all, is but one instance of deliberate stipulation.

The Sophistic nature-convention dichotomy is often criticized for being simplistic; many social scientists will say that human behavior is the product neither of nature alone nor of nurture alone but of an interaction between them. Such criticism, however, leaves the nature-convention dichotomy very much in place. The history of science suggests that no amount of criticism can defeat an existing theory; only an alternative theory can defeat an existing theory. Perhaps Aristotle's trichotomy offers just such an alternative. What I hope to show is: first, that this trichotomy is deeply rooted in Aristotle's thought; second, that Aristotle's account of nature, custom, and stipulation needs revision in the light of the modern natural and social sciences; and third, that the shortcomings of Aristotle's social theory derive largely from his failure to employ this trichotomy consistently.

---

ingenii, exercitatio dicendi, ratio aliqua (*Pro Archias*). See "*Physis, Meletē, Epistēmē*," in *Transactions and Proceedings of the American Philological Association* 40 (1909): 185–201.

The Logic of Nature, Custom, and Stipulation: As Interdefinable

In an attempt to transcend the *nomos-physis* antithesis, Plato and Aristotle develop a complex analogy between art and nature known as natural teleology.[6] If nature were understood on the model of an artisan whose works are the rational product of a single mind, and if nature were seen to employ the most efficient means to the best ends, then nature and art would be reconciled because one is deemed analogous to the other. As W. K. C. Guthrie puts it, "a genuine reconciliation between *nomos* and *physis* could only be effected, as Plato effected it, by seeing in nature not a series of accidents but the product of a supreme designing mind."[7] Art or convention is the imitation of nature, but only because nature is assumed to imitate art. Certainly the Platonic-Aristotelian natural teleology is one way to reconcile *physis* and *nomos*, but it is by no means the only way.[8]

In addition to his familiar metaphor describing nature as a craftsman, Aristotle is famous for his metaphorical descriptions of custom as both "second nature" and "unwritten law." Before we examine the circle of metaphors that define nature, custom, and stipulation, we should first consider the question: what is the status of metaphor within Aristotle's philosophy generally? Speaking of the poet, Aristotle praises the mastery of metaphor as a sign of genius (*Poet.* 1459a5); but speaking of the rules of definition and of dialectical argument, he condemns metaphor because "a metaphorical expression is always obscure" (*Top.* 139b34; *An. Post.* 97b37). As we saw in chapter 2, Aristotle is quite right about the obscurity of metaphors: a metaphor is obscure not only because it is an abbreviated analogy, but because it is an abbreviation that may stand for several different analogies. To interrogate a metaphor we must describe the underlying analogy—as Aristotle does when he points out that the metaphor "the sunset of life" is based on the analogy "as old age is to life, so is evening to day" (*Poet.* 1457b22).

6. According to Heinimann, the *physis-technē* antithesis was one variant of the *physis-nomos* antithesis; see *Nomos und Physis*, 105 and 155.

7. W. K. C. Guthrie, *A History of Greek Philosophy* (Cambridge: Cambridge University Press, 1962–1981), 3:73. Confer J. P. Maguire on Plato's view of nature: "The universe is regarded as a product of *technē*, and the basic assumption is that the Divine Craftsman operates in identically the same manner as the human craftsman." See "Plato's Theory of Natural Law," *Yale Classical Studies* 10 (1947): 172.

8. One major shortcoming of natural teleology is that it eliminates history from nature: if natural order is a function of efficient design, if organisms are perfectly adapted to their niches, then history is irrelevant. Darwin pointed precisely to organisms that are poorly adapted to their niches to show that nature is the product of history, not efficient design.

Unfortunately, Aristotle does not subject his own circle of metaphors defining nature, custom, and law to such analysis.[9] If he had, he would have seen, for example, that it is misleading to define custom as "unwritten law" because customs do not become law by virtue of being written down.[10] In the case of his metaphor of natural craftsmanship, however, Aristotle does explore its underlying analogy. In response to the objection that nature cannot pursue a goal because nature does not deliberate, Aristotle replies that art does not deliberate either (*Phys.* 199b27). This reply may not be very plausible, but it does reveal that Aristotle is aware of the complex analogy that underlies his metaphor of natural craftsmanship: nature is to an organism as a craftsman is to an artifact. Unfortunately, Aristotle does not generally interrogate the analogies that underlie his circle of metaphors; he thus runs afoul of his own rules prohibiting the use of metaphors in dialectical argument.

Perhaps the most influential and controversial member of Aristotle's circle of interdefinables is his metaphor "natural law." That Aristotle should develop an analogy between nature and law is not surprising since natural order was first understood on the model of the stipulated legal order. The word *kosmos* originally signified the legal order of society before it came to mean the order of the natural universe; Aristotle uses both *eukosmia* and *eunomia* to refer to a good legal order.[11] In the first document in the history of Western philosophy, Anaximander develops an elaborate analogy between the natural cycle of the seasons and the legal cycles of transgression and retribution. This fragment (DK 12A9) is the first expression of natural law because Anaximander describes the uniformities of nature as just

9. Either Aristotle was not aware that his descriptions of nature, custom, and law are metaphorical or he knew them to be metaphors, but did not think them based on an analogy. Aristotle thought that only some metaphors are based on analogy, whereas actually all metaphors are condensed analogies—as can be seen with the examples Aristotle gives of allegedly nonanalogical metaphors (see *Poet.* 1457b7ff).

10. Just as customs can be written, so laws can be unwritten. Law differs from custom not by being written, but by being stipulated; and law can be stipulated orally. Thus Edward Sapir: "Law can emerge from custom long before the development of writing and has demonstrably done so in numerous cases" ("Custom," in the *Encyclopedia of the Social Sciences* [New York: Macmillan, 1930], 661). In one place, Aristotle anticipates the anthropologists: "Before men knew the art of writing they used to sing their laws in order not to forget them" (*Prob.* 919b37).

11. Werner Jaeger, *Paideia* (New York: Oxford University Press, 1944), 1:110. Charles Kahn says: "It may be that, from the beginning, *kosmos* was applied to the world of nature by conscious analogy with the good order of society" (*Anaximander and the Origins of Greek Cosmology* [New York: Columbia University Press, 1960], 223).

(*dikē*).[12] Indeed, the Greek word for natural cause (*aitia*) is a legal term for guilt—the cause is guilty of the effect.[13] G. E. R. Lloyd points out that the legal analogy extended not only to cosmology but also to physiology: in the Hippocratic writings health was defined as a state of equal rights (*isonomia*) between parts of the body.[14]

The dilemma that Aristotle inherited from his predecessors is how to reconcile the Milesian analogy between nature and law with the Sophistic antithesis between the internal constraints of nature and the external compulsion of law. Aristotle's famous distinction between nature and art embodies the Sophistic opposition between intrinsic natural motion and extrinsic compulsion: natural things, such as organisms, have an internal principle of motion whereas artifacts, such as tools, are compelled by an external agent (*Phys.* 192b12). But how can nature and law be analogous if internal natural constraint is antithetical to external legal compulsion? Aristotle finds the solution to his dilemma in custom or habit (*ethos*). Since both the Milesian analogy and the Sophistic antithesis neglect the role of custom in mediating nature and law, Aristotle's claim that custom (*ethos*) is analogous both to nature (custom is the internal constraint of habit) and to law (customs are conventional) enables him to defend the Milesian analogy from the Sophistic antithesis.

> We should consider the organization of an animal to resemble that of a city well-governed by laws [*eunomia*]. For once order [*taxis*] is established in a city, there is no more need of a separate monarch to preside over every activity; each man does his own work as assigned, and one thing follows another because of habit [*ethos*]. In animals this same thing

12. "And the source of coming-to-be for existing things is that into which destruction, too, happens, according to necessity; for they pay penalty and retribution to each other for their injustice according to the ordinance of time." According to Kahn's interpretation of this fragment, "the elements feed one another by their own destruction, since what is life to one is death for its reciprocal. The first law of nature is a *lex talionis*: life for life" (*Anaximander and the Origins of Greek Cosmology*, 183).

13. Hans Kelsen sees the word *aitia* as central to the early Greek conception of natural law: "It is significant that the Greek word for cause, *aitia*, originally meant guilt: the cause is guilty of the effect, is responsible for the effect. . . . One of the earliest formulations of the law of causality is the famous fragment of Heraclitus: 'If the Sun will overstep his prescribed path, then the Erinyes, the handmaids of justice, will find him out.' Here the law of nature still appears as a rule of law: if the Sun does not follow his prescribed path he will be punished" (*Pure Theory of Law*, ed. Max Knight [Berkeley: University of California Press, 1970], 84).

14. G. E. R. Lloyd, *Magic, Reason, and Experience* (Cambridge: Cambridge University Press, 1979), 248.

happens because of nature: specifically because each part of them, since they are so ordered, is naturally disposed to do its own task.[15]

What Aristotle is saying here is that once stipulated laws become habitual, they operate with the same internal constraint as nature—habit is, after all, second nature. In other words, by becoming habitual, law becomes natural. Only after touring his circle of interdefinability does Aristotle arrive at natural law.

The Logic of Nature, Custom, and Stipulation: As a Progressive Hierarchy

Aristotle's circle of analogies appears to transcend the antithesis of nature and convention by describing the analogical resemblances between nature, custom, and law. But we must carefully distinguish an apparent transcendence from a real transcendence: this circle of analogies will not bear critical scrutiny because these analogies do not capture what is distinctive about natural, customary, and stipulated order. The constraints of custom are distinct from the constraints of nature just as the constraints of law are distinct from the constraints of either nature or custom. The circle of interdefinability shows us that our three concepts are related; the progressive hierarchy shows us how they are related.

One way of describing the logic of nature, custom, and stipulation is to posit a genus, such as order (*taxis*), and to describe nature, custom, and stipulation as three coordinate species of the genus. But this genus-species logic, as we saw in chapter 2, has two principal shortcomings: the first is that the genus "order" is more or less empty and does not add any information to the *differentiae* nature, custom, and stipulation; the second is that if we see nature, custom, and stipulation merely as the coordinate species of the genus, we have not indicated their serial and progressive relations. Yet Aristotle implicitly claims that nature is prior to custom and custom is prior to stipulation.

Aristotle's development of the genus-species logic of classification is well known; what is not well known is that Aristotle also offers an alternative logic of classification. This logic of progressive hierarchy is most clearly illustrated by Aristotle's analysis of the hierarchy of plant, animal, and human souls; but Aristotle also applies this progressive hierarchy to the classification

---

15. *MA* 703a29. Translation from Martha Nussbaum, *Aristotle's De Motu Animalium* (Princeton: Princeton University Press, 1978).

of integers, the categories of being, and political constitutions.[16] In every instance of such a progressive hierarchy, the prior members of the series can exist without the subsequent members, but the subsequent members presuppose the prior members.[17] Although Aristotle makes use of this alternative logic of classification, he does not develop a general logical definition of the progressive hierarchy.[18]

Thomas Aquinas was the first to argue explicitly that Aristotle treats nature, custom, and stipulation as a progressive hierarchy.[19] By examining our trichotomy in a variety of contexts, we will see that this progressive hierarchy is pervasive in Aristotle's thought; I will follow Aquinas's lead by making explicit what is only implicit in Aristotle. First, for Aristotle, nature, custom, and stipulation articulate the hierarchy of the *scala naturae*: "Animals lead for the most part a life of nature [*physis*], although in lesser particulars some are influenced by habit [*ethos*] as well. Man has reason [*logos*], in addition, and man only" (*Pol.* 1332b4). The logic of Aristotle's analysis of the hierarchy of species parallels the logic of his hierarchy of souls. Just as the sensitive soul includes the vegetative, so the habit of higher animals includes the nature of lower animals; and just as the rational soul includes the sensitive soul, so human reason includes animal habit.

Second, nature, custom, and stipulation form the same progressive hierar-

16. For Aristotle's use of a progressive hierarchy in classification see: in the case of souls, *DA* 414b20–415a13; in the case of integers, *Met.* 999a6; in the case of categories of being, *NE* 1096a17; and in the case of constitutions, *Pol.* 1275a35.

17. If one wishes to retain the genus-species framework, one can distinguish between a true *genus univocum* such as "animal" and an empty *genus analogum* such as "soul" or "order." See R. D. Hicks, *Aristotle: De Anima* (Cambridge: Cambridge University Press, 1907), 185. But the shortcomings of generic definition are well described here by D. W. Hamlyn: "An account of figure in general or soul in general . . . will be uninformative about figures and souls, not just in the way that any generic definition is uninformative about the details of the things to which it is applied, but also because it will omit the crucial point that figures and souls form a progression" (*Aristotle's De Anima II and III* [Oxford: Clarendon Press, 1968], 94).

18. Rulon Wells offers a formal Aristotelian definition of this alternative logic of classification: "But what if the structure is that A has just one positive property, the generic property, and B has two positive properties, the generic property and also a *differentia specifica*?" ("Criteria for Semiosis," in *A Perfusion of Signs*, ed. Thomas A. Sebeok [Bloomington: Indiana University Press, 1977], 9).

19. As Aquinas says in his commentary on Aristotle's discussion of this trichotomy: "*Quare hoc oportet consonare inter se, scilicet naturam, consuetudinem, et rationem: semper enim posterius praesupponit prius*" (*In Libros Politicorum Aristotelis Expositio*, ed. Raymundi Spiazzi [Turin: Marietti, 1951], 386).

chy in individual development as they do in the scale of nature: ontogeny recapitulates phylogeny. Aristotle says (*Met.* 1047b31) that there are three kinds of human faculties (*dynameis*): those that are innate (*suggenēs*), those that come by practice (*ethos*), and those that come from teaching (*mathēsis*). These three faculties form a hierarchy: "Nature's part [*physis*] evidently does not depend on us . . . while argument [*logos*] and teaching [*didakē*], we may suspect, are not powerful with all men, but the soul of the student must first have been cultivated by means of habits [*ethos*]" (*NE* 1179b21).[20] Our nature is given at birth, but our natural instincts are trained through habits; teaching invites us to reflect on our habits and perhaps to stipulate new habits.

Third, this hierarchy plays the same role in the political development of a community as it does in the moral development of an individual. The first task of a legislator, says Aristotle, is to regulate the biological nature of the citizens through eugenics (*eugeneia* or *aretē genous*);[21] his second task is to instill the proper habits in each citizen through an educational regime aimed at developing the right political disposition (*euhexia politikē*);[22] his final task is to reflect on his first two tasks by studying political science. "We have already determined what natures [*physeis*] are likely to be most easily moulded by the hands of the legislator. All else is the work of education; we learn some things by habit [*ethizomenoi*] and some by instruction [*akouontes*]" (*Pol.* 1332b8).[23] Given the centrality of the nature, custom, and stipulation trichotomy to Aristotle's analysis of the scale of nature, individual virtue, and political virtue, it is surprising that most commentators interpret this triad solely in terms of individual *paideia*.[24]

20. J. A. Stewart ably illustrates the progression of nature, custom, and stipulation in the moral development of an individual: "This natural tendency to refrain from acts of intemperance is strengthened by education till it begins to attract its possessor's attention, and he makes 'intemperance' and 'temperance' *objects of moral reflection* in relation to other objects of moral experience" (*Notes on the Nicomachean Ethics of Aristotle* [Oxford: Clarendon Press, 1892], 2: 105). Thus Aristotle says that the young are guided more by character (*ēthos*) than by *logos*; whereas the old are guided more by *logos* than by character (*Rhet.* 1389a33 and 1390a16).

21. *Pol.* 1334b30ff. On the primacy of eugenics, see Jean Aubonnet, *Aristote: Politique* (Paris: Belles Lettres, 1960–1986), 3.1:242n; and Stewart, *Notes on the Nicomachean Ethics of Aristotle*, 2:105, 461.

22. *Pol.* 1336a4. On *euhexia politikē* see Jules Tricot, ed., *Aristote: La Politique* (Paris: J. Vrin, 1982), 541n.

23. "Now in men reason [*logos*] and mind [*nous*] are the end [*telos*] towards which nature [*physis*] strives, so that the birth and training in custom [*ethos*] of the citizens ought to be ordered with a view to them" (*Pol.* 1334b15).

24. See Aubonnet, *Aristote: Politique*, 3.1:243n; Tricot, *Aristote: La Politique*, 522n.

In addition to these passages illustrating the triadic logic of nature, custom, and stipulation, there are several passages illustrating the dyadic transitions from nature to custom and from custom to stipulation. Concerning the transition from nature to custom, Aristotle often says that *ethos* makes use of the potentialities of human biology: "There are some gifts which by nature [*physis*] are made to be turned by habit [*ethos*] to good or bad" (*Pol.* 1332b3). Aristotle is not saying that humans are by nature good or bad; this is not naturalism. Aristotle is saying that nature affords various potentialities, which are turned by habit into good or bad.

Aristotle also describes the transition from custom to stipulation in various ways: first, he tells us that a young man does not have enough experience to study political science because habitual actions are the subject matter of political reflection (*NE* 1095a1); second, he asserts that one cannot have practical wisdom (*phronēsis* or *orthos logos*) apart from good moral habits (*ēthikē aretē*);[25] finally, Aristotle even describes his own philosophical reflection as the critical articulation of customary modes of thought.[26] If we combine the dyadic transition from nature to custom with the dyadic transition from custom to stipulation, we arrive at our triadic hierarchy.

Revising Aristotle: Nature

Greek philosophy from the beginning set reality in opposition to appearance, knowledge in opposition to mere opinion. Philosophy was understood to be a search for what is ultimately real, inherent, and immutable in the world of

---

25. *NE* 1144b32. Stewart ably describes the transition from *ethos* to *logos*: "Phronesis, or the 'Practical Reason,' does not appear fully in a man till 'good habits' have been formed—till the manifold of his sensible nature has been reduced to the *orthos logos*. Reason grows with its object. It is evolved as the moral agent takes increased pleasure in good actions—called 'good' at first only by anticipation, in relation to a future *orthos logos* in him, or still latent Reason. Reason is thus the Habit of Habits" (*Notes on the Nicomachean Ethics of Aristotle*, 1:206).

26. "Now some of these views have been held by many men and men of old, others by a few persons; and it is not probable that either of these should be entirely mistaken, but rather that they should be right in at least one respect or even in most respects" (*NE* 1098b26). Aristotle employs two sources for the study of ethics: "the *ethos* of society and the *endoxoi andres*." See Edward Ryan, "Aristotle's *Rhetoric* and *Ethics* and the *Ethos* of Society," *Greek, Roman, and Byzantine Studies* 13 (1972): 292. "We find in the procedure of Aristotle a resonance of modern phenomenological methods in which forward progress is measured by one's success in explicating the truth mediated through an unreflected, pre-philosophical experience" (J. D. Monan, *Moral Knowledge and Its Methodology in Aristotle* [Oxford: Clarendon Press, 1968], 104).

appearance. It is of great moment that the early Greek physiologers used the term *nature* (*physis*) to refer to the essential character of things, as we still do when we speak of the "nature of things." For Empedocles, the *physis* of things is the permanent elements; for Democritus, it is atoms and the void; for Plato, it is soul; for Aristotle, nature is "the essence [*ousia*] of things that have a principle of movement in themselves qua themselves" (*Met.* 1015a13). Although *physis* also meant the process of growth and development, most scholars now agree that the primary meaning of *physis* was not growth but essential form or character.[27] Of course, the study of growth and development was often thought to be the key to the understanding of essence, as when Aristotle says: "*Physis* in the sense of coming-to-be is the path to *physis* [in the sense of essential form]" (*Phys.* 193b12). Yet Aristotle criticized his predecessors for their emphasis on growth and generation rather than on essential form: "For the process of generation exists for the sake of the complete being [*ousia*], not the being for the sake of generation" (*PA* 640a11–19). Aristotle's view that the cosmos is eternal and ungenerated may have led to his more static view of *physis* as form and essence (*Phys.* 193a30, 193b1).

Because of this original identification of nature with essential reality, it is not surprising that custom and stipulation are constantly being reduced to nature in European thought. As we saw in chapter 2, the pervasive appeal to nature has always been profoundly ambiguous: something can be natural because it is causally determined by natural processes or because it is formally analogous to nature. This ambiguity is especially deep-seated in Aristotle's

27. Ever since Aristotle tried to link *physis* with *genesis* (*Met.* 1014b17), many commentators have followed W. A. Heidel by arguing that *physis* originally meant growth. W. D. Ross, however, follows John Burnet by arguing that "it seems doubtful whether *physis* ever had this meaning of 'birth' or 'growth.'" Ross further accepts Burnet's etymological argument that *physis* derives from the verb *phu* (which like the Latin *fu* means "to be,") and not from the verb *phýomai* ("I grow"). More recently, Charles Kahn attempts to reconcile the dispute between Heidel and Burnet. Kahn rejects Burnet's etymology but agrees with him that "the usual sense of *physis* in Greek literature is not 'growth,' but 'form, character, nature (of a given thing).'" Yet Kahn also insists that *physis* had a derivative sense of "origin and growth": "The choice of just this term [*physis*] to designate the true nature of a thing (in preference to such conceivable alternatives as *eidos* or *morphē*) clearly reflects the importance attached to the process of development." For Heidel, see "*Peri Physeōs*: A Study of the Conception of Nature among the Pre-Socratics," *Proceedings of the American Academy of Arts and Sciences* 45 (1910): 96–97. For Burnet, see *Early Greek Philosophy* (New York: Meridian Books, 1957), appendix. For Ross, see *Aristotle's Metaphysics*, vol. 1 (Oxford: Clarendon Press, 1924), at 1014b17. For Kahn, see *Anaximander and the Origins of Greek Cosmology*, 200–3.

explicit doctrines of nature and the natural. For example, Aristotle describes the polis as natural for two very different reasons: first, because man shares with other animals a social instinct (*hormē koinōnia*); second, because the polis is self-sufficient (*Pol.* 1252b28, 1261b10). Similarly, some forms of slavery are natural: first, because some people are born with deficient minds and/or bodies; second, because the master-slave relation mirrors the relation between soul and body (*Pol.* 1254a22, 34). In the first sense of "natural," a man is causally determined to be a slave if his innate biological disposition is slavish; and the polis is causally determined because people have an innate social instinct. In the second sense of "natural," slavery is natural because the relation between master and slave is formally analogous to the relation between soul and body; in the same way, the self-sufficiency of the polis is analogous to the self-sufficiency of individual organisms.

Aristotle never explicitly distinguishes these two senses of "natural," but his terminology betrays an implicit—though inconsistent—distinction. The significance of this distinction was first recognized by the sixth-century commentator Simplicius; curiously, his insight has all but vanished from modern scholarship. At *Physics* 193b35, Aristotle says that the property of fire to be carried upward is both by nature (*physei*) and according to nature (*kata physin*). In his commentary on this passage, Simplicius says that everything that is caused by natural essence (*physikē ousia*), including birth defects and illness, is *physei* but that only what happens according to nature's plan (*boulema tēs physeōs*) is *kata physin*. The upward motion of fire, for example, is both caused by nature (*physei*) and is in accordance with nature's plan (*kata physin*); by contrast, birth defects and illness are caused by nature (*physei*) but are not in accordance with nature's plan (*kata physin*)—they are, in fact, contrary to nature (*para physin*). Of the larger set of things by nature (*physei*), then, some are in accordance with nature (*kata physin*) whereas others are contrary to nature (*para physin*).[28]

When Aristotle wants to contrast the internal principle of motion by nature with the external principle of motion by law, he contrasts the instrumental datives *physei* and *nomō*; the natural, understood as that which is opposed to

<hr />

28. See *Simplicii in Aristotelis Physicorum Libros Quattuor Priores Commentaria*, ed. Hermann Diels (Berlin: G. Reimer, 1895), 270.35–271.24. In his commentary on *Physics* 197b32ff, W. D. Ross uses Simplicius's distinction to explicate Aristotle's argument that spontaneous generation is both *physei* and *para physin*. See Ross, *Aristotle's Physics* (Oxford: Clarendon Press, 1936), 524.

the conventional, is *physei*. "Thus in things that derive their motion from themselves, e.g. all animals, the motion is natural [*physei*]" (*Phys.* 254b14). But when Aristotle wants to compare the teleology of nature to that of art he uses the expression *kata physin*; the natural understood by analogy to the conventional, then, is *kata physin*.[29]

Aristotle uses *physei* to distinguish natural causation not only from stipulated causation (in art and law) but also from customary causation: "The incontinent, then, seems to be bad by custom [*ethei*], but the intemperate by nature [*physei*]. Therefore, the intemperate is the harder to cure. For one custom [*ethos*] is dislodged by another [*ethei*], but nothing will dislodge nature [*physis*]" (*MM* 1204a1). Here we find a clear statement of natural causal determinism: natural causes are fixed and universal.[30] Similarly, some forms of slavery and patriarchy are natural in the sense of causally determined by nature (*Pol.* 1252a31, 1254b12): a man biologically suited to use his mind is a master by nature (*physei*), whereas a man biologically suited to use his body is a slave by nature (*physei*); the male is biologically stronger than the female by nature (*physei*). When speaking of the efficient causes of nature, then, Aristotle uses the term *physei*.

Aristotle uses the expressions *kata physin* and *para physin* to develop analogies between nature and convention. Indeed, W. A. Heidel is surely right to argue that the two expressions have no proper sense apart from a teleological interpretation of nature.[31] The phrase *kata physin* is a metaphor for a complex analogy between the teleology of art and of nature: the craftsman realizes his goal *kata technēn* just as nature realizes its goal *kata physin* (*Phys.* 193a32). Both art and nature operate as if in accordance with a plan (*kata logon*). Because Aristotle often compares nature to a craftsman,[32] it makes sense to describe physical or biological phenomena as either contrary or according to nature's plan: "Since everything that depends on the action of

29. *Physis* is opposed to *technē*: *Meteor.* 390b14; *GA* 734a31, b21. *Physei* is opposed to *nomō*: *NE* 1094b16, 1133a30, and 1133b21; *Pol.* 1253b20, 1254a14, 1255a1. *Kata physin* is compared to *kata technēn*: *Phys.* 199a18, 193a32, 199a34; *GA* 767a17; *Pol.* 1333a23.

30. "But these are the two marks by which we define the natural [*physei*]—it is either that which is found with us as soon as we are born, or that which comes to us if growth is allowed to proceed regularly, e.g., grey hair, old age, and so on" (*Eud.* 1224b31). In modern terms, the natural (*physei*) is genetically determined.

31. Heidel, "*Peri Physeōs*," 100.

32. Nature subordinates means to ends with the same efficiency as a craftsman: *Phys.* 199b27f. Nature does nothing in vain: *Pol.* 1256b20; *Cael.* 271a33; *DA* 432b21 and 434a31.

nature is by nature [*kata physin*] as good as it can be, and similarly everything that depends on art [*kata technēn*] . . . " (*NE* 1099b21).[33] Aristotle extends his analogy between art and nature quite far: mistakes occur, for example, *kata physin* just as they do *kata technēn* (*Phys.* 199a34). Aristotle is not saying that nature actually deliberates over a plan (he even denies that an artisan deliberates); rather, he is saying that we should interpret the structure of an organism as if it were designed efficiently in accordance with a plan or goal.

Although Aristotle is far from consistent in his use of these two expressions for nature, we can make sense of many passages only if we recognize an implicit distinction between them. When, for example, he says that "in the realm of nature occurrences take place which are even contrary to nature [*para physin*]" (*Mem.* 452a30), he would be contradicting himself if he did not distinguish two senses of "natural." The same applies when he says (*Pol.* 1254a34–b2) that the rule of the mind over the body is natural (*kata physin*), whereas the rule of the body over the mind is unnatural (*para physin*), even though both are by nature (*physei*). And when Aristotle says (*IA* 706a19, b10) that man is the most natural of animals (*kata physin*), he can only mean that man is the most perfect product of natural craftsmanship. Finally, Aristotle often says that what is forced or compulsory (*bia*) is contrary to nature (*para physin*); this seems odd to moderns, since we often associate the laws of physics with force and compulsion.[34] A volcano, by forcing the heavy rock upward, would be an example of motion *para physin* that is nonetheless *physei*.

We might consider why the implicit distinction between these two very different senses of "nature" is not made explicit by Aristotle or most of his commentators. The reason is that by Aristotle's standards, what is *physei* and what is *kata physin* typically coincide: the statistically normal is usually normative.[35] Thus Aristotle can say that marriage is both *physei* and *kata physin*

33. Nature always chooses the best: *OY* 469a27; *GC* 336b27; *PA* 658a23; *IA* 704b16 and 711a16. Nature makes nothing superfluous: *PA* 691b4 and 694a15.

34. On *bia* as *para physin*, see *Phys.* 215a1; *Cael.* 300a23; *GA* 788b27; *Met.* 1015b15. There seem to be several reasons for Aristotle to define force as contrary to nature: first, Aristotle contrasts *physei* to *nomō*, and like the Sophists, he associates force with legal constraint (see *Pol.* 1253b20); second, force is assumed to be rare, and thus not "always or for the most part"; third, those things *kata physin* are analogous to an intentional ends-means teleology, whereas *bia* is blind compulsion contrary to nature's intention.

35. "But then we must look for the intentions of nature [*kata physin*] in things which retain their nature [*physei*], and not in things which are corrupted" (*Pol.* 1254a34). In other words, the normative must be sought in the normal.

since marriage is both normal and normative; similarly, Aristotle says that the upward motion of fire is both *physei* and *kata physin* (*NE* 1162a16; *Phys.* 192b35). Since it is very difficult to distinguish phenomena that co-vary, we must look for those cases where the two senses of "natural" diverge. The polis is an example of such divergence, since the polis is statistically rare yet normative: it is not *physei* in the sense of "always or for the most part" but is *kata physin*.[36] Monstrosities are another case where the senses of "nature" diverge: monsters are contrary to nature's intention (*para physin*), but they are natural (*physei*) in the sense of causally determined by nature. In the case of monsters, even the two senses of causal nature (*physei*) diverge: monsters are part of nature's causal nexus, but they are not caused "always or for the most part."[37]

Which of Aristotle's two main expressions for "natural" is compatible with his nature, custom, and stipulation hierarchy? Since Aristotle uses both expressions to reduce social institutions to nature and the natural, neither is genuinely compatible with his progressive hierarchy. Social institutions are neither causally determined by nature (*physei*) nor in accordance with nature's plan (*kata physin*). The expressions *kata physin* and *para physin* reflect a teleological view of nature based on an analogy between the stipulated order of a plan and the order of nature. Something can be according to or contrary to nature only if nature is defined in terms of stipulated order; however, our progressive hierarchy is precisely an effort to escape from this circle of interdefinability. To describe social order by analogy to natural order obscures all that is distinctive of customary and stipulated order. If we are to revise Aristotle's doctrines of nature so that they are compatible with contemporary natural science, then we will have to drop Aristotle's notion that some phenomena are in accordance with nature and some contrary to it. Far from being thought con-

36. The divergence of the two senses of "natural" in the case of the polis is what generates the paradox noted by Jaakko Hintikka: "How can he claim that the city-state, polis, exists by nature? Occasionally he says that natural is that which happens always, or in most cases. Yet he does not suggest that people always and everywhere or even in most cases organize themselves into city-states." See "Some Conceptual Presuppositions of Greek Political Theory," *Scandinavian Political Studies* 2 (1967): 21. Nature as causal nexus (*physei*) is usually "that which happens always or for the most part" (see *Rhet.* 1369a35); the polis is natural because it is analogous to the optimal design of nature. Even if there were only one polis in existence, it would be natural "since everything that depends on the action of nature is by nature [*kata physin*] as good as it can be" (*NE* 1099b21).

37. *GA* 770b9 and 767b5. Thus when Simplicius distinguishes between *physei* and *kata physin*, he refers to deformity and disease.

trary to nature, violent motion and monstrosities are now regarded as central to our understanding of natural processes.

On the other hand, the concept of nature as a causal nexus (*physei*) is compatible with our hierarchy only if we treat the relation of nature to custom and stipulation as one of potency to act. Nature provides the causal powers that are made actual by habit and reason. Thus Aristotle tells us: "Neither by nature [*physei*], then, nor contrary to nature [*para physin*] do excellences arise in us; rather we are adapted by nature to receive them, and are made perfect by habit" (*NE* 1103a23). Moral and intellectual self-realization is not caused by nature (*physei*), nor does it reflect (or contradict) nature's plan (*kata physin*); rather, we have the natural power (*dynamis physei*) to become excellent. If we read this passage in conjunction with the passage where Aristotle says that moral and intellectual excellence requires nature, custom, and reason, then we must conclude that Aristotle's progressive hierarchy requires a notion of natural potential (*dynamis physei*) that is distinct both from what is simply caused by nature (*physei*) and from what is analogous to nature (*kata physin*).

Only by carefully distinguishing Aristotle's notion of natural potential (*dynamis physei*) from his notion of nature's plan (*kata physin*) can we make sense of his highly elliptical discussion of natural justice (*NE* 1134b17–1135a5). Aristotle begins by saying that "of political justice [*dikaion*], part is natural [*physikon*] and part is legal [*nomikon*]." Here Aristotle hopes to transcend the Sophistic antithesis of *nomos-physis* by saying that political justice involves both, but he neglects the crucial role of custom in mediating nature and law. He should have said that political justice is the joint product of nature, custom, and law. Natural justice (*dikaion physikon*), he says, is "that which everywhere has the same force [*dynamis*] and does not exist by people's thinking this or that" (1134b19); again, he says, "what is natural [*physei*] is unchangeable and has everywhere the same force [*dynamis*] as fire burns both here and in Persia" (1134b25). But if what is just or right by nature (*physei*) is a rational potency to be actualized by custom and stipulation (as fire is not), then what is just by nature (*physei*) must be changeable. Indeed, Aristotle then goes on to say that "with us there is something that is just even by nature [*physei*], yet all of it is changeable, but still some is by nature [*physei*] some not by nature." For example, "by nature [*physei*] the right hand is stronger, yet it is possible that all men should come to be ambidextrous." Nature, in short, gives us the power to be either right-handed or ambidextrous; realizing that power is a function of custom and stipulation.

Since we commonly assume, like the Sophists, that nature is fixed whereas conventions change, Aristotle's claim that natural justice is as changeable as legal justice has created an interpretative quandary.[38] If we look at his language, however, we see that Aristotle has said only that what is natural (*physei*) has the same potential (*dynamis*) everywhere, not the same actuality or force (*energeia*).[39] Nature gives every society a set of natural potentialities for justice, but different social customs actualize different natural powers: one society will base justice on physical strength, another on natural kinship, another on sexual differences. Natural justice changes in the sense that the particular natural potentialities employed by custom and stipulation vary over time and space.[40]

Aristotle, however, is not content to let nature provide us with the potential for justice; he goes on to say that nature has a standard or norm for justice: "There is but one [constitution] which is everywhere by nature [*kata physin*] the best" (*NE* 1135a5). His use of the expression *kata physin* reveals that quite a different sense of nature is at work here, nature as a hierarchy of ends. Natural justice (*dynamis physei*) is a power actualized by the historical contingencies of custom and stipulation; the naturally best constitution (*kata physin*) reduces custom and stipulation to nature's plan. J. J. Mulhern, however, conflates what is natural *physei* with what is natural *kata physin*: he says that just as natural justice can vary from place to place, so the best constitution can also vary.[41] Harry Jaffa, by contrast, implicitly recognizes the distinction

38. Jules Tricot follows Stewart by arguing that natural justice changes for the same reason that nature changes—because there are exceptions to "always or for the most part." See Tricot, ed., *Aristote: Ethique à Nicomaque* (Paris: J. Vrin, 1983), 251n; and Stewart, *Notes on the Nicomachean Ethics of Aristotle*, 1:495.

39. Ross, followed by Ostwald, renders *dynamis* as "force." J. J. Mulhern rightly points to Aristotle's discussion of *dynamis* in *DI* (22b36ff), where Aristotle clearly states that (in Mulhern's words) "while most irrational capabilities [*dynameis*], like that of fire to burn, are capabilities for one actualisation only, the same rational capability will be a capacity for more than one actualisation." See Mulhern, "*Mia monon pantachou kata physin hē aristē*," *Phronēsis* 17 (1972): 267.

40. Although they do not notice the import of the term *dynamis*, Leo Strauss and Harry Jaffa see that natural justice is changeable. "The nature of things and not convention then determines in each case what is just. This implies that what is just may very well differ from city to city and from period to period" (Strauss, *Natural Right and History* [Chicago: University of Chicago Press, 1953], 102). "There is no rule of precept of natural right, according to Aristotle, which may not change with circumstances" (Jaffa, *Thomism and Aristotelianism* [Chicago: University of Chicago Press, 1952], 184).

41. "Thus different places may have different naturally best constitutions and may even have different natural justice" (Mulhern, "*Mia monon pantachou . . .* ," 268).

here between what is *kata physin* and what is *physei*: "What is naturally best is distinct from what is naturally right." What is best *kata physin* is always and everywhere the same, but what is right *dynamis physei* depends on the particular customs and circumstances.[42]

Revising Aristotle: Custom

Customs, as we saw in chapter 2, are social patterns of behavior with normative import; customs are rooted in individual habit, but they reside in collectivity. Customs are not the sum of individual habits; rather, we participate in customs through our individual habits. Customs are the indissoluble unity of natural habit and social convention; they cannot be assimilated to individual habits or to stipulated laws. Because Aristotle's Greek lacked a word for this concept of custom, he tends to split the unity of custom into individual habit (*ethos*) on the one side and social convention (*nomos*) on the other. Unfortunately, *ethos* can refer to either habit or custom: Aristotle has no way of distinguishing between idiosyncratic habit and social custom. Similarly, *nomos* can refer to either law or custom: Aristotle cannot distinguish between conventions stipulated by a single mind (law) and conventions derived from unreflective social traditions (custom). *Ethos* and *nomos* are not, strictly speaking, ambiguous terms; they are genuinely vague.[43] Their essential vagueness leads Aristotle to assimilate the habitual aspect of custom (*ethos*) to nature as "second nature" and to assimilate the normative aspect of custom (*nomos*) to stipulation as "unwritten law."[44]

Aristotle's discussion of the relation of legal stipulation to custom reveals his twofold reduction of custom to natural habit and to law. In one place Aristotle says that "legislators make the citizens good by forming habits [*ethē*] in them, and this is the wish of every legislator" (*NE* 1103b2). Aristotle has in mind here the formation of the right habits in the citizenry through political control of education. In another place, Aristotle says that the legislator "should

---

42. Jaffa, *Thomism and Aristotelianism*, 183.

43. An ambiguous term has two precise meanings that are distinguished by context: "to rent" is ambiguous because it can mean to lease from someone or to someone. A vague term has no precise meaning.

44. On Aristotle's notion of *ethos* as "second nature," see Gerhard Funke, *Gewohnheit* (Archiv für Begriffsgeschichte), Band 3 (Bonn: H. Bouvier, 1961), 48–53; on Aristotle's notion of *ethos* as "unwritten law," see Rudolf Hirzel, *Agraphos Nomos* (Leipzig: B. G. Teubner, 1900), 1–34.

make laws, both written and unwritten, which will contain all the preservatives of states" (*Pol.* 1319b38). In both passages, Aristotle is trying to make the same point, namely, that good laws require the support of good customs; but his notion that the legislator can stipulate the right customs or even habits reveals the absence of a concept of custom as the accumulated fund of tradition.[45]

The absence of a clear distinction between social custom and individual habit leads Aristotle to describe the transmission of custom purely as a function of individual habituation. Thus when Aristotle says that there are three things that make men good (*physis*, *ethos*, *logos*), he usually interprets *ethos* not as the process whereby an individual is patterned after a particular set of social customs, but as the process of individual habituation removed from any specific customary context. The customs of aristocratic Athens are presupposed by Aristotle's account of moral training and thereby become invisible.[46] Thus he often says that education (*paideia*) requires careful habituation (*ethizein*); this habituation, by his account, is not socially specific but is guided simply by reason (*logos*).[47]

Aristotle comes closest to acknowledging the specific customary basis of moral habituation in his comments on the importance of the law and the regime for moral education. Democratic regimes and aristocratic regimes, he says, create different types of character.[48] "But it is difficult to get from youth up a right training for excellence if one has not been brought up under the right laws [*nomoi*]" (*NE* 1179b32). Still, we cannot be sure whether he is speaking here of the right customs or the right laws.

Perhaps the clearest evidence that Aristotle has reduced custom to habit are his many comments on the habituation (*ethizein*) of brute animals (*HA* 588a16–633b9). Because he uses the same term (*ethos*) to describe both the habits of animals and the customs of men, Aristotle is unable to distinguish the habituation of brute animals from the acculturation of humans.[49] Although, as

45. Thomas Pangle says: "There is in Greek no clear sense of a 'social' realm of custom that is quasi-independent of politics and legal authority" (*The Laws of Plato* [New York: Basic Books, 1980], 511n).

46. "Custom did not challenge the attention of social theorists because it was the very stuff of their own thinking: it was the lens without which they could not see at all" (Ruth Benedict, *Patterns of Culture* [1934] [Boston: Houghton Mifflin, 1959], 9).

47. *NE* 1179b24; 1180a3; *Pol.* 1332b11; 1334b15.

48. *Pol.* 1310a15.

49. Thus Aristotle discusses a barbarian custom simply as biological habituation without any attention to the customary realm of meaning: "Hence many barbarians have a custom [*ethos*] of

anthropologists have shown, the profoundly complex semiotics of human custom has no counterpart among brute animals, Aristotle must differentiate men from animals on the basis of reason (*logos*) alone (*Pol*. 1332b5).

Aristotle is famous for his doctrine that habit is "second nature."

> If, then, the mind has not moved in an old path, it tends to move to the more customary [*synētheia*]; for custom [*ethos*] now assumes the role of nature [*physis*]. Hence the rapidity with which we recollect what we frequently think about. For as one thing follows another by nature [*physei*], so too that happens by custom [*synētheia*], and frequently creates nature (*Mem*. 452a26).[50]

In other words, habits and customs can be so deeply embedded that they become indistinguishable from nature. Indeed, modern biologists agree that there is continuity between natural instinct and learned habit. But what Aristotle's analogy between the natural and the customary conceals is the particular customary context within which habits are formed. Human nature is not the product of local customs in the way that human habits are. Moreover, Aristotle's notion of custom as "second nature" obscures the fundamental role of history in the constitution of custom: any adequate theory of custom presupposes a notion of long-term linear temporal continuity—what we call history. Habits bear the imprint of the history of the individual whereas customs bear the imprint of the history of society. For Aristotle, however, individual organisms and societies have developmental cycles of birth and death but no history.[51]

Individuals, in Aristotle's view, have development and growth but not history. Individual plants and animals are born potentially mature: the growth from potential to actual maturity, from *dynamis* to *energeia*, is an unfolding of what was already there (*entelecheia*). Growth for Aristotle is prospective and predictable: we know that the acorn will unfold into an oak tree, that the infant will unfold into a man—except in rare accidents. History, however, is

---

plunging their children at birth into a cold stream. . . . For human nature should be early habituated [*ethizein*] to endure all which by habit [*ethizein*] it can be made to endure; but the process must be gradual" (*Pol*. 1336a15).

50. "Habits [*ethē*] also are pleasant; for as soon as a thing has become habitual [*ethos*], it is virtually natural [*physei*]" (*Rhet*. 1370a5). See *NE* 1152a30.

51. According to Aristotle, nature has no history because it is eternally immutable. On the eternal *kosmos*, see *Meteor*. 352b17 and 353a14; *Cael*. 270b14. On the eternal fixity of the species, see *GA* 731b31ff.; *GC* 338b11; *DA* 415a25ff.

not an unfolding from potentiality to actuality: historical progression is unpredictable and is intelligible only in retrospect. There is order to history but it is not the prospective order of growth; rather it is the retrospective order of inheritance, genealogy, and narrative.

Aristotle says that we are born with the potential to become good; and if we develop the right habits in youth, then we will realize a stable moral disposition (*hexis*) known as character (*ēthos*): "Character [*ēthos*] derives from custom [*ethos*]; for it is called moral [*ēthikē*] excellence because it is the result of accustoming [*ethizein*]."[52] *Ethos* is usually rendered "habit" here because the issue is the development of the individual and not the social system of norms. What is inadequate about this doctrine of the moral *hexis* or character is that it assumes that our moral habits are like our physical growth: we develop while we are young, and then we reach the state of natural maturity and stop.[53] Modern psychology questions this assumption that habits ever attain a stable state; rather habits are always in the process of being created, modified, and augmented. Aristotle seems to see human character on the model of animal temperament: a small repertoire of behaviors that quickly stabilize.[54] Human habits bear the imprint of a life history rather than the mere unfolding of growth. What, then, is the relation between habit and character? John Dewey nicely defines character as the interpenetration of various habits; a strong character is one whose various habitual modes of behavior are integrated. Character is a process not a state.[55]

If individual life for Aristotle is a cycle of growth, maturity, and death, so too is social life. One reason why Aristotle rarely notices the historical dimension of custom is that for him, history lacks continuity: the human species is eternal, but cycles of natural disasters force humans to re-create civilization from scratch over and over.[56] Every art, every philosophy, every political

52. *MM* 1186a1. See *NE* 1103a14 and *Eud.* 1220a38. Aristotle's etymologies reveal the absence of a genuine concept of history: "Observe the etymological theory implied by the use of *para* (*ēthos para to ethos*). The Greeks did not think of words as 'derived' from other words, but as deflexions or declensions from a normal form" (John Burnet, *The Ethics of Aristotle* [London: Methuen, 1900], 74n).

53. Thus Aristotle emphasizes the importance of youthful habituation, for once the growth process is distorted, it is too late to achieve full maturity (see *NE* 1103b24).

54. Indeed, Aristotle ascribes psychological character (*psychēs ēthos*) to brute animals: *PA* 692a22 and 650b35.

55. John Dewey, *Human Nature and Conduct* [1922] (New York: Modern Library, 1957), 37.

56. On the eternality of the human species: *GA* 732a1; on the cycles of natural catastrophes: *Meteor.* 352b15 and 353a14. Stewart suggests that Aristotle's cyclical view of history leads him

regime, has developed to its natural limit many times and perished (*Met.* 1074b10; *Pol.* 1329b25). The modern theory of custom assumes that any cultural configuration is the product of a continuous genealogical path from earliest times; yet Aristotle tends to see customs as life cycles of growth, maturity, and decay.[57] This assimilation of custom to natural cycles is evident in Aristotle's account of the history of tragedy: "It was, in fact, only after a long series of changes that the movement of tragedy stopped on its attaining to its natural [*physis*] form" (*Poet.* 1449a10).[58] In keeping with the growth imagery, Aristotle even says that tragedy and comedy already existed potentially in Homer before they unfolded over time (*Poet.* 1449a1).[59]

If the diachronic dimension of custom is assimilated to natural growth, then the synchronic dimension of custom is assimilated to stipulation. The order of custom—think of language—emerges spontaneously from the myriad usages of individuals: every person who participates in a customary practice contributes to the shape of that custom. Aristotle, however, usually assumes that any customary order is the product of individual design (*MA* 703a30). Myths are ascribed to an original author; family customs are ascribed to the father (*Pol.* 1252b22, 1269b28). Most significant, Aristotle ascribes political and legal institutions to individual lawgivers (*nomothetai*).[60]

---

to reduce custom to habit: just as every epoch begins from scratch, so each individual develops habits from scratch (*Notes on the Nicomachean Ethics of Aristotle*, 1:171).

57. There are suggestions, nonetheless, in Aristotle of cultural history, as opposed to cultural cycles: "For in the case of all discoveries the results of previous labours that have been handed down from others have been advanced bit by bit by those who have taken them on . . . the celebrities of today are the heirs (so to speak) of a long succession of men" (*SE* 183b16ff).

58. The history of philosophy is a natural unfolding or maturation: "For the earliest philosophy is, on all subjects, like one who lisps, since in its beginnings it is but a child" (*Met.* 993a15).

59. "An important part of Aristotle's theory of the origins of the dramatic genres, tragedy and comedy, is that their 'forms' or essences were grasped and foreshadowed by Homer before they actually came into being as genres" (Gerald Else, *Aristotle's Poetics* [Ann Arbor: University of Michigan Press, 1970], 86n).

60. See *Pol.* 1271b30, 1329b7, 1253a30, 1333b7. "The foundation of colonies, under ready-made laws, doubtless gave plausibility to this view, which in itself however is quite in keeping with the peripatetic doctrine of discontinuous civilization" (Stewart, *Notes on the Nicomachean Ethics of Aristotle*, 1:171). This tendency is not unique to Aristotle: "It is interesting to see how the Greeks in fact tended to postulate individual law-givers like Solon or Lycurgus as creators of their constitutions" (Hintikka, "Some Conceptual Presuppositions of Greek Political Theory," 20).

Revising Aristotle: Stipulation

The transition from custom to stipulation has two related aspects: the habitual becomes the object of reflection; and the social system of custom becomes the object of an individual synoptic mind. Stipulated order, as the unity of reflection and synoptic totalization, is best captured in Greek by the term *logos*. This is why Aristotle says that when we act according to *logos* we act not according to unreflective custom but according to a deliberately stipulated norm.[61]

Stipulation is an act of rational will, as can be discerned in the history of translation of Aristotle's *logos* from Thomas Aquinas's *ratio* (reason) to John Poinsot's *placitum* (stipulation). Just as Francisco Suárez had emphasized the fundamental role of the will in the act of law-giving, so his student Poinsot emphasized the role of the will in stipulation generally. For when I stipulate a rule of grammar, a recipe, or a law, I make a rational maxim in the imperative mood; it is an act of the rational will. This willful or imperative dimension is only implicit, however, in Aristotle's *logos*; we must revise, then, his concept of stipulation.

Recall Aristotle's claim that it is not *physis* or *ethos* that distinguishes man from the brute animals but *logos* (*Pol.* 1332b5). What does this mean? Aristotle seems to mean that man alone can deliberate to make a rational choice (*prohairesis*); indeed, he denies that any other animal is capable of rational choice (*Eud.* 1226b21). Unfortunately, this does not seem to be true: members of other species, especially primates, appear to engage in deliberation and to make choices about the satisfaction of desires based on consideration of alternatives. What distinguishes man is not the exercise of reason but the will to form what Harry Frankfurt calls "second-order desires." Man alone has the capacity for the reflective self-evaluation of his desires and the capacity to stipulate new desires. The essence of being a person, says Frankfurt, lies not in reason (*logos*) but in the structure of the rational will (*placitum*).[62] It is on these grounds that I take the liberty of rendering Aristotle's *logos* as stipulation.

61. According to Burnet, to act *kata logon* is "to act not merely 'by a rule' but consciously 'with a rule'" (*Ethics of Aristotle*, 37n).

62. "In maintaining that the essence of being a person lies not in reason but in will, I am far from suggesting that a creature without reason may be a person. For it is only in virtue of his rational capacities that a person is capable of becoming critically aware of his own will and of forming volitions of the second order. The structure of a person's will presupposes, accordingly, that he is a rational person" (Harry Frankfurt, "Freedom of the Will and the Concept of a Person," *Journal of Philosophy* 68 [1971]: 11–12).

Aristotle, like the legal positivists, often insists upon a very close relation between law and individual stipulation. He emphasizes, for example, the synoptic unity of legal stipulation: *nomos* is always the result of *phronēsis*— either the *phronēsis* of the individual lawgiver or the *phronēsis* of the assembly acting as one mind.[63] Unlike other forms of stipulation, "the law [*nomos*] has compulsive power, while it is at the same time an account [*logos*] proceeding from a sort of practical wisdom [*phronēsis*] and intellect [*nous*]" (*NE* 1180a21). Not only is law a species of *logos*, but *logos* is often personified as a lawgiver: *logos* commands, orders, and defends. Since *logos* often means "a rule," and since *nomos* is the embodiment of reason, Aristotle has difficulty distinguishing *logos* from *nomos*.[64] *Nomos* is Aristotle's chief exemplar of rational stipulation.

Nomos has a precise meaning in terms of rational stipulation but becomes vague when it is taken to include the order of custom. Just as in history law grew out of custom, so the meaning of *nomos* evolved from meaning primarily custom to meaning primarily stipulation.[65] The early understanding of *nomos* is beautifully captured in Pindar's ode *Nomos Basileus*: "*Nomos*, king of all, mortals and immortals, brings on with sovereign hand what is most violent and makes it just." The precise meaning of the term *nomos* here has been contested since the time of Herodotus; but there is now some agreement that Pindar is referring to custom in the sense of customary reverence toward the deeds of gods and heroes—no matter how unjust those deeds might be.[66] In-

---

63. According to Martin Ostwald: "There is universal agreement, as far as I know, that this noun [*nomos*] is derived from the same root as *nemō*, whose basic concept involves a 'distribution' or 'assigning' of some kind" (*Nomos and the Beginnings of the Athenian Democracy* [Oxford: Clarendon Press, 1969], 9). To which Guthrie adds: "That is to say, it presupposes an acting subject—believer, practitioner or apportioner—a mind from which the *nomos* emanates" (*History of Greek Philosophy*, 3:55).

64. On *logos* as lawgiver, see *NE* 1114b29, 1115b19, 1117a8, 1119a20, 1125b35, 1138b20. On *logos* as "rule," see John Burnet, "On the Meaning of *Logos* in Aristotle's *Ethics*," *Classical Review* 28 (1914): 6. On the general relation of *nomos* to *logos* see René Gauthier and Jean Jolif, *L'Ethique à Nicomaque* (Louvain: Publications Universitaires, 1970), 2:149; and Jacqueline Romilly, *La loi dans la pensée grecque* (Paris: Belles Lettres, 1971), 173ff.

65. According to Ostwald, *nomos* does not refer to law until the fifth century: during the fifth century, *nomos* replaces *thesmos* as the term for law. Where *thesmos* meant arbitrary legal stipulation, *nomos* meant the legal stipulation of custom: "*Thesmos* envisages it [a statute] as being imposed upon a people by a lawgiver legislating for it, while *nomos* looks upon a statute as the expression of what the people regard as a valid and binding norm" (*Nomos and the Beginnings of the Athenian Democracy*, 55).

66. "The fact of experience, then, to which Pindar gave expression in this poem is that a

deed, that cruel and even violent customary practices are often revered is a profound and disturbing fact.

Unfortunately, as *nomos* gradually came to refer to law proper it retained its earlier meaning as custom. The profound vagueness of *nomos* undermines many Aristotelian discussions of social conventions. Aristotle says, for example, that money (*nomisma*) "exists not by nature but by law [*nomos*]" (*NE* 1133a29). Does money arise, then, from customary usage or from legal stipulation? The Scholastics translated *nomos* as *lex*, leading them to confuse legal-tender money with money as a medium of exchange created by usage.[67] Actually, of course, to explain an institution like money we must make use of all three of our categories: money makes use of the natural properties of precious metals or paper, money arises out of customary usage, and money can be stipulated as legal tender.[68]

The conflation of law and custom in *nomos* also undermines Aristotle's legal theory. He says that "laws [*nomoi*] are enacted concerning all matters" (*NE* 1129b14).[69] But does Aristotle mean to say that all norms of justice and right are legally stipulated by the sovereign? He seems to confirm this interpretation: "The law [*nomos*] does not command a man to kill himself, and what it does not command it forbids" (*NE* 1138a7).[70] Bentham and Austin, as we saw in chapter 2, similarly asserted that all binding norms—whether customary or legal—derive from sovereign stipulation. To effect this assimilation of custom to law they invoke the principle that "whatever the sovereign per-

---

basic popular attitude, that is, the common acceptance of a traditional belief as a valid and binding conviction, is king; in other words, that it has absolute, unchallengeable, and legitimate power, both among men and among the gods." For this translation and interpretation of Pindar's ode (frag. 169), see Martin Ostwald, "Pindar, *Nomos*, and Heracles," *Harvard Studies in Classical Philology* 69 (1965): 125. Guthrie agrees that Pindar's *nomos* essentially means custom; see *History of Greek Philosophy*, 3:131. For ancient interpretations of this ode, see Herodotus, *History of the Greek and Persian Wars* 3.38, and Plato, *Gorgias* 484B.

67. Eric Roll, *A History of Economic Thought* (Englewood Cliffs, N.J.: Prentice-Hall, 1956), 34.

68. Stewart, in his note on this passage, insists that money is natural, not conventional: "It is as 'natural' i.e. as *necessary*, that standard coins should be made of a precious metal, as that knives should be made of a hard metal" (*Notes on the Nicomachean Ethics of Aristotle*, 1:463). Stewart, like Aristotle, assumes that an institution like money must be either natural or conventional: the Sophistic (and sophistical) antithesis between nature and convention lives on.

69. Gauthier and Jolif suggest that Aristotle must be referring to Sparta! See *L'Ethique à Nicomaque* 2:339.

70. Gauthier and Jolif comment: "*Cette assertion surprenante a reçu un assez bon nombre d'explications*" (ibid., 2:423).

mits, he commands"—which is but the converse of Aristotle's "what the law does not command it forbids."

However, is it plausible to say of law that it makes enactments on all matters and that therefore what it does not command it forbids? I suggest that it is more plausible to interpret these passages in terms of custom rather than in terms of law. Custom, unlike law, very nearly does "make enactments on all subjects," which is why it is clearly false to say that what the law does not command, it forbids; or in contemporary terms, whatever the sovereign permits, he commands. Law, by contrast, is the deliberate enforcement of those customs deemed central to public order; the law is silent on most matters. True, custom is also silent on some matters of private behavior; but concerning social behavior, it is very nearly the case that whatever custom does not command, it forbids.[71]

If *nomos* were simply ambiguous we could substitute the term *custom* for what is almost always translated as *law*.[72] The confusion generated by the passages above, however, is no simple ambiguity: the relation between custom and law in *nomos* is profoundly vague. These passages are not simply referring to custom because terms such as *enactments*, *command*, and *forbid* refer to legal stipulation. Only law, as the product of an individual mind, can "enact" or "command" or "forbid"; customs habituate or constrain. Thus *nomos* refers in these and other passages to both law and custom—which is to say neither.

In some places, Aristotle does implicitly distinguish law from custom. For example, in one interesting passage (*Pol.* 1324b12–22), Aristotle contrasts the custom (*ethos*) of the barbarous nations to the law (*nomos*) of civilized nations, suggesting that law emerges out of custom. In the same vein, he says that "customary laws [*kata ta ethē*] have more weight, and relate to more important matters, than written laws and a man may be a safer ruler than the written law, but not safer than the customary law" (*Pol.* 1287b5). The upshot of this passage is that law, far from growing out of custom, can be a threat to custom.

71. As Stewart rightly comments: "Custom or fashion does not tell Oxford undergraduates to go down to the River in academic dress; it therefore forbids them to do it. Nor do the Statutes of the University tell them; but the Statutes do not therefore forbid them. The Statutes are neutral in this matter, as in many other matters in which fashion takes a side" (*Notes on the Nicomachean Ethics of Aristotle*, 1:390).

72. This is Stewart's suggestion; and "custom" is undoubtedly an improvement over "law" in the above passages.

Unfortunately, in the final analysis, *ethos*, like *nomos*, is vague: in some cases, we do not know whether Aristotle is contrasting law to custom or to habit. "For the law [*nomos*] has no power to command obedience except that of habit [*ethos*], which can only be given by time, so that readiness to change from old law to new law weakens the power of law" (*Pol.* 1269a20). Is Aristotle making the sociological argument that laws require support from customary mores, or the psychological argument that people obey the law only out of habit? Either way, his arguments are not persuasive. Customs are enforced by every member of society who practices them; laws are enforced by specialized legal professionals. Although it is easier to enforce laws that are based on custom, laws are often enforced contrary to custom or to reconcile conflicts in custom. And legal sanctions provide a strong incentive to obey the law regardless of its relation to habit.

Nowhere is the opacity of Aristotle's circle of metaphors greater than in his discussions of the unwritten law (*agraphos nomos*). What makes these discussions so opaque is that the same metaphor of "unwritten law" conceals several very different underlying analogies. Rudolf Hirzel observes that Aristotle describes unwritten law alternatively as customary law, as divine law, and as natural law: "*Die Sache bleibt, die Namen wechseln.*"[73] I submit, however, that it is more accurate to say that the nominal continuity of the metaphor "unwritten law" conceals a profound conceptual discontinuity of underlying analogies: "*Der Name bleibt, die Sachen wechseln.*" Moreover, it is in this discussion of unwritten law that Aristotle not only explicitly refers to natural law but does so in a way that anticipates Stoic and Thomistic natural law doctrine.[74]

To begin with, Aristotle is famous for his description of custom as "unwritten law." When he says that "written laws depend on force while the unwritten do not" (*Rhet.* 1375a16), he means to distinguish legal from customary sanctions; similarly, when he says that a legislator should institute both written and unwritten laws (*Pol.* 1319b40), he means that a legislator must be concerned not just with the stipulation of laws but also with inculcation of customs. When he uses the metaphor "unwritten law" to describe custom, then, the underlying analogy is: written law is to unwritten law as law is to custom.

73. Hirzel, *Agraphos Nomos*, 3.

74. Strauss (*Natural Right and History*) and Jaffa (*Thomism and Aristotelianism*) are right to distinguish sharply Aristotle's natural justice from Aquinas's natural law; but because they totally neglect Aristotle's discussion of natural law in the *Rhetoric*, they overstate the distance between Aristotle and Aquinas.

Just when we think that unwritten law means custom, we find this passage: "Law [*nomos*] is either special [*idios*] or general [*koinos*]. By special law I mean that written law which regulates the life of a particular community; by general law, all those unwritten principles which are supposed to be acknowledged everywhere" (*Rhet.* 1368b7). How can this universal unwritten law be custom, when customs are notoriously local? What we find here is that "unwritten law" implies a very different analogy: written law is to unwritten law as the local (*idios*) is to the universal (*koinos*). That we are no longer describing custom is evident when we realize that this is the same analogy underlying Aristotle's distinction between legal justice and natural justice (*NE* 1134b18): legal justice is to natural justice as the local is to the universal.[75] Recall that natural justice has everywhere the same potential but not the same actuality or validity; the general law (*koinos nomos*), however, has the same validity everywhere.

Aristotle illustrates this universal unwritten law: "for instance, gratitude to, or requital of, our benefactors, readiness to help our friends, and the like" (*Rhet.* 1374a24); in short, says Aristotle, this is the law described by Antigone as the divine and eternal unwritten laws (*nomina theōn*).[76] Aristotle here interprets the metaphor "unwritten law" according to a completely new analogy: written law is to unwritten law as the human is to the divine. What makes the unwritten law more timeless, more universal, and more important than written law is that it comes from the gods.[77] In addition to this universal unwritten law, Aristotle identifies a particular unwritten law, a local supplement to the written code of law, known as equity (*epieikes*) (*Rhet.* 1374a27).[78] Equity

75. E. M. Cope explicitly identifies these concepts: *physikon dikaion* = *koinos nomos* just as *nomikon dikaion* = *idios nomos*. "Natural justice is law because it is right, conventional justice is right because it is law" (Cope, *An Introduction to Aristotle's Rhetoric* [London: Macmillan, 1867], 241–42).

76. On the meaning of the divine unwritten law in the *Antigone* (ll. 454–57), see Ostwald, *From Popular Sovereignty to the Sovereignty of Law* (Berkeley: University of California Press, 1986), 153.

77. Socrates refers to this divine unwritten law in Xenophon's *Memorabilia* 4.4. On the theological origins of Greek thought about unwritten law, see Hirzel, *Agraphos Nomos*, 32–35: "*Aus dem göttlichen allgemeinen Gesetz, wie wir sehen, war eine menschliche particulare Sitte geworden*"; and Ostwald, *From Popular Sovereignty to the Sovereignty of Law*, pp. 94–108 and chap. 3.

78. "Here therefore this second, subordinate kind of *agraphos nomos* is said to mean equity, the modification or mitigation of the rigour of the law . . . or particular decision adapted to the special occasion where the written general laws fail to meet the case" (Cope, *Introduction to Aristotle's Rhetoric*, 243).

enables the written law to be interpreted in accordance with local customary notions of justice and fairness (see *NE* 1137b8).[79]

Aristotle's signal contribution to legal theory was to transform these traditional concepts of unwritten law into a doctrine of natural law. In his discussion of Sophocles' *Antigone*, Aristotle says that when Antigone spoke of the divine unwritten laws, she meant the natural law (*Rhet.* 1373b10, 1375a32). Although Antigone had contrasted positive law to divine law, Aristotle interprets this as a contrast of positive law to natural law. In addition to all the previous analogies underlying the metaphor "unwritten law," Aristotle adds a momentous new one: written law is to unwritten law as positive law is to natural law. Once Aristotle transmuted "unwritten law" into "natural law," the doctrine of natural law would henceforth embody all of the attributes of the analogies underlying the metaphor "unwritten law"—thus it is that natural law came to be associated with what is customary, what is universal, and what is divine. "Universal law is the law of nature [*kata physin*]. For there really is, as everyone to some extent divines [*manteuomai*], a natural justice and injustice that is common to all, even to those who have no association or covenant with each other" (*Rhet.* 1373b3). Aristotle's use of the verb "to divine or prophesy" (*manteuomai*) reveals the theological origin of his doctrine of natural law. By transforming divine law into natural law, Aristotle is simply completing the project of the pre-Socratic *physikoi* who had already "deliberately enthroned Nature in the place of God."[80] Indeed, Aristotle's view that law is the rational stipulation (*logos*) of a mind implies that the natural law emanates from some kind of mind: the expression *kata physin* implies *kata logon*. If nature did not somehow promulgate this law, then how can all people "divine" it in their hearts?

Moreover, Aristotle goes on to suggest that the particular unwritten law, the principles of equity, also belongs to natural law: "We must urge that the principles of equity are permanent and changeless, and that the universal law does

---

79. As Max Hamburger says: "And this is the nature of the equitable, a correction of law where it is defective owing to its universality." Hamburger illustrates the role of equity by citing the Swiss Civil Code of 1907: "When there is no statutory rule applicable to the case, the judge ought to decide according to customary law" (*Morals and Law* [New Haven: Yale University Press, 1951], 98 and 99n).

80. "The transfer of the functions and attributes of the ancient gods to *physis* by the philosophers of the sixth and fifth centuries eventually so charged Nature with personality that the Socratic teleology was a foregone conclusion. From Plato onwards, with few exceptions, philosophers proceed with the synthesis: the gods act according to the laws of nature, and Nature assumes the divinity of the gods" (Heidel, "*Peri Physeōs*," 94–95).

not change either, for it is the law of nature [*kata physin*], whereas written laws often do change" (*Rhet.* 1375a30). Aristotle does not directly make equity a part of natural law, but he clearly establishes a close connection between the "permanent and changeless" principles of equity and the equally immutable laws of nature.[81] What is certain is that Roman jurisprudence followed Aristotle's view that "equity is as eternal as human nature itself"—as is evident in the expression *aequitas naturalis*.[82]

Aristotle's description of the universal unwritten law as *kata physin* in the *Rhetoric* (1373b6, 1375a32) anticipates Stoic and Thomistic natural law in a way that his discussion of what is just by nature (*physei*) in the *Ethics* does not. His doctrine of what is natural (*physei*) lacks the attributes of rationality present in his doctrine of what is according to nature (*kata physin*). Aristotle does not have a full-blown theory of natural law because he does not have a full-blown theory of divine personality as the source of legal stipulation. But Aristotle's notion of a law that is *kata physin* implies that nature has a rational plan; and Aristotle's notion that everyone can "divine" this law suggests that natural law is promulgated in something like human conscience.[83] Since it is not until Suárez that we find a theory of rational will as the source of law, even Thomas Aquinas lacks a truly full-blown theory of divine personality as the source of natural law.[84] Aristotle's natural teleology embodies enough elements of personality to ground a rudimentary doctrine of natural law.

Aristotle has completed the circle of interdefinability: custom is both "second nature" and "unwritten law"—and unwritten law is the law of nature!

81. As Hamburger says: "This juxtaposition of equity and the universal law of nature and the immutability common to them reveal the close kinship between the two concepts" (*Morals and Law*, 100).

82. On the role of equity in Latin natural law jurisprudence, see Hirzel, *Agraphos Nomos*, 5–10.

83. Aristotle's view of natural law seems to draw on a personification of nature voiced by Demosthenes, who said of a moral precept that "nature herself has decreed it in the unwritten laws and in the hearts of men." See Guthrie, *History of Greek Philosophy*, 3:118.

84. After dismissing the discussion of natural law in the *Rhetoric* as mere forensics, Jaffa says: "The reason why there is no mention of natural law in Aristotle may be gathered from Thomas' own definition of law: 'Law is nothing else than a certain ordinance of reason for the common good, by him who has the care of the community, and promulgated.'" According to Jaffa, Aristotle cannot have a doctrine of natural law because he meets only two of four criteria. By this logic Thomas Aquinas cannot have a doctrine of natural law because he does not meet all the criteria of Suárez's definition of law. See Jaffa, *Thomism and Aristotelianism*, 168–69.

Part Three

An Aristotelian Critique of Classical Political Economy

Karl Marx rightly defined "classical political economy" as the school of thought beginning with the seventeenth-century writer William Petty, branching into physiocracy, and reaching full articulation in the period from Adam Smith to Marx himself.[1] What Marx did not observe is that the expression "political economy" is ironic: this school of thought sought above all to remove the economy—especially production—from the realm of moral and political debate. Far from understanding economics in terms of political deliberation or legal stipulation, classical political economy systematically reduced economics to a technical quest for efficiency in accordance with natural laws.

Classical political economy is a creature of seventeenth century, and although the seventeenth century prided itself on its rejection of Aristotle, what we actually find in this period is largely an elaboration of Aristotle's conceptual scheme. Just as Aristotle explicitly claimed that production is governed solely by technical reason, so the political economists reduced the moral dimension of the division of labor to technical efficiency; and just as Aristotle often described the division of labor between men and women, between master and slave, as natural, so the political economists reduced the customary and stipulated dimensions of the division of labor to nature.

What unifies this twofold reduction is Aristotle's concept of the economy of nature: for example, since the division of labor is efficient it must be natural—after all, "nature makes nothing in vain." Far from rejecting the teleo-

1. According to Ronald L. Meek: "Physiocracy and the type of theory propounded by Smith and his followers are best regarded, I suggest, as two different species of the genus Classicism" (*The Economics of Physiocracy*, ed. Ronald L. Meek [London: George Allen and Unwin, 1962], 347).

logical concept of the economy of nature, the seventeenth century employed this concept in biology as well as in physics. Natural theology inferred the existence of divine economizing from the efficient adaptation of each organism to its niche; and the principle of least action in physics—also called the principle of natural economy—assumed that all natural motion follows the most efficient path. Nothing is more Aristotelian about classical political economy than the view that because nature economizes the economy must be natural.

By defining its object of inquiry as the "economy," classical political economy was, it seems, destined to a twofold reduction of the division of labor to technique and to nature. Since *economy* (*oikonomia*) means "household management," the metaphor "political economy" stems from an implicit analogy between the management of a household and the management of a society. This analogy was intended not to politicize the domicile but to domesticate the polity. In this sense classical political economy is more Platonic than Aristotelian because although Plato often compared the *technē* of household management to the *technē* of politics, Aristotle rejected any reduction of politics to household management.[2] In short, the choice of the expression "political economy" had a profound effect in defining the character of classical political economy. In the first comprehensive English treatise on political economy, James Steuart defined the new science: "What oeconomy is in a family, political oeconomy is in a state."[3] The notion of "social housekeeping" was at the center of classical political economy in its mercantilist, physiocratic, Smithian, and Marxist phases.[4]

---

2. Thus Hannah Arendt claims that "according to ancient thought on these matters, the very term 'political economy' would have been a contradiction in terms." See *The Human Condition* (Chicago: University of Chicago Press, 1958), 29. Actually, however, in Greek thought we often find an analogy drawn between the *oikos* and the *polis*: "Given the association of the ideas of political and domestic economy which appears time and again in the works of Plato and Xenophon, the parallel between state and family was doubtless on occasion drawn more explicitly" (Thomas Cole, *Democritus and the Sources of Greek Anthropology* [Western Reserve University: American Philological Association, 1967], 133). For Plato's comparison of *oikos* and *polis*, see *Meno* 73A and 91A, *Protagoras* 318E; for Aristotle's critique of this analogy, see *Pol.* 1252a5 and 1255b15.

3. James Steuart, *Principles of Political Oeconomy* (London: A. Millar and T. Cadell, 1767), 1:1 Similarly, James Mill writes: "Political Economy is to the State, what domestic economy is to the family" (*Elements of Political Economy* [London: Baldwin, Cradock, and Joy, 1826], 1).

4. On the notion of political economy as "social housekeeping"—especially evident in the

Although political economy defines market equilibrium as the unintended outcome of diverse individual transactions, the very concept of a national "economy" or "economizing" presupposes a collective subject that acts to maximize social welfare. Thus Adam Smith's view that political economy is a "branch of the science of a statesman or legislator" is at war with his own theory of an autonomous market order. According to Gunnar Myrdal, to describe the unintended result of innumerable individual transactions as "social economizing" is to fall into the trap of the "communistic fiction," that is, positing a collective subject where there is none.[5] Of course, Marxist socialism is perfectly compatible with the "communistic fiction" of political economy because if the entire society is organized into a single household or a single firm, then political economizing is perfectly possible.[6] The very notion of a political economy, then, points inexorably to socialism—which is why champions of the free market have rejected the name "economics" ever since the logician Richard Whately offered the name "catallactics" for the science of market exchange.[7]

The notion that political economy is social housekeeping serves admirably to define economics as a technical rather than a moral or political science. The art of household economizing is a straightforward technical exercise in selecting the most efficient means to the ends selected by the head of the household. The authority of the father traditionally eliminated political conflict over the ends of domestic economy. The polity can economize only if we assume an analogous paternal authority and the absence of conflict over the goals of economic life: political economy, in short, is possible only in the absence of politics.[8] J. G. A. Pocock rightly grasps the apo-

---

German *Volkswirtschaftslehre*—see Gunnar Myrdal, *The Political Element in the Development of Economic Theory* [1954], trans. Paul Streeten (New York: Simon and Schuster, 1969), chap. 6.

5. Myrdal, *Political Element in the Development of Economic Theory*, 145.

6. On Marxist socialism as a single-firm economy, see Ugo Pagano, *Work and Welfare in Economic Theory* (Oxford: Basil Blackwell, 1985), 45.

7. Whately's term "catallactics" (1838) from the Greek *katallattein* (to exchange) has been championed in our time by Ludwig von Mises and F. A. Hayek. See Hayek, *The Fatal Conceit*, ed. W. W. Bartley (Chicago: University of Chicago Press, 1988), 112.

8. Some contemporary feminists criticize this technical view of even the domestic economy by arguing that the conflict of interests within the family leads to a political economy in the household. So where the classical political economists sought to domesticate the polity, feminists seek to politicize the domicile. See Nancy Folbre, "Exploitation Comes Home: A Critique of the Marxian Theory of Family Labor," *Cambridge Journal of Economics* 6 (1982).

litical nature of what is called classical political economy: "It replaced the *polis* by politeness, the *oikos* by the economy."⁹ Indeed, we still refer to the national economy as the "domestic" economy.

Given this obvious reduction of economics to the technical art of house-keeping, it is surprising to find a commentator arguing that because Smith defines political economy as a "branch of the science of a statesman or legis-lator," he must hold a political theory of the economy.¹⁰ What Smith means by this expression is simply that the statesman should economize in the polity (through trade surpluses, for example) as if it were a household. What Smith clearly does not mean is that the statesman should subject the ends of eco-nomic activity to political debate. Marx's model of the communist economy is precisely such a patriarchal household in which central planning will enable the "head" of the economy to maximize social welfare by allocating resources among competing uses.¹¹ Indeed, since a household economy maximizes the utility of the head of the household alone, both Smith and Marx end up by turning to Robinson Crusoe as a model of economic activity. Marx will explicitly compare the single-firm communist economy to the single-person economy of Robinson Crusoe.

Not content with defining political economy as a technical art, our econo-mists went on to define political economy as a natural science of society. Although Smith defines political economy as a "branch of the science of a statesman," the whole purpose of the *Wealth of Nations* is to show that the best way for a nation to economize is, for the most part, to keep statesmen from interfering with the market. By locating the economy in the realm of society, however, and by insisting on the autonomy of social life, the classical political economists were able to banish politics from the economy.¹² The state would

9. Pocock, "Cambridge Paradigms and Scotch Philosophers," in *Wealth and Virtue*, ed. Istvan Hont and Michael Ignatieff (Cambridge: Cambridge University Press, 1983), 242.

10. See Adam Smith, *The Wealth of Nations* [1776], ed. R. H. Campbell, A. S. Skinner, and W. B. Todd (Oxford: Oxford University Press, 1979), 4 (introduction): 428. Donald Winch cites this passage to prove that Smith has a truly political understanding of the econ-omy in his *Adam Smith's Politics* (Cambridge: Cambridge University Press, 1978), 12.

11. On Marxist communism as a household writ large, see William James Booth, "The New Household Economy," *American Political Science Review* 85 (1991): 59-76, and Alec Nove, *The Economics of Feasible Socialism* (London: George Allen and Unwin, 1983), 39.

12. As Thomas Hodgskin says of political economy: "It is not, as is generally supposed, a meddling, factious, ambitious science,—not a *political* science, prescribing regulations for society, or dictating duties to men" (*Popular Political Economy* [London: Charles Tait, 1827], 38–39).

still have a role regulating certain aspects of economic activity, but the division and deployment of labor, for example, would no longer be subject to political deliberation as it was with medieval guilds.

It was no accident that the economy became identified with the social realm: the term *societas* in Roman law refers to a private contractual partnership of individuals; the *universitas* (corporation), by contrast, refers to an association incorporated by a sovereign authority. *Societas* belongs strictly to the private law of contracts (*ius privatum*); *universitas* belongs to the public law of incorporation (*ius publicum*). Thus the early modern theory of the state as a "social contract" represents a profound legal and philosophical confusion: the state is by definition a corporation, not a society.[13] Or, put differently, once the state became defined as a *societas*, it was a mere redundancy to argue that it arose from a contract. The notion that the economy is a *societas*, however, makes perfect sense because a society is a contractual partnership.

Therefore, over time, the expression "social economy" came to replace the expression "political economy" in the works of classical political economy. Indeed, the political economists were the first theorists to demarcate the realm of "society" as a system of relations distinct from the realm of "politics": the chief contribution of political economy to philosophy is its doctrine of society, not its doctrine of the state. We thus find the curious phenomenon of treatises on "political economy" that explicitly define their subject matter as "social economy."[14]

Once the economy was located in society and once it was understood that many forms of social cooperation arise spontaneously—that is, without being legally stipulated—social economy could be defined as a natural science. Because economic processes are not the product of deliberate stipulation but the unintended result of myriad interactions, the economy was thought to be subject to natural law. And so classical political economy achieved its final and most perfect articulation by defining economics not as a political but as a

13. "How came it about that political theory, which went to the lawyers for most of its ideas, borrowed the contract of partnership rather than the apparently far more appropriate act of incorporation?" (Frederic W. Maitland, "Introduction" [1900], in Otto Gierke, *Political Theories of the Middle Age* [Cambridge: Cambridge University Press, 1938], xxiii).

14. Thus Jean-Baptiste Say: "Political economy is nothing else than social economy." *Cours complet d'économie politique* (Paris: Guillaumin, 1840), 1. J. S. Mill follows Say by defining political economy as the "science of social economy" (*Essays on Some Unsettled Questions of Political Economy* [London: John W. Parker, 1844], 135).

natural science: "Political economy is a natural, not a political science, and must not be left exclusively to statesmen."[15] Nor can this naturalism be ascribed to capitalist apologetics, since the above citation is from Thomas Hodgskin—a radical Ricardian socialist. Given the curiously apolitical character of "political economy," it is not surprising that our political economists treated the division of labor as either the inevitable product of efficient housekeeping or as the equally inevitable expression of human nature.

15. As Hodgskin says: "The whole system of social production must be considered, like the solar system, as a part of the universe, which man may observe and know, but cannot regulate" (*Popular Political Economy*, 261–63). J.-B. Say similarly claims that political economy is to the social body what physiology is to the natural body—and the social body, he adds, is a living body just like the human body. See *Cours complet d'économie politique*, 1. J. S. Mill defines political economy as "the science which treats of the production and distribution of wealth, so far as they depend upon the laws of human nature" (*Essays on Some Unsettled Questions of Political Economy*), 133.

Chapter 5

The Social and the Technical Division of Labor
in Classical Political Economy

The Division of Labor as Technical Productivity

The importance of the division of labor in economic life has been appreciated since the time of Plato and Xenophon. What then is distinctive of the treatment of this "eternal commonplace of economics" (Joseph Schumpeter) in classical political economy? It is the analysis of the social division of labor solely in terms of physical efficiency. Our economists all insist that an increased division of labor produces more output with the same input. They treat the social division of labor as but a special case of the more general maxim of instrumental reason: namely, that given an end (maximum output) we seek the best means (minimum input).

However, as we saw in chapter 1, it is very difficult to show in a specific instance that increasing the social division of labor leads to more output for the same input. To show unequivocally that a detailed division of labor is more efficient, two conditions must hold: first, ends and means must be separable, so that we can compare different divisions of labor as means to the same end of maximum output; and second, our ends-means relation must be isolated from intervening variables, so that the effects of an increased division of labor can be independently measured. In the first chapter we showed how these two conditions are related: the only way for ends and means to be even provisionally separated is if their relation can somehow be isolated from the intervening causal and semiotic networks.

The classical political economists endeavored mightily to show with precision that the increased social division of labor had such univocal effects on output; and they did this by attempting to isolate and measure the independent effect of the social division of labor on productivity. Such a strategy of experimental isolation and control makes sense in the case of the technical division of work into tasks, but the social division of workers cannot be isolated from the intervening linguistic and psychological systems of meaning. By treating the social division of labor as a mere means to greater production, economists neglected the fact that a detailed division of labor, by eroding the morale of workers, might undermine productivity itself; for the same reason, a less detailed and more humane division of labor, by improving morale, could well enhance productivity. Because the productivity of the social division of labor is inseparable from the question of worker morale, and because the morale of workers is inseparable from the moral significance of work, the social division of labor cannot be reduced to the technical division of tasks.

In response to Socrates' question, "Who would do a finer job, one man practicing many arts, or one man one art?" Plato argues for specialization on two different grounds (*Republic* 370B–C). First, specialization makes efficient use of differences in natural aptitudes: "One man is naturally fitted for one task, and another for another." But Plato also argues that specialization is preferable in and of itself, even if one assumes no differences in natural aptitude. "And further, it's also plain, I suppose, that if a man lets the crucial moment in any work pass, it is completely ruined." Plato is arguing that in every trade one must be attentive to the objective sequence of tasks if the work is to be performed properly. If a man attempts to be both a baker and a fisherman, then the cake will burn while the fish are biting, or the fish will swim away while the cake comes out of the oven. Plato's emphasis here on the efficiency of specialization per se — apart from the Sophistic controversy about whether skill is natural or conventional — is the first attempt to isolate the technical relation between the division of labor and productivity.[1]

Plato says that specialization produces goods in greater quantity (*Republic* 370C) and of greater quality, but he emphasizes quality: Socrates asks whether a specialist would do a *finer (kalliōn)* job. Xenophon also argues that

---

1. Joseph Schumpeter denies the importance of Plato's emphasis on the efficiency of specialization per se: "He [Plato] elaborates on this eternal commonplace of economics with unusual care. If there is anything interesting in this, it is that he (and following him, Aristotle) puts the emphasis not upon the increase of efficiency that results from division of labor *per se* but upon the increase of efficiency that results from allowing everyone to specialize in what he is by nature best fitted for" (*History of Economic Analysis* [New York: Oxford University Press, 1954], 56). Yet it is precisely Plato's emphasis on the efficiency of specialization per se that is his most original contribution to the theory of the division of labor.

"he who devotes himself to a very highly specialized line of work is bound to do it in the best possible manner [*arista poiein*]."[2] Ever since Dugald Stewart and Karl Marx pointed out the contrast between the ancient quest for greater quality and the modern quest for greater quantity, commentators have argued that the ancients did not treat the division of labor in terms of technical efficiency. But one can perfectly well measure efficiency in terms of quality where there is agreement about the ordinal ranking of degrees of quality: one can, in short, maximize quality just as one can maximize quantity. Comparisons of efficiency require only ordinal, not cardinal, commensurability. For the ancients, increasing the division of labor is efficient because with the same labor inputs, one gets a higher quality of output.[3]

When we turn to the early modern period, theorists begin to emphasize not the quality, but the cheapening, of commodities that results from specialization. William Petty was the first to observe that "Cloth must be cheaper made, when one Cards, another Spins, another Weaves, another Draws," etc.[4] In this respect, as in others, Marx was right to praise Petty as the father of classical political economy.[5] By focusing on the reduction of price, Petty has advanced

2. Xenophon, *Cyropedia*, trans. Walter Miller (London: William Heinemann, 1914), 8.2.5. In the same passage he says: "And it is, of course, impossible for a man of many trades to be proficient in all of them [*kalōs poiein*]."

3. Dugald Stewart was the first theorist to grasp the fundamental contrast between the ancient and the modern accounts of the division of labor: "What Xenophon lays the chief stress on, is the effect of this division in improving the *quality* of the articles produced, whereas the circumstance which has chiefly attracted the attention of Mr. Smith and other modern writers is its astonishing effect in increasing their *quantity*" ("Lectures on Political Economy" [1810], in *The Collected Works of Dugald Stewart*, vol. 8, ed. Sir William Hamilton [Edinburgh: Thomas Constable, 1853], 312). Marx essentially follows Stewart on this point: "In most striking contrast with this accentuation of quantity and exchange-value, is the attitude of the writers of classical antiquity, who hold exclusively by quality and use-value" (*Capital*, vol. 1 [1867] [New York: International Publishers, 1967], 14.5.344). William James Booth agrees with Marx that the ancients did not view the division of labor in terms of increasing productivity, which he defines in terms of quantity (*pleiō*); see his "Economies of Time," *Political Theory* 19 (February 1991): 9–12. What these comments overlook is that productivity can be measured in terms of quality or quantity. The ancients and the moderns emphasize a different maximand, but they share a similar logic of maximization.

4. William Petty also says that the division of labor in watch-making means that "the Watch will be better and cheaper, than if the whole Work be put upon any one Man" (*The Economic Writings of Sir William Petty* [1676–1690], ed. Charles Henry Hull [Cambridge: Cambridge University Press, 1899], 1:260 and 2:473).

5. According to Marx, "classical political economy" begins with Petty and ends with Ricardo. See "A Contribution to the Critique of Political Economy" [1859], in *Collected Works*,

the quest for a precise measurement of the efficiency of a greater division of labor.[6]

Although improvements in quality are debatable and difficult to measure, a reduction in price seems to be empirically demonstrable and quantifiable. For the first time, the effects of a greater division of labor appear to be empirically verifiable; however, the complexity of economic processes undermines this appearance of experimental control. Often a greater division of labor does not simply produce the same product for a lower cost and price; a greater division of labor often produces a different product. A watch custom-made by a single artisan is a unique work of art; watches mass-produced through the detailed division of labor are all standard. In many cases, the greater division of labor cheapened commodities in both senses of "cheap"—lower price and lower quality. Moreover, a reduction in the price of a commodity does not afford a stable basis for comparison and measurement, since all prices are relative to other prices—including the price of money. If all commodities become cheaper, then no commodity is cheaper, for cheapness is relative.[7] Thus we still have not found our absolute standard of comparison to measure the efficiency of an increasing social division of labor.

Adam Smith's signal contribution to the theory of the division of labor was to propose such an absolute standard of comparison by arguing that a greater division of labor produces a greater quantity of goods. Whereas other writers had suggested in a vague way that specialization produces more goods, Smith alone went to great lengths to quantify the precise numerical improvement in productivity per man due to the division of labor.[8] We find in Smith's work a

---

vol. 29 (New York: International Publishers, 1987), 292. Marx says of Petty: "What from the outset distinguishes Petty's conception of the division of labour from that of classical antiquity is his grasp of its influence on the exchange value of the product, on the product as commodity—its cheapening" ("Economic Manuscript of 1861–63," in *Collected Works*, vol. 30 [New York: International Publishers, 1988], 286).

6. Petty's discussion of cheapened goods is picked up by Joseph Harris in *An Essay upon Money and Coins* (London: G. Hawkins, 1757), 21, and by Josiah Tucker in "Instructions for Travellers" [1757], in *Josiah Tucker: A Selection from His Economic and Political Writings*, ed. Robert L. Schuyler (New York: Columbia University Press, 1931), 241.

7. The development of the labor theory of value was precisely an attempt to provide an invariant standard with which one could measure absolute cheapening over time; but in the absence of an explicit theory of value, Petty and others were not able to specify whether cheapening was to be measured in real or in merely nominal terms.

8. I emphasize the originality of Smith's contribution here because there is a consensus

significant shift from the 1762–63 *Lectures on Jurisprudence* to the 1776 *Wealth of Nations*. In the *Lectures*, Smith emphasizes both the greater number of goods produced as well as the cheapening of the goods: "By the division of the work, 10, 20, or 40 times the quantity of work is done which is done when the hands are fewer, and the more highly the work is divided the cheaper it will always be."[9] In the *Wealth of Nations*, however, the issue of the cheapening of commodities disappears from his discussion of the division of labor. The contrast between the two works is especially clear in the case of a passage that appears in both works—but with one significant change. In the *Lectures*, we read: "This increase of the stock of commodities, and the cheapness of work arising from the division of work, has three causes."[10] In the *Wealth*, however, we read: "This great increase of the quantity of work, which, in consequence of the division of labour, the same number of people are capable of performing, is owing to three different circumstances."[11] Neither Smith nor his commentators ever take note of this significant shift in the terms of analysis.[12] In short, Smith's achievement is to quantify the increased physical productivity due to the detailed social division of labor.[13]

Since Smith's emphasis on the sheer physical productivity of the division of labor became the model for all subsequent discussion, we should consider briefly why Smith rejects Xenophon's appeal to improved quality and Petty's

---

among historians of economic thought that Smith contributed nothing original to the theory of the division of labor. Marx first expressed the view that "Adam Smith has not established a single new proposition relating to the division of labor" (*Capital*, 1:14.3.329n. Marx's view is echoed by Edwin Cannan, *A Review of Economic Theory* (London: P. S. King and Son, 1929), 96; Schumpeter, *History of Economic Analysis*, 187; and Eric Roll, *A History of Economic Thought* (Englewood Cliffs, N.J.: Prentice-Hall, 1956), 104.

9. Adam Smith, *Lectures on Jurisprudence* [1762–1766], ed. Ronald L. Meek, D. D. Raphael, and P. G. Stein (Oxford: Oxford University Press, 1978), 344.

10. Ibid., 345.

11. Adam Smith, *The Wealth of Nations* [1776], ed. R. H. Campbell, A. S. Skinner, and W. B. Todd (Oxford: Oxford University Press, 1979), 1:1.17.

12. At the level of economic processes, of course, the cheapening of commodities is often simply the result of the greater quantity produced. But at the level of economic theory, the shift from explaining productivity in terms of cheapening to explaining it in terms of quantity is quite significant.

13. Smith's numerical examples are speculative rather than empirical; they vary from the *Lectures* to the *Wealth*. In the *Lectures*, we have eighteen workers making 36,000 pins per day, or 2,000 pins per worker per day; in the *Wealth* we have ten workers making 48,000 pins per day, or 4,800 pins per worker per day.

appeal to the cheapening of commodities. Smith is quite explicit about why he rejects appeals to quality: "Quality, however, is so very disputable a matter, that I look upon all information of this kind as somewhat uncertain."[14] The technical superiority of the division of labor cannot be based on debatable standards of quality; we need an objective and quantifiable measure of productivity. Indeed, Smith's rejection of quality illustrates the larger story of the history of science as the quest for intersubjectively verifiable knowledge that is not based on particular interpretive traditions. Smith's turn to the quantitative is driven by the quest for objective knowledge not subject to moral, cultural, or political dispute.

Between the *Lectures* and the *Wealth*, Smith seems to have realized that the cheapening of commodities is just as disputable a standard as is the quality of commodities. In the *Lectures*, Smith argues that the cheapening of commodities will increase profits so that "each branch of trade will afford enough both to support the opulence and give considerable profit of the great men, and sufficiently reward the industry of the labourer."[15] If it were true that cheapened commodities benefit all men equally, then we would have consensus about our standard of productivity; but Smith became aware that cheapened commodities leading to increased profits need not benefit the workers. Why should the capitalist share his profits with the workers? "I do not mean that the profits are divided in fact precisely in the above manner [i.e., divided with workers], but that they may be divided in such manner."[16] Because the benefits of cheapened commodities are thus subject to dispute, Smith takes physical productivity to be the only objective and indisputable measure of the technical superiority of the division of labor. Smith was so sure that quantity represented a technically unimpeachable standard that he even argues for the division of philosophical labor on the grounds that it increases the quantity of knowledge.[17] Of course, in the case of knowledge it is all too evident that sheer quantity will not serve as the sole standard of progress, since the quality of knowledge is also, presumably, important.[18] But if the production of knowledge is no mere question

14. Smith, *Wealth of Nations*, 1:11.261.

15. Smith, *Lectures on Jurisprudence*, 343.

16. Smith, "Early Draft of Part of *The Wealth of Nations*," in *Lectures on Jurisprudence*, 566.

17. "Each individual becomes more expert in his own peculiar branch, more work is done upon the whole, and the quantity of science is considerably increased by it" (Smith, *Wealth of Nations*, 1:1.22).

18. We can now see why the quest for an objective standard of comparison in academic pro-

of physical efficiency, this is equally true, though less obvious, of the production of commodities.

Smith: The Reduction of the Social to the Technical Division of Labor

Smith's efforts to define the division of labor in terms of physical productivity, as opposed to improved quality or the cheapening of commodities, became the basis for Marx's historical materialism. By showing that it produces an ever-greater quantity of goods, Smith made the division of labor into the universal and transhistorical engine of economic progress. What Joseph Schumpeter says of Smith's emphasis on the division of labor is more or less true of classical political economy generally: "With Adam Smith it is practically the only factor in economic progress."[19] Improvements in the quality of goods are subject to culturally specific criteria; similarly, the cheapening of commodities is possible only in an exchange economy. But the production of a greater and greater quantity of goods seems to provide a world-historical criterion by which all social and economic progress can be measured. Indeed, the very notion of economic progress presupposes such a universally valid metric by which such progress can be measured. Socialism can be the fulfillment of capitalism only if both economic systems are subject to the same criterion of physical productivity. Smith's project was to show that the ever-increasing division of labor is both the cause and the index of the growing wealth of nations; Marx extends Smith's project by arguing that the division of labor is the measure of all historical progress: "How far the productive forces of a nation are developed is shown most manifestly by the degree to which the division of labor has been carried."[20]

As we discovered in chapter 1, there is no doubt that the technical division of labor—by analyzing a process into its components—greatly enhances the

---

motion increasingly focuses on the verifiable quantity of published output as opposed to the disputable quality of output.

19. Schumpeter, *History of Economic Analysis*, 187.

20. Marx, "The German Ideology" [1846], in *Collected Works*, vol. 5 (New York: International Publishers, 1976), 32. Jon Elster comments: "Like Weber and Durkheim, Marx thus saw the progress of history up to the present as one of constant differentiation" (*Making Sense of Marx* [Cambridge: Cambridge University Press, 1985], 113). This is true, but one must add that all three men are following Adam Smith's lead.

efficiency of labor; but whether this analysis requires a corresponding social division of laborers—assigning each worker to a single task—is quite doubtful. The classical political economists all accepted Smith's arguments that the minute social division of laborers is a technical requisite of efficient industrial production. Nonetheless, Smith's arguments do not bear scrutiny.

That Smith could cast a spell over two centuries of social science with his tale of the pin factory is one of the most curious chapters of modern intellectual history. As Fernand Braudel comments: "From the time of Adam Smith, economists regarded the idea [of division of labor] as something akin to Newton's law of gravity."[21] Yet Smith's arguments, far from being based on some *experimentum crucis*, are based on the literary topos of the pin factory. The extraordinary influence of Smith's rendition of this tale must be ascribed in large measure to the willful suspension of disbelief.

The use of a pin factory to illustrate the division of labor has its origins in the economic treatise of Ernst Ludwig Carl (1682–1743). A German nobleman writing in French, Carl wrote the first general work on the role of the division of labor in economic life.[22] It is not known whether Smith drew his material from Carl directly or indirectly through other sources.[23] What is known is that Smith directly derived his discussion of the eighteen distinct operations leading to the production of a pin from the *Encyclopédie* of Denis Diderot and Jean Le Rond d'Alembert.[24] Indeed, Smith tells us that he chose the example of pin-

21. Fernand Braudel, *The Perspective of the World*, trans. Sian Reynolds (New York: Harper and Row, 1984), 592. "Smith's discussion of the division of labour was so widely accepted by his economist-successors that it was largely taken for granted and rarely critically discussed" (P. D. Groenewegen, "Adam Smith and the Division of Labour: A Bicentenary Estimate," in *Adam Smith: Critical Assessments*, vol. 3, ed. John Cunningham Wood [London: Croom Helm, 1984], 561).

22. See Ernst Ludwig Carl, *Traité de la richesse des princes et de leurs Etats, et des moyens simples et naturels pour y parvenir* (Paris, 1722–23). Carl's seminal treatise was rediscovered in the 1930s by the German historian Anton Tautscher. See his "Ernst Ludwig Carl und Adam Smith," *Weltwirtschaftliches Archiv* 54 (1941). For a recent assessment of Carl's importance, see Terence Hutchison, *Before Adam Smith* (Oxford: Basil Blackwell, 1988), 163: "His *Treatise* is remarkable as one of the earliest comprehensive and systematic expositions of the subject, and, more specifically, for its early and important insights into the nature and implications of the division of labor. As such, it deserves an important place in the history of economic thought."

23. Anton Tautscher argues that Smith must have read Carl because of the considerable parallels in language and phrasing; see his "Ernst Ludwig Carl und Adam Smith." Hutchison, however, believes that Smith could have drawn on Carl indirectly through Diderot's *Encyclopédie*; see *Before Adam Smith*, 163 and 397n.

24. See Denis Diderot and Jean Le Rond d'Alembert, *Encyclopédie* (Paris, 1755), s.v. "Art"

making because it is a trade "in which the division of labour has been very often taken notice of." Thus Smith is developing a literary topos more than he is making empirical observations or conducting an experiment.[25] Of course, just because pin-making was a commonplace illustration in Smith's day does not in itself have any bearing on the truth of his claims for the division of labor; but perhaps the very familiarity of this example to Smith and his successors helps to explain how it has largely escaped critical scrutiny.

Smith's thought experiment comparing the productivity of ten detail workers with ten independent artisans reveals his ignorance of the actual methods of guild labor: "Those ten persons, therefore, could make among them upwards of forty-eight thousand pins in a day. Each person, therefore, making a tenth part of forty-eight thousand pins, might be considered as making four thousand eight hundred pins in a day. But if they had all wrought separately and independently, and without any of them having been educated to this peculiar business, they certainly could not each of them have made twenty, perhaps not one pin in a day."[26] Smith gives us a patently biased comparison here since the independent artisans are working, he says, "without any of them having been educated to this peculiar business"; thus we cannot say whether the superiority of the detail laborers is due to the division of labor per se or simply to their experience at the trade—hardly a controlled experiment! Moreover, Smith has his artisans making pins one at a time, that is, going sequentially through each of the eighteen operations for each individual pin. Yet no artisan would ever resort to such an inefficient mode of operation; artisans almost always organize work into batches: they would cut wire for four thousand pins, then straighten them all, then point them all, etc. With such batch production one has at the end of the day not one or twenty completed pins but rather four thousand half-completed pins. Smith's comparison of

---

and "Epingle." The French Encyclopedists in turn drew heavily on the article "Pin" in Ephraim Chambers, *Cyclopedia* (London, 1728). In Chambers we read: "They reckon twenty-five workmen successively employed in each pin, between the drawing of the brass-wire, and the sticking of the pin in the paper."

25. Yet Smith's pin-making example is still treated by commentators as if it were an empirical case study. E. G. West, for example, tells us that Smith's claims about the division of labor are "supported by one major empirical study, of the famous pin-factory" ("Adam Smith's Two Views on the Division of Labor," in *Adam Smith: Critical Assessments*, vol. 3, ed. John Cunningham Wood [London: Croom Helm, 1984], 162).

26. Smith, *Wealth of Nations*, 1:1.15.

these modes of production has persuasive force only if the reader is completely ignorant of the actual methods of craft production—which may explain the enormous influence of this example on two centuries of economists and social theorists.[27]

Smith cites three specific reasons why the social division of labor increases productivity: (1) the increase of the dexterity of the worker; (2) the saving of time lost in passing from one species of work to another; and (3) the invention of machinery to facilitate labor. Let us consider these in order. "First, the improvement of the dexterity of the workman necessarily increases the quantity of work he can perform, and the division of labor, by reducing every man's business to some one simple operation, and by making this operation the sole employment of his life, necessarily increases very much the dexterity of the workman."[28] Since the purpose and the effect of such a detailed division of labor is to remove the skill of the worker and to limit him to "one simple operation," it is hard to see how the division of labor improves the dexterity of the worker. If the workman is indeed limited to "one simple operation," then he will reach maximum dexterity in a few days—in which case he will be ready to learn a new operation.[29] Smith treats the acquisition of skills as a zero-sum game in which if I learn a new skill, I lose my old one; actually, the opposite is more generally true: skills build upon one another, like learning languages.[30]

27. For a discussion of the foibles of academic theorizing about labor from a writer who is also a skilled craftsman, see Harry Braverman, *Labor and Monopoly Capital* (New York: Monthly Review Press, 1974), 106n.

28. Smith, *Wealth of Nations*, 1:1.17–18.

29. According to Kenneth Arrow: "Learning associated with repetition of essentially the same problem is subject to sharply diminishing returns. . . . To have steadily increasing performance, then, implies that the stimulus situations must themselves be steadily evolving rather than merely repeating" ("The Economic Implications of Learning by Doing," *Review of Economic Studies* 29 [June 1962]: 155–56). What we actually know about the acquisition of skill, then, shows that the detailed social division of labor represents a profound waste of human learning potential.

30. "But, when the manual dexterity requisite for the practice of any art can be attained in so short a time, it cannot matter much to the society or to the individual, whether the workmen have to learn one or several arts. Besides, the acquisition of any difficult art very much facilitates the attainment of any other. . . . Hence a good workman in any trade, displays comparatively but trifling awkwardness in applying himself to any other" (John Rae, *The Sociological Theory of Capital* [1834], ed. Charles Whitney Mixter [New York: Macmillan, 1905], 239–40). "Nor can I bring myself to believe, that . . . the dexterity of the workman in performing this one operation would be at all impaired, though he should also have acquired a few other accomplishments of a similar nature: that the drawer of the wire would be less fitted for his employ-

Second, Smith argues that specialization enables the pin-maker to work continuously because he is not interrupted by changing tasks: "The advantage which is gained by saving the time commonly lost in passing from one sort of work to another, is much greater than we should at first view be apt to imagine it. It is impossible to pass very quickly from one kind of work to another, that is carried on in a different place, and with quite different tools."[31] Here we find a characteristic failing of Smith's analysis: in his simple technical view of means and ends, incessant exertion means greater productivity; yet from a broader moral perspective, we can see that such monotonous exertion may well undermine the morale of workers and thereby reduce productivity.[32] Moreover, Smith's concern here with the time lost in passing from one type of work to another reflects his confusion of the technical and the social division of labor. If a worker were to attempt to make one pin at a time, he would, no doubt, spend a great deal of time moving from one operation to another; but if he divides the work technically into batches, then the time lost moving between operations will generally shrink to insignificance.[33] Time is saved chiefly by the technical division of work, not by the social division of workers.

"Third, and lastly, every body must be sensible how much labour is facilitated and abridged by the application of proper machinery. . . . I shall only observe, therefore, that the invention of all those machines by which labour is so much facilitated and abridged, seems to have been originally owing to the division of labour." Smith's discussion of the relation between the division of labor and the invention of machinery is especially confused. Smith offers two very different accounts of the effects of the division of labor on invention.

---

ment, if he changed occupations for a day or two with the cutter or pointer of the pin" (Stewart, "Lectures on Political Economy," 314).

31. Smith, *Wealth of Nations*, 1:1.18.

32. J. S. Mill eloquently corrects Smith on this point: "It is a matter of common experience that a change of occupation will often afford relief where complete repose would otherwise be necessary, and that a person can work many more hours without fatigue at a succession of occupations, than if confined during the whole time to one. Different occupations employ different muscles, or different energies of the mind, some of which rest and are refreshed while others work" (*Principles of Political Economy* [1871], ed. Sir William Ashley [New York: Augustus Kelley, 1976], 127).

33. "To save 'the time that is commonly lost in passing from one species of work to another' it is necessary only to continue in a single activity long enough that the set-up becomes an insignificant proportion of total work time. . . . Saving of time implies *separation* of tasks and *duration* of activity not *specialization*" (Steven A. Marglin, "What Do Bosses Do?" [1974], in *The Division of Labour*, ed. André Gorz [Brighton: Harvester Press, 1976], 18).

First, he tells us that most productive machines are "originally the inventions of common workmen, who, being each of them employed in some very simple operation, naturally turned their thoughts towards finding out easier and readier methods of performing it."[34] It is ironic that Smith, who argues in book 5 that the division of labor degrades the mental faculties of workers, should here find them so inventive. Although Smith is famous for his analysis of the incentives governing economic behavior, he never considers what possible incentive a worker might have to invent a machine that may replace him. Indeed, the very institution of wage labor serves as a profound disincentive to the innovative efforts of workers.[35]

Smith's second claim concerning invention is that the division of labor leads to the emergence of a special trade of philosophers or men of speculation "whose trade it is, not to do any thing, but to observe every thing; and who, upon that account, are often capable of combining together the powers of the most distant and dissimilar objects."[36] Thus even the emergence of generalists is attributed to the growth of specialization! Yet whereas innovation in the first case was the product of a mind directed toward a single object, here innovation is the product of a mind surveying diverse objects.

Unfortunately, neither account accurately depicts the true logical and historical relation between the division of labor and the invention of productive machinery. Dugald Stewart was the first theorist to grasp correctly the precise connection between the division of labor and the deployment of machinery. The division of labor, by analyzing a complex operation into a series of simple motions, makes possible the introduction of machines.[37] The invention of pro-

34. Smith, *Wealth of Nations*, 1:1.19–20.

35. Dugald Stewart rightly observes that "the workman has no motive to exert his ingenuity in multiplying machines, as in doing so, though he may accelerate the process of the manufacture, yet he does not abridge his own day's labour; and indeed there is even a probability that he may throw himself and his companions out of employment" ("Lectures on Political Economy," 317).

36. Smith, *Wealth of Nations*, 1:1.21.

37. "The obvious effect of the division of labor in any complicated mechanical operation is, to analyse that operation into the simplest steps which can be carried on separately. . . . Now, it is only by resolving an operation into its simplest elements, that this separation can be made, so as to force on the attention of the mechanist, in their simplest forms, those particular cases where his ingenuity may be useful" (Stewart, "Lectures on Political Economy," 319). "It is generally agreed that Adam Smith . . . missed the main point. The important thing, of course, is that with the division of labour a group of complex processes is transformed into a succession of simpler processes, some of which, at least, lend themselves to the use of machinery" (Allyn Young, "Increasing Returns and Economic Progress," *Economic Journal* 38 [1928]: 530).

ductive machinery is thus an unintended by-product of the division of labor—all of which sounds like grist for the invisible-hand mill!

The role of the division of labor as a stimulus to invention is well illustrated by the development of the digital computer.[38] The French mathematician G. F. Prony came across Smith's *Wealth of Nations* purely by chance in 1784. As he read the first chapter on the division of labor in pin-making, he was struck with the realization that logarithms could be produced through a division of mental labor. Through analysis of the complex calculations into a series of simple stages involving addition and subtraction, the tables of logarithms were produced in large part by workers who knew no mathematics beyond simple arithmetic. Charles Babbage, reading an account of Prony's construction of mathematical tables through this division of mental labor, decided to substitute machinery for the lowest echelon of workers performing the simplest operations. What impressed Babbage most about Prony's computational process was not the efficiency of the technical division of a complex task into simple components, but the social division of workers into various levels of mathematical skill: Prony saved a lot of money by using low-wage workers to perform simple calculations and thus economized on the use of high-wage mathematicians. Babbage, an exemplary Victorian figure, saw his computer primarily as a device for saving money.[39]

Thus Babbage was the first theorist to grasp the specifically capitalist logic of the social division of labor. He realized that the capitalist seeks not to maximize pins but to minimize costs—and thereby to maximize profit. The social division of labor, in short, does not produce more pins or more logarithms, but more profits—it saves not time but money. Babbage argued that Smith overlooked "the most important and influential cause" of the social division of labor: "that the master manufacturer, by dividing the work to be executed into

38. On the sources of Charles Babbage's invention of the computer, see Babbage, *On the Economy of Machinery and Manufactures* [1835] (New York: Augustus Kelley, 1963), 191–201; and Richard Romano, "The Economic Ideas of Charles Babbage," *History of Political Economy* 14 (1982).

39. "We have seen, then, that the effect of the division of labour, both in mechanical and in mental operations, is, that it enables us to purchase and apply to each process precisely that quantity of skill and knowledge which is required for it: we avoid employing any part of the time of a man who can get eight or ten shillings a day by his skill in tempering needles, in turning a wheel, which can be done for sixpence a day; and we equally avoid the loss arising from the employment of an accomplished mathematician in performing the lowest processes of arithmetic" (Babbage, *On the Economy of Machinery and Manufactures*, 201).

different processes, each requiring different degrees of skill or of force, can purchase exactly that precise quantity of both which is necessary for each process; whereas, if the whole work were executed by one workman, that person must possess sufficient skill to perform the most difficult, and sufficient strength to execute the most laborious, of the operations into which the art is divided."[40] Babbage developed a numerical example based, of course, on pin-making, to show that even if we assume that skilled artisans could make as many pins per day as unskilled detail workers, it would save the employer a lot of money to divide the task among unskilled workers. In short, Babbage shows that Smith's attempt to explain the social division of labor in terms of a technical standard of physical productivity is misguided: what drives the capitalist division of labor is not the trans-historical quest for maximum physical output but a socially and morally specific quest for maximum profitability.

A look at a contemporary pin factory in Britain proves the superiority of Babbage's theory of productivity over Smith's. Productivity has increased 167 times over the two centuries since Smith's day, showing how wildly exaggerated was Smith's estimate that the division of labor alone had increased productivity 240 times. Automated pin-making machines are responsible for most of the massive long-run increase in productivity. What we find in this factory is not a detailed division of labor, but the rotation of simple tasks among unskilled workers supervised by an administrative staff: the divorce of conception from execution economizes on skilled labor just as Babbage expected.[41]

Babbage's claim that the social division of labor must be explained in terms of economic rather than technical efficiency decisively undermines Smith's efforts to define technical efficiency apart from a specific social context. Are we then to conclude that the social division of labor, although not necessarily technically more efficient, is more profitable? Whereas Smith asserted that the advantage of the division of labor is the enhancement of the

40. Ibid., 175. The "Babbage Principle" is clearly anticipated by Josiah Tucker, who developed a numerical example to show that having a child assist a man in making buttons saves money by economizing on the high-wage labor of the man. See "Instructions for Travellers," 242. Since Smith had a copy of Tucker's work in his library, it is surprising that Smith never grasped the true economic motive behind the division of labor.

41. On Smith's claim for a 240-fold increase due to division of labor, Clifford Pratten says (with considerable understatement): "This, however, seems very high." Pratten goes on to say: "The recent experience of rotation of operations suggests that the division of labor *per se* was less effective than Smith suggested." See Pratten, "The Manufacture of Pins," in *Journal of Economic Literature* 18 (March 1980): 95.

skill of the worker, Babbage proved that the division of labor is advantageous to the individual capitalist because it enables him "to create a vast number of jobs that do not require any specific skill."[42] It may be profitable for an individual firm to trap workers in unskilled jobs, but whether the creation of unskilled jobs is profitable for the economy as a whole is another question: there is reason to believe that the market systematically underinvests in training workers because the firm doing the training may not reap most of the rewards of skilled labor.[43] The division of labor, far from illustrating the beneficence of the invisible hand, turns out to illustrate a process whereby individual firms are enriched while society is impoverished.

A final illustration of the impossibility of determining the technical efficiency of labor apart from its moral and social context concerns the role of authority in the capitalist firm. The social division of labor in a factory affords managers greater control over the work process and greater discipline over the workers. "The essence of the factory is discipline—the opportunity it affords for the direction of and coordination of labour."[44] Historical studies suggest that factories did not initially produce goods more cheaply than other methods; they were simply more profitable than other methods for their capitalist owners.[45] Once a process that was formerly integrated by the skill of a craftsman is broken up into parts and distributed to different workmen, the problem of coordination arises. Having lost control over the productive process, workers are subject to the authority and discipline of the employer. "To devise and administer a successful code of factory discipline, suited to the necessities of factory diligence, was the Herculean enterprise, the noble achievement of Arkwright. . . . It required, in fact, a man of a Napoleon nerve and ambition, to subdue the refractory tempers of work-people accustomed to irregular paroxysms of diligence."[46] Smith noted the tendency of masters to dominate their employees ruthlessly, but this never led him to consider whether the great productivity of the pin factory might be as much due to the intensity of

42. For a contemporary economic analysis of the Babbage principle, see Ugo Pagano, *Work and Welfare in Economic Theory* (Oxford: Basil Blackwell, 1985), 13.

43. According to Arrow, "The presence of learning means that an act of investment benefits future investors, but this benefit is not paid for by the market. Hence, it is to be expected that the aggregate amount of investment under the competitive model . . . will fall short of the socially optimum level" ("Economic Implications of Learning by Doing," 168).

44. David Landes, cited in Marglin, "What Do Bosses Do?" 28.

45. See Charles Sabel, *Work and Politics* (Cambridge: Cambridge University Press, 1984), 38.

46. Andrew Ure, *The Philosophy of Manufactures* (London: Charles Knight, 1835), 15–16.

labor as to the division of labor.[47] Just as Smith never saw the degradation of workers as an obstacle to productivity, so he also never saw the domination of workers as a cause of productivity: indeed, both cases reflect his profound blindness to the moral dimension of production.

Marx: Division of Labor and Technological Determinism

Smith poses the fundamental dilemma for classical political economy: if the inexorable march of economic progress requires an increasingly fragmented social division of labor, then socially productive powers can increase only at the expense of individual productive powers; society can be enriched only if the individual is impoverished. Marx's achievement is to bring this dilemma to its logical apotheosis; his failure is never to have seen that for any given technical division of labor (and, indeed, for any given technology) there is a variety of efficient social divisions of labor. The integrity of Marx's thought is rent asunder by a tragic dilemma he found inescapable: his deeply held convictions about the dignity of human labor, his hopes for a future society in which "labor is life's prime want," are shattered by his assent to the inexorable logic of the increasing division of labor. This champion of *homo faber* gradually abandons the quest for the humanization of work and pins his hopes on automation and the escape from work. Just as Aristotle said that if shuttles would weave by themselves we would not need slaves, so Marx looks to automated technology to free men from the necessity of labor. In the end, as we shall see, Marx reverts to the Aristotelian view that whereas production is the realm of necessity, leisure alone is the realm of moral freedom.

Marx could not develop an analysis of productive labor and technology as the realm of moral freedom because he never wavers from his Smithian conviction that the technical division of tasks logically entails the social division of workers. Despite his formidable capacity for skeptical contempt, Marx accepts Smith's parable of the pin factory, comparing a detail worker to an artisan: "Consequently, he [the detail worker] takes less time in doing it, than the artificer who performs a whole series of operations in succession."[48] Marx's

47. "It is important to emphasize that the discipline and supervision afforded by the factory had nothing to do with efficiency, at least as this term is used by economists. Disciplining the work force meant a larger output for a greater input of labour, not more output for the same input" (Marglin, "What Do Bosses Do?" 36).

48. Marx, *Capital*, 1:14.2.321. "The division of labour is a particular, differentiated, further

characterization of the artisan reveals that he shares Smith's ignorance of the actual processes of craft production. Marx's belief in the logical necessity of the social division of labor is especially evident in his concept of the "iron law of proportionality." This concept first appears as the "principle of multiples": "the principle that the different operations are not only distributed between different workers but according to certain numerical proportions."[49] Even Smith allows that of the eighteen operations in pin-making, "the same man will sometimes perform two or three of them"; but Marx sees an ironclad one-to-one correspondence between the individual tasks and the individual workers. In *Capital*, the principle of multiples becomes the iron law of proportionality: that is, "a fixed mathematical relation or ratio which regulates . . . the relative number of labourers, or the relative size of the group of labourers, for each detail operation."[50]

Given Marx's belief that the social division of labor within a firm is "a fixed mathematical relation" and is "experimentally established," it is not surprising that he also regards it as uniquely efficient. Yet as we saw in chapter 1, experiments in job design have shown that there is usually a variety of efficient divisions of labor; the actually existing division of labor is almost never experimentally established, but is simply the product of customary rules of thumb.

Marx's faith in the optimal efficiency of the social division of labor blinds him to the most obvious shortcoming of detail labor—the enormous costs of coordination. Fragmented divisions of labor, whether in the factory or in the office, require large supervisory staffs. Yet Marx repeatedly asserts that coordination costs do not exist: "The increase in productive power achieved through simple cooperation and the division of labour costs the capitalist nothing."[51] This astonishing view is rooted in Marx's conviction that the social division of labor is simply the technical application of modern science; and the growth of science, he says, is a "free gift" to the capi-

---

developed form of cooperation, a powerful means of heightening the productive power of labour" (Marx, "Economic Manuscript of 1861–63," 264).

49. "If, e.g. 10 workers are needed for various operations, the number of persons employed must be a multiple of 10" (Marx, "Economic Manuscript of 1861–63," 320 and 288).

50. Marx, *Capital*, 1:14.3.327.

51. "The social productive power which arises from cooperation is a free gift" (Marx, "Economic Manuscript of 1861–63," 321 and 260). By contrast, a contemporary economist says: "Much of economics deals with the problem of coordination posed by complex divisions of labor" (Louis Putterman, *Division of Labor and Welfare* [Oxford: Oxford University Press, 1990], 29).

talist.[52] Marx's boundless confidence in the efficiency of the existing patterns of the social division of labor prevents him from seeing the possible competitive advantage in reducing coordination costs through alternative social divisions of labor.[53]

Furthermore, aside from routine coordination costs, detail labor is quite vulnerable to disruption and sabotage. Where each worker is an interdependent part of the productive whole, one worker's mistake or sabotage threatens the entire productive process. Yet Marx argues that the continuity of the technical division of tasks somehow necessitates the continuity of the socially divided workers: "It is clear that this direct dependence of the operations, and therefore of the labourers, on each other, compels each one of them to spend on his work no more than the necessary time, and thus a continuity, uniformity, regularity, order, and even intensity of labour of quite a different kind, is begotten."[54] If the technical continuity of an assembly line truly compelled social continuity, then the auto industry, for example, would never experience slowdowns, stoppages, sabotage, sit-down strikes, and work-to-rule.[55] It is lucky that trade unions do not share Marx's view that the technical integration of tasks determines the social integration of workers.

Marx's profound confidence in the efficiency of the planned coordination of labor in a firm is matched by his profound suspicion of the efficiency of

52. "Such an increase in productive power, a kind of machinery which does not cost capital anything, is the division of labor. . . . Another productive force which costs it nothing is scientific power" (Marx, "Grundrisse" [1857–58], in *Collected Works*, vols. 28–29 [New York: International Publishers, 1987], 29:149).

53. Marx does, however, distinguish between simple coordination costs, which are the inevitable by-product of all large-scale cooperation, and the costs of exercising authority over workers where there is antagonism between capitalist and worker. See *Capital*, 1:13.313–14. Marx argues that workers' cooperatives avoid the costs associated with exercising capitalist authority over workers and thus cooperatives have a competitive advantage. See *Theories of Surplus Value* [1862–63], vol. 3 (Moscow: Progress Publishers, 1963), 356. What Marx does not consider is the reduction of simple coordination costs through alternative social divisions of labor.

54. Marx, *Capital*, 1:14.3.326.

55. Actually, the converse of Marx's statement is closer to the truth: the famous Trist and Bamforth study of coal mining shows that the continuity of the technical division of tasks often depends of the social continuity of workers. In other words, if one shift of workers prepares the coal face for blasting and another shift does the blasting, there had better be some continuity of workers across both shifts to ensure the smooth integration of the two tasks. "Differentiation gives rise to the need for social as well as technological integration" (E. A. Trist and K. W. Bamforth, "Some Social and Psychological Consequences of the Longwall Method of Coal-Getting," in *Organization Theory*, ed. D. S. Pugh [Harmondsworth: Penguin Books, 1971], 362).

market coordination of labor in society as a whole. As Ugo Pagano observes, Marx exaggerates the costs of market coordination and ignores the costs of planning coordination.[56] This defect in Marx's analysis is of considerable importance since Marx bases his arguments for the productive superiority of communist planning on his analysis of capitalist planning within a firm: he claims that communism can achieve the planning efficiency for a whole society that capitalism provides for a single firm. It is difficult to know whether Marx's prior commitment to socialism blinded him to the costs of capitalist planning or whether this blindness led to his commitment to socialist planning. What is certain is that whatever the costs of the detailed division of labor in the capitalist firm, they are likely to be greatly magnified in the Marxist model of single-firm communism. In short, Marx has too much confidence in the efficiency of the capitalist firm and too little confidence in the efficiency of the capitalist market.

In *Capital*, Marx describes the profound transformation of the labor process from the Smithian era of manufacture (meaning handicraft) to his own era of machinery and modern industry. In contrast to the simple determinism of manufacture, where the social division of labor is determined by the technical, Marx sees a two-stage determinism in modern industry: first, the design of technology is determined by the technical division of tasks, and second, the social division of labor is then determined by the technology. As early as 1847 we find Marx claiming that technology determines the social division of labor, an argument that he develops in detail in *Capital*: "Labour is organised, is divided differently according to the instruments it has at its disposal. The hand-mill presupposes a different division of labour from the steam-mill."[57] As we noted in chapter 1, there are two specific points of slippage that derail this determinism: first, there is a variety of efficient technologies for any given technical division of tasks; second, there is a variety of efficient social divisions of labor for any given technology.

It is important to note that Marx is not committed to a "technological" determinism in the sense that machine technology is an autonomous force that determines all the other forces and relations of production. For Marx, the design and deployment of machinery is itself determined by the objective requirements of the technical division of labor into discrete tasks. As soon as production is technically divided into simple and repetitive tasks, machinery

56. Pagano, *Work and Welfare in Economic Theory*, 58.

57. Marx, "The Poverty of Philosophy" [1847], in *Collected Works*, vol. 6 (New York: International Publishers, 1976), 166 and 183.

can replace the detail worker. Just as Marx argues that there is only one efficient social division of labor, so he also argues that there is only one efficient design for the machinery that would replace detail workers.[58] In other words, just as the iron law of proportionality determines the number of detail workers for every task in manufacture, so this same law determines the number of "detail machines" for every task.

Moreover, Marx argues that there is a technological imperative requiring that machinery eliminate the need for human labor at every stage of production. In manufacture, says Marx, it was imperative to isolate each stage of the productive process into detail labor; in machine production, by contrast, it is equally imperative to ensure a seamless continuity from raw materials to a finished product.[59] What Marx ascribes to the logic of technique, however, is actually a logic of social control. The use of machinery to circumvent all human skill, far from being a technological imperative, in many cases reduces efficiency by failing to utilize the judgment and creativity unique to human beings.[60] The quest for total automation is often a quest for control over recalcitrant workers more than a quest for efficiency. Moreover, machine technology is quite flexible about how tasks are combined: some machines take a process through a series of operations from start to finish; others simply stamp out parts to be assembled later. There is no technical imperative that determines how machinery synthesizes a group of tasks.

Given that Marx thus attributes both the design and deployment of machinery to the technical requisites of production, it is not surprising that he goes on to argue that the social division of labor is determined in turn by the objective needs of technology. "In its machinery system, Modern Industry has a productive organism that is purely objective, in which the labourer becomes a mere appendage to an already existing material condition of production."[61]

---

58. "When Marx argued that firms knew only the practice they were currently using, he did so because he thought that at any given moment of time there was only one efficient technique in existence" (Jon Elster, *Explaining Technical Change* [Cambridge: Cambridge University Press, 1983], 163).

59. "In Manufacture the isolation of each detail process is a condition imposed by the nature of division of labor, but in the fully developed factory the continuity of those processes is, on the contrary, imperative" (Marx, *Capital,* 1.15.1.359–60).

60. For a discussion of the disasters in production caused by the attempt to remove all human input, see Harley Shaiken, *Work Transformed* (New York: Holt, Rinehart and Winston, 1984), 190–216.

61. Marx, *Capital,* 1:15.1.359.

Here the laborer adapts himself to the objective technological environment; but is not technology itself adapted to the laborer? Since all technologies are designed with a user in mind—they are supposed to be "user-friendly"—technologies embody social assumptions about the skill and responsibility of those users. Marx, however, denies that technology is shaped by the perceived subjective needs of its users; he claims that technology is determined simply by the objective demands of the technical division of labor.[62] Speaking of machinery, Marx says: "Here, the process as a whole is examined objectively, in itself, that is to say, without regard to the question of its execution by human hands, it is analysed into its constituent phases; and the problem, how to execute each detail process, and bind them all into a whole, is solved by the aid of machines, chemistry, etc."[63] The question is whether these alleged necessities of science and efficiency are not actually the exigencies of social domination.

As we saw in chapter 1, technology is the interface between the technical and the social division of labor: technology translates a task or group of tasks into a job for an individual or group of individuals. Studies of the design and deployment of productive technology, however, reveal that at every stage of development social choices are made—usually to reduce the autonomy of workers and to increase the authority of management. When technology is controlled by its users—as is medical technology—it serves to augment rather than to replace the skill of the user. The power tools of a modern crafts-

62. "The machine is a uniting of the instruments of labour, and by no means a combination of different operations for the worker himself" (Marx, "Poverty of Philosophy," 186). This view is defended by John McMurtry: "Technological relations," he says, "never involve persons as such, but only labor-powers. Thus the same technological relations obtain on an assembly line, whether the labor-power places are filled by one set of individuals or by n sets of individuals acting in turn" (*The Structure of Marx's World View* [Princeton: Princeton University Press, 1978], 73n). McMurtry is right to assert that for any technology there is a variety of possible social divisions of labor; but he is wrong to assert that technology does not embody assumptions about the social division of labor: the assembly line was designed for detail workers—which is why it prevents some modes of the social division of labor, such as team production. McMurtry confuses technology, as the interface between the technical and social division of labor, with the technical division of labor itself.

63. Marx, *Capital*, 1:15.1.359. Marx repeatedly insists that technology is simply the embodiment of modern science: "The principle which it pursued, of resolving each process into its constituent movements, without any regard to their possible execution by the hand of man, created the new modern science of technology. The varied, apparently unconnected, and petrified forms of the industrial process now resolved themselves into so many conscious and systematic applications of natural science to the attainment of given useful effects" (ibid., 1:15.9.456–57).

man, for example, increase the productivity of labor while they augment the skill of the worker. Technology can usually be designed either to circumvent or to augment the skill of the operative. As Harry Braverman says, "Machinery embraces a host of possibilities, many of which are systematically thwarted, rather than developed, by capital."[64]

Marx's theory of technology serves to obscure completely the moral and political dimension of production. As he observes modern industry, Marx sees "the technical subordination of the workman to the uniform motion of the instruments of labour," rather than the political subordination of workers to the managers and engineers who design and deploy technology. Marx often comments that machinery is a weapon deployed by capitalists to break strikes, but to say that the introduction of machinery reflects politics is not the same as saying that the design and deployment of machinery reflects politics. Politics is the realm of freedom, and Marx never suggests that "machinery embraces a host of possibilities."

Marx even describes technology as the embodiment of science itself.[65] What hope is there for the social transformation and humanization of work if the worker is being oppressed by science? Perhaps if Marx had not hypostatized "science" as some abstract agent of history, he would have seen that "science" can serve many diverse interests: "When capital enlists science in her service, the refractory hand of labour will always be taught docility."[66]

Although in most places Marx describes the effects of machinery on the worker as dehumanizing, in some places he looks to machinery to humanize labor.[67] In both cases, however, he attributes these effects not to the social

64. See Braverman, *Labor and Monopoly Capital*, 230. Marx's comment that "in its machinery system, Modern Industry has a productive organism that is purely objective" is decisively refuted by studies of technology by Harry Braverman, David Noble, and Harley Shaiken.

65. Just as Marx sees science as an agent of production, so he also describes the machine as an agent: "In no respect does the machine appear as the means of labour of the individual worker. Its *differentia specifica* is not at all to mediate between the activity of the worker and the object, as is the case with the means of labour. On the contrary, the worker's activity is posited rather as merely mediating the labour of the machine, its action upon raw material—he watches over it and guards against obstructions" ("Grundrisse," 82). From the fact that the worker does not control the machine, Marx concludes that the machine controls the worker. But such dialectical reversals obscure the essential political fact that the capitalist controls both the machine and the worker.

66. Andrew Ure, cited in Marx, "Economic Manuscript of 1861–63," 342.

67. On the dehumanizing effects of machinery, see Karl Marx and Friedrich Engels, "The

choices of design, but to a technological imperative. "But the employment of machinery does away with the necessity of . . . the constant annexation of a particular man to a particular function."[68] In this view, machinery is teleologically directed toward abolishing the detailed division of labor. Indeed, Marx sees a fundamental contradiction between the technical requirements (or *telos*) of modern technology and the detailed division of labor: "Modern Industry, indeed, compels society, under penalty of death, to replace the detail-worker of today . . . by the fully developed individual, fit for a variety of labours."[69] Because it is designed to remove all skill from the worker, modern automation does often enable workers to rotate from one unskilled task to another, but this hardly constitutes the creation of "the fully developed individual."

Of course, Marx's view of technology as liberator is simply the inversion of his view of technology as oppressor: both views share the same fundamental defect, namely, the assumption that technology determines the social division of labor. Marx treats technology as an inexorable and natural force that shapes society alternatively for good or for evil; he almost never considers the way in which social custom and social interests shape technology. Although technology can change the social division of labor in unforeseen ways, a given technology is almost always adaptable to a variety of uses and is, therefore, largely the product of social choice. For Marx, by contrast, technology is literally "out of control": he says that it "imposes itself after the manner of an overpowering natural law, and with the blindly destructive action of a natural law."[70] If technology dehumanizes workers, however, it is not because it is out of control, but because it is out of their control.

Since Marx insists that the social division of labor and technology are strictly determined by the objective technical requirements of modern production, it is not surprising that from his earliest writings he sometimes loses hope for the humanization of work and looks instead to the liberation from

---

Manifesto of the Communist Party" [1848], in *Collected Works*, vol. 6 (New York: International Publishers, 1976), 490: "He [the worker] becomes an appendage of the machine, and it is only the most simple, most monotonous, and most easily acquired knack, that is required of him." Marx makes exactly the same observation in *Capital*, 1:15.4.398.

68. Marx, *Capital*, 1:15.4.397. "What characterizes the division of labour in the automatic workshop is that labour has there completely lost its specialised character. . . . The automatic workshop wipes out specialists and craft-idiocy" (Marx, "Poverty of Philosophy," 190).

69. Marx, *Capital*, 1:15.9.458.

70. Ibid.

work. It is striking to note that at the very same time that Marx was developing his view that human beings realize their essential nature through labor he was also calling for the abolition of labor.[71] Marx's lifelong musings about the abolition of labor evolve from utopian fantasy to economic prognosis. Although Marx sometimes suggests that automation will create a more humane division of labor, ultimately he looks to automated machinery to create free time from labor. Marx even sees capitalism as the unwitting agent of communist utopia by its deployment of labor-saving technology: "Capital in this way—quite unintentionally—reduces human labor, the expenditure of [human] energy, to a minimum. This will be to the advantage of emancipated labour and is the condition for its emancipation."

Marx's naive faith in technology is evident in his belief that "the saving of labour time is equivalent to the increase of free time."[72] In other words, Marx assumes that even in capitalism, advances in productivity will always be translated into reductions of the workweek. Yet although technology can create the possibility for an increase of free time, technology cannot itself create free time. The translation of productivity into free time is a moral and political question, not a technical one.

In the third volume of *Capital* Marx distinguishes production as the realm of necessity from leisure as the realm of freedom. "In fact, the realm of freedom actually begins only where labour which is determined by necessity and mundane considerations ceases; thus in the very nature of things it lies beyond the sphere of actual material production." In Aristotelian fashion, Marx identifies moral reason with leisured action and technical reason with production. The moral humanization of labor is not only empirically improbable, it is now logically impossible. "Beyond it [the realm of necessity] begins that development of human energy which is an end in itself, the true realm of freedom, which, however, can blossom forth only with this realm of necessity as its basis."[73] Marx has democratized Aristotle's polis: instead of slaves pro-

71. "It is one of the greatest misapprehensions to speak of free, human, social labour, of labour without private property. 'Labour' by its very nature is unfree, inhuman, unsocial activity. . . . Hence, the abolition of private property will become a reality only when it is conceived as the abolition of 'labour'" (Marx, "On Frederich List's Book" [1845], in *Collected Works*, vol. 4 [New York: International Publishers, 1975], 278–79). "The subjection of separate individuals to the division of labor can only be removed by the abolition of private property and of labor itself." See Marx, "German Ideology," 77.

72. Marx, "Grundrisse," 29:87 and 97.

73. Marx, *Capital*, vol. 3 [1894] (New York: International Publishers, 1967), 48.820.

ducing in order to create freedom for the moral action of the few, we have automation producing in order to create moral freedom for all. In both cases, production is not a part of but a condition for moral and political freedom. As Richard Winfield observes: "In this way the leisure of the *polis* citizen becomes the free time of the emancipated proletarian."[74]

The Paradox of Marxist Taylorism

Although Marxists throughout the twentieth century have championed the scientific management of Frederick Taylor, some of the most profound critics of Taylorism also claim the authority of Marx. How could a movement that identified with the industrial proletariat champion the most systematic degradation of work ever conceived—especially when Taylorism met violent opposition from workers? Not only did Leninist regimes adopt Taylorist methods of organizing work, but Marxist movements within capitalist economies also welcomed "scientific management" as a sign of progress.[75] Marxist Taylorism is a disturbing illustration of the profound practical consequences of theoretical inquiry.

The root of the problem lies in Marx's distinction between the material and the social aspects of economic life. Instead of arguing that there is a technical and a moral dimension to economic life, Marx insists that a certain "material" realm of economic life reflects technical and natural necessity, whereas the "social" realm of economic life reflects moral and political freedom. So, for example, Marx says: "Machinery is no more an economic category than the bullock that drags the plough. Machinery is merely a productive force." In this view machinery is a material phenomenon that becomes a social or political phenomenon only when it becomes the property of a capitalist. Similarly, Marx describes the social division of labor in Smith's pin factory as a material relation that only becomes a social relation when workers are subject to the authority of capital—as G. A. Cohen puts it, "not all relations between men are social." Marx attacked J. S. Mill's distinction between the immutable laws of production and the socially specific laws of distribution, but Cohen rightly argues that Marx merely reproduces this distinction.[76] Marx's "forces

74. Richard D. Winfield, *The Just Economy* (New York: Routledge, 1990), 75.

75. Antonio Gramsci argues that Taylorism is rational and should be widely implemented in *Selections from the Prison Notebooks*, ed. and trans. Quintin Hoare and Geoffrey Nowell Smith (New York: International Publishers, 1971), 309–12.

76. For Mill's distinction between production and distribution, see his *Principles of Politi-*

of production" represent the objective technical requisites of the economy, which are not subject to social transformation, whereas his "relations of production" represent the authority hierarchies in the firm, which are subject to social transformation. Just as Mill argues that production belongs to the sciences of nature and engineering, whereas distribution belongs to political economy, so Marx regulates the forces of production to other disciplines: "Political economy," he says, "is not technology." Marx describes technology and the division of labor as "free gifts" of scientific progress that, like all things free, lie outside of political economy.[77]

Marx thus places a great deal of emphasis on the distinction between the "horizontal" social division of labor, which belongs to the technical forces of production, and the "vertical" authority structure, which belongs to the social relations of production. As we have seen, Marx regards the horizontal mode of cooperation to be a gift of science; by contrast, he regards the vertical authority structure of the firm to be an expense generated mainly by class conflict. Put differently, the social division of labor may be the unfortunate by-product of progress, but only the authority structure of the firm can be despotic.[78] In his analysis of the vertical relations of authority, Marx is careful to distinguish the technical authority necessary for the coordination of socially divided labor from the political authority necessary to overcome class antagonism. Unfortunately, in his analysis of the horizontal division of labor, he does not make a similar distinction between the specialization necessary for efficient production and the specialization imposed to advance the authority of management.

---

cal Economy, "Preliminary Remarks" and book 2, chap. 1. For Marx's attack on Mill, see "Grundrisse," 28:25. As G. A. Cohen says: "Mill's distinction between production and distribution resembles Marx's distinction between subsocial and social dimensions of the economy" (Karl Marx's Theory of History [Princeton: Princeton University Press, 1978], 108).

77. On machinery and the division of labor as part of the material forces of production, see "Poverty of Philosophy," 183; "Contribution to the Critique of Political Economy," p. 292; "Grundrisse," 28:24. On technology and the division of labor as free gifts of modern science, see "Grundrisse," 29:149.

78. Cohen follows Marx by distinguishing "work relations" from "social relations" on the grounds that social relations alone involve "rights or powers vis-à-vis other men"; Elster sees Marx as distinguishing between the "technical" (i.e., in my terms, social) and the "capitalist" division of labor. I have attempted to show, however, that "work relations" themselves reflect social rights and powers and that the "technical" division of workers may reflect a "capitalist" mode of domination. See Cohen, Karl Marx's Theory of History, 94, and Elster, Making Sense of Marx, p. 246.

Marx says that machinery and the division of labor are material, not social, phenomena for the same reason that a black person is a material, not a social, phenomenon. In his view, a black person becomes a slave only under specific social relations, just as machinery and the division of labor become enslaving only under capitalist social relations. The phenomenon of Marxist Taylorism, however, decisively refutes this argument. Although it is undeniable that a black person becomes a slave only under specific social circumstances, machinery and the detailed division of labor are just as oppressive under socialism as under capitalism. What Marx called the "forces of production" are strategies of domination that lend themselves to capitalist, fascist, and communist "relations of production."[79] If the relations of production truly correspond to the forces of production, then how is it that the same forces are found within such radically diverse relations of production?

Jon Elster is right to ask: "Should not Taylorism count as a productive force?" Marx, in fact, anticipated the rise of a science of work that would analyze human labor into fundamental laws of mechanical motion; like Taylor, Marx saw productive labor as a branch of "the science of mechanics" rather than as a branch of political economy.[80] Just as neoclassical economists followed Mill's advice to leave production to the natural and engineering sciences, so Marxist economists followed Marx's advice to focus their critique on the relations of production rather than on the forces of production. Given the enormous body of Marxist economic analysis of such topics in distribution and exchange as value theory, crisis theory, and property relations, it is astonishing to note that after Marx's *Capital* (1867) there is no significant Marxist analysis of the forces of production until Braverman's *Labor and Monopoly Capital* (1974).[81] Although Marx saw the labor process as a Rosetta stone for

79. Jon Elster suggests a test for distinguishing the forces from the relations of production: "The productive forces should be defined so that, when the relations of production change, there is no *immediate* change in the productive forces employed [because] technical rationality dictates that the existing productive forces should be retained." See *Making Sense of Marx*, 246. By this test, Taylorism is a mere force of production since it remained constant when the relations of production (property relations) changed from capitalism to communism. Whether this is due to the sheer technical superiority of Taylorism or due to a universal interest in domination is a question Elster does not address.

80. "Technology also discovered the few main fundamental forms of motion, which, despite the diversity of the instruments used, are necessarily taken by every productive action of the human body; just as the science of mechanics sees in the most complicated machinery nothing but the continual repetition of the simple mechanical powers" (Marx, *Capital*, 1:15.9.456).

81. "It is one of the interesting paradoxes in the history of Marxism that Marx's analysis of

deciphering the hieroglyphs of capitalism, Marxists for over a century left the study of the labor process to "bourgeois" sociologists such as Elton Mayo, Georges Friedmann, and James Bright. Ironically, these bourgeois analysts had much less confidence in the efficiency of Taylorism than did such orthodox Marxists as Ernest Mandel.

If Marxism has consistently championed Taylorism, then how could the most far-reaching critique of Taylorism come from a self-described Marxist? Of course, the paradox vanishes if Braverman turns out not to be a Marxist. Braverman says that one reason why there is no body of Marxist literature on the labor process is "the extraordinary thoroughness and prescience with which Marx performed his task"; but he goes on to say that "Marxists adapted to the view of the modern factory as an inevitable if perfectible form of the organization of the labor process." Yet if Marx had really been so prescient in his analysis of labor, then how could Marxists have so easily accepted the modern factory as the inevitable form of the organization of labor?

Braverman's profound concern for the dignity of labor and pride of workmanship, his notion of work as the unity of "conception and execution," his moral outrage about the "degradation of labor," stem not from Marx but from John Ruskin.[82] By showing that machinery does not represent a natural or technical necessity but is a reified social relation, Braverman claims that he is simply extending Marx's analysis of commodity fetishism. But Braverman's approach must differ significantly from Marx's, if only because Braverman has inspired a vast body of empirical and theoretical work on the labor process—much of which has jettisoned any connection with Marxism.[83]

---

the labour process, as formulated in *Capital*, had until recently remained largely unchallenged and undeveloped" (Michael Burawoy, *The Politics of Production* [London: Verso, 1985], 21). Braverman notes that "there is simply no continuing body of work in the Marxist tradition dealing with the capitalist mode of production" (*Labor and Monopoly Capital*, 9).

82. As Burawoy says, "We should beware of Braverman's humility before Marx" (*Politics of Production*, 21). Braverman cites Ruskin's *Stones of Venice* on the division of labor but conceals his own profound debt to Ruskin, who speaks so eloquently of "this degradation of the operative into a machine" because of "two mistaken suppositions: the first, that one man's thought can be, or ought to be, executed by another man's hands; the second, that manual labour is a degradation, when it is governed by intellect" (*The Stones of Venice*, vol. 2 [London: Smith, Elder and Co., 1853], chap. 6). The subtitle of Braverman's *Labor and Monopoly Capital* is "The Degradation of Work in the Twentieth Century."

83. See, e.g., David Noble, *Forces of Production* (New York: Alfred Knopf, 1984) and Shaiken, *Work Transformed*.

Smith: Moral Sentiment and Technical Reason

Many theorists, such as Hannah Arendt, Jürgen Habermas, and Louis Dumont, have demonstrated that Marx collapsed Aristotle's distinction between *praxis* and *poiēsis*: occasionally Marx uses *praxis* to refer to productive labor; more often, though, he uses "production" to encompass all realms of human action.[84] Marx's model of the craftsman who transforms himself by transforming the material world became his model for all of human action. When, for example, Marx saw in automated technology the emancipation of the proletariat, he was looking to *poiēsis* to provide the liberation possible only on the basis of *praxis*.

Just as Marx seems to reduce *praxis* to *poiēsis*, so Smith reduces *phronēsis* to *technē*. Did Smith's reduction prepare the way for Marx's? Or do these parallel reductions reflect a deeper current in modern intellectual history? Adam Smith's *Theory of Moral Sentiments* is generally, and rightly, regarded as a treatise on the moral, and not the intellectual, virtues. Nonetheless, by explicitly collapsing *phronēsis* into *technē*, Smith does implicitly develop a doctrine of the intellectual virtues—namely, that ends-means analysis is restricted to the choice of the most efficient means to a given end. Since the ends of conduct are given by the moral sentiments, moral reason is restricted to the instrumental selection of "prudent" means. Indeed, as *phronēsis* became *prudentia* in Latin and "prudence" in English, the meaning of the term has been considerably transformed: the *Oxford English Dictionary* now defines a prudent person as "sagacious in adapting means to ends." *Phronēsis*, in short, has now become *technē*.

David Hume had prepared the way for the assimilation of prudence to art (*technē*): "'Tis impossible to execute any design with success, where it is not conducted with prudence and discretion. . . . All the advantages of art are owing to human reason; and where fortune is not very capricious, the most considerable part of these advantages must fall to the share of the prudent and sagacious."[85] Here prudence means precisely the artful adaptation of means to

---

84. Marx rarely uses the term *praxis*, but when he does "it may range from bodily labor of the most humble sort to political revolutions." See Nicholas Lobkowicz, *Theory and Practice* (Notre Dame: University of Notre Dame Press, 1967), 419. As for "production," Marx says: "Religion, family, state, law, morality, science, art etc., are only particular modes of production, and fall under its general law." See "Economic and Philosophic Manuscripts of 1844," in *Collected Works*, vol. 3 (New York: International Publishers, 1975), 297.

85. David Hume, *A Treatise of Human Nature* [1740], ed. L. A. Selby-Bigge (Oxford: Clarendon Press, 1978), 610.

ends—whatever those ends might be. For Aristotle, *technē* involves above all foresight and the ability to predict the course of events—which is why the *technai* were given to men by Prometheus (foresight). Where a course of action is not predictable—where, in Hume's words, fortune is capricious— we must rely on *phronēsis*.

Adam Smith was writing at a time when "prudence" was in transition between *phronēsis* and *technē*; indeed, Smith distinguishes between a superior and a lesser prudence in a way that roughly corresponds to Aristotle's distinction between *phronēsis* and *technē*. As an illustration of lesser prudence, Smith argues that the division of labor is not the product of deliberate foresight and intention, but rather is an accidental by-product of the human urge to truck, barter, and exchange: "No human prudence is requisite to make this division."[86] Prudence here exactly corresponds to *technē*. In general, an individual's concern with his own well-being involves lesser prudence: "The care of the health, of the fortune, of the rank and reputation of the individual . . . is considered as the proper business of that virtue which is commonly called Prudence."[87]

Smith was well aware, however, that this lesser prudence bore little resemblance to the Aristotelian *phronēsis*, which is most perfectly realized as *politikē aretē*: "We talk of the prudence of the great general, of the great statesman, of the great legislator. . . . This superior prudence, when carried to the highest degree of perfection, necessarily supposes the art, the talent, and the habit or disposition of acting with the most perfect propriety in every possible circumstance and situation."[88] Just as Aristotle's *phronēsis* includes and transcends *technē*, so Smith's superior prudence "necessarily supposes the art" of the lesser prudence. Speaking of the superior prudence, Smith says: "It necessarily supposes the utmost perfection of all the intellectual and of all the moral virtues."[89] Unfortunately, this superior prudence, because it is restricted to the deliberations of great political and military leaders, plays no role in

86. Smith, *Lectures on Jurisprudence*, p. 351.

87. Smith, *The Theory of Moral Sentiments* [1759], ed. D. D. Raphael and A. L. Macfie (Oxford: Oxford University Press, 1979), 6:1.213. The editors of the *Wealth of Nations* note that in this chapter of *The Theory of Moral Sentiments*, Smith consistently treats prudence as the means to the goal of social status: "Here Smith argued that if the pursuit of social status was the real objective of the drive to better our condition, then the means to this end are foresight and sacrifice—in short prudence" (Smith, *Wealth of Nations*, 2:3.338n).

88. Smith, *Theory of Moral Sentiments*, 6:1.216.

89. Ibid.

Smith's analysis of the moral virtues. We are left, then, with a doctrine of prudence restricted to the artful selection of means to ends discerned by the moral sentiments. Joseph Cropsey rightly asks of Smith's prudence: "The reconstruction of prudence to exclude moral discrimination left a vacuum in the chamber of the excellences. If not prudence, then what attribute enables the individual to distinguish in detail between the better and the worse course of action?"[90] The Aristotelian *phronēsis*, by contrast, being both a moral and an intellectual virtue, evaluates the interaction of ends and means in a unified course of action.

Thus, Smith's articulation of the reduction of *phronēsis* to *technē* in prudence is an implicit theory of intellectual virtue; but Smith's most original and significant contribution to the theory of intellectual virtue is his discovery of the theory of "displacement of goals."[91] As we saw in chapter 1, this theory refers to the propensity of moral agents to treat the means to an end as the end itself. Although this concept is usually attributed to Wilhelm Wundt, Smith anticipated Wundt's discovery by a century—Wundt's later discovery, however, was probably independent of Smith's. What is of special interest here is the close connection of this concept with "the invisible hand."

Smith argues that a well-designed machine is attractive because of the splendid fit between its form and its function, between its mechanical means and its functional end. "But that this fitness, this happy contrivance of any production of art, should often be more valued, than the very end for which it was intended . . . has not, so far as I know, been yet taken notice of by any body." Watches, says Smith, are intended to inform us of the time, but they are often valued simply as splendid mechanisms. "Nor is it only with regard to such frivolous objects that our conduct is influenced by this principle; it is often the secret motive of the most serious and important pursuits of both private and public life." Power and riches, for example, are actually only means to bodily and social security, but they are often pursued as ends in themselves—even when they become threats to our security. But were wealth not sought as an end in itself, were it sought only within the rational bounds of prudent comfort, society would never progress. "It is this deception which

90. Joseph Cropsey, *Polity and Economy* (The Hague: Martinus Nijhoff, 1957), 42.

91. Thus Cropsey is not quite justified in claiming that *Theory of Moral Sentiments* "is entirely a discussion of moral virtue and contains no systematic treatment of or reference to intellectual excellence except . . . in the case of a prudence deliberately shrunken in scope from its traditional estate" (*Polity and Economy*, 8).

rouses and keeps in continual motion the industry of mankind." Moreover, this irrational pursuit of wealth causes the rich to employ the poor and thereby to redistribute wealth: "They [the rich] are led by an invisible hand to make nearly the same distribution of the necessaries of life, which would have been made, had the earth been divided into equal portions among all its inhabitants, and thus without intending it, without knowing it, advance the interest of society, and afford means to the multiplication of the species."[92] Thus the famous "invisible hand," which is usually referred to as the "law of unintended effects," is actually the consequence of what Wundt calls "the preponderance of the means over the end,"—that is, the specific mechanism whereby means become treated as ends.

Although Smith's "invisible hand" has come to be seen as the consequence of market exchange alone, Smith's use of the invisible hand in *The Theory of Moral Sentiments* is more general: the invisible hand governs the consequences of the "displacement of goals" both in economic and in political life. "The same principle, the same love of system, the same regard to the beauty of order, of art and contrivance, frequently serves to recommend those institutions which tend to promote the public welfare."[93] In the case of public policy, Smith cites the example of government mending roads sheerly for the beauty of the network rather than for the purpose of promoting transportation. Whether bureaucrats pursuing the enlargement of government, or entrepreneurs pursuing the enlargement of wealth, all people tend to lose sight of their true ends and come to regard mere means as ends.[94] And the invisible hand uses all of these displacements to advance the commonweal.

This mechanism of the displacement of goals has considerable import for moral conduct, for it shows us that ends and means cannot be separated: we ought then to be careful how we choose our means—since they are likely to become our ends. Smith, however, does not develop this concept in terms of

---

92. Smith, *Theory of Moral Sentiments*, 4:1.179–84.

93. Ibid., 185. Smith continues: "The perfection of police, the extension of trade and manufactures, are noble and magnificent objects. . . . They make part of the great system of government, and the wheels of the political machine seem to move with more harmony and ease by means of them. We take pleasure in beholding the perfection of so beautiful and grand a system."

94. "Useful means are valued first for the ends at which they aim, but then we are charmed by the beauty of their sheer efficiency, and this pleasure, Smith believes, plays a major part in sustaining economic activity and political planning. Smith legitimately took pride in his originality on this last point." See "Editors' Introduction" in Smith, *Theory of Moral Sentiments*, 14.

moral reason but in terms of the invisible hand of providence. Instead of viewing the displacement of goals as evidence of the inseparability of means and ends in moral conduct, Smith treats this phenomenon as evidence of the beneficence of providence, which directs our displacement of goals to the common good. Where *phronēsis* was once responsible for harmonizing the ends and means of conduct, now it is providence. Smith's reliance on providence instead of *phronēsis* is evident in his confidence that the consequences of the displacement of goals are always desirable. But surely the pursuit of money or power, whether in the market or in government, often has undesirable consequences. We are all too familiar with the corporate or governmental bureaucrat who follows the rules even where they frustrate the goals of the organization.

Still, the effects of the invisible hand are more ambiguous than is commonly thought—or than Smith perhaps intended. Smith considers the problem of capital flight: will a free capital market lead investors to send capital abroad in search of the highest return? Smith argues that we need not be concerned about capital flight because investors will tend to prefer domestic industry: "He generally, indeed, neither intends to promote the publick interest, nor knows how much he is promoting it. By preferring the support of domestick to that of foreign industry, he intends only his own security; and by directing that industry in such a manner as its produce may be of the greatest value, he intends only his own gain, and he is in this, as in many other cases, led by an invisible hand to promote an end which was no part of his intention."[95] This passage has always been taken to be an illustration of how the self-interested action of individuals is transmuted into the common good by the magic of the market. According to orthodox economic analysis, however, the preference exercised here for domestic over foreign industry serves to distort the world capital market and to reduce the total welfare of the human community. Smith's invisible hand, by keeping capital at home, promotes mercantilist more than free-market principles.[96] By preferring to invest in his own nation, the investor promotes the interest of his own society at the expense of other societies. Thus Smith has unwittingly acknowledged that the invisible hand produces mixed effects.

95. Smith, *Wealth of Nations*, 4:2.456.

96. In other places, Smith acknowledges the need to intervene in the market for reasons of national defense, but there is no mention of such considerations here.

Division of Labor, Providence, and Moral Theodicy

The seemingly inexorable degradation of labor led both Smith and Marx to a profound pessimism about the future of the working classes in capitalist society. Capitalism, in their view, is an economic and technological juggernaut beyond anyone's control. What is especially fascinating about this historical pessimism is that it led both Smith and Marx to a providential optimism. Deeply pessimistic about the potential for moral and political deliberation to remedy the evils of the division of labor, Smith and Marx turned to providence to bring about the salvation denied to human endeavor. The turn to providence helps to account for the strange confidence of our economists that despite the apparent evils of the division of labor, this is the best of all possible modes of production.

Ever since the Stoics first developed the notion of providence (*pronoia*), the division of labor has been associated with providential design. Jacob Viner charts the history of the ancient tradition concerning the role of providence in establishing the territorial division of labor: "(1) providence favors trade between peoples as a means of promoting the universal brotherhood of man; (2) to give economic incentives to peoples to trade with each other providence has given to their respective territories different products." Just as trade presupposes a territorial division of labor, so exchange within a society presupposes a social division of labor. Thus, differences in natural talents, like differences in natural resources, are the basis for trade.[97] Providence plays two complementary roles in Smith's account of the division of labor: first, the propensity to truck and barter, which gives rise to the division of labor, is planted in men by providence; second, the invisible hand of providence guarantees that the division of labor benefits all men.

Once the assumption is made that the division of labor is part of the providential order, it simply will not do to argue that such an institution benefits some and harms others. Instead of acknowledging the contingent mix of good and evil in the division of labor, our political economists develop a theodicy to

97. This view stems from Libanius, the fourth-century Stoic teacher of Basil and Chrysostom. Ben Franklin (in 1729) related the territorial division of labor to the social division of labor: "As Providence has so ordered it, that not only different countries, but even different parts of the same country, have their peculiar and most suitable productions, and likewise that different men have geniuses adapted to a variety of different arts and manufactures" (cited in Jacob Viner, *The Role of Providence in the Social Order* [Philadelphia: American Philosophical Society, 1972], 32 and 41).

show that what appears to be evil is in reality good. Christian theologians had long attempted to account for the existence of evil in a world governed by divine providence. Ever since Augustine, however, most theologians have believed that God's perfect freedom means that divine providence must be largely inscrutable to human reason—meaning that the divine rationale for evil is beyond human comprehension. Gottfried Leibniz's *Theodicy* represents a revival of the Stoic confidence that divine providence must conform to the laws of reason. Once Leibniz had made providence subject to the "principle of sufficient reason," it was but a short step to make history subject to rational human understanding. Just as *Theodicy* argued that all the apparent evils of the world are in reality necessary conditions for the goodness of the whole, so the "sociodicy" of classical political economy sought to justify particular social evils by showing how they are necessary to the welfare of society as a whole.[98] What links the *Theodicy* of Leibniz to the sociodicy of classical political economy is that they both characterize evil not in moral but in instrumental terms. Evil becomes a necessary means to a greater good.

Jon Elster argues that the sociodicy of Marx is analogous to the *Theodicy* of Leibniz but that no sociodicy can be legitimately deduced from Leibniz: "There is no reason why the best of all possible worlds should also include the best of all possible societies."[99] The moral justification of the division of labor from Smith to Marx reflects a profound commitment to moral sociodicy: both friends and foes of capitalism have felt compelled to justify the evils of the division of labor, even though they also eloquently condemned those evils. Marx's appeal to a moral sociodicy is especially ironic since he explicitly condemns the "economic theodicy" of bourgeois apologists for capitalism.[100]

Although Smith was well aware that the detailed division of labor led to the physical and moral degradation of workers, he often insists that the division of

98. A sociodicy is not a secularization of Leibniz's Christian theodicy (as Elster suggests) since Leibniz's rationalism is no more Christian than Marx's. "In the modern form given it by Leibniz, theodicy is already outside any theological function; it does indeed belong to the protest of the Enlightenment against the God of will and His *potentia absoluta*" (Hans Blumenberg, *The Legitimacy of the Modern Age* [Cambridge: MIT Press, 1983], 58).

99 "Indeed, the whole point of the theodicy is that suboptimality in the part may be a condition for the optimality of the whole, and this may hold also if the part in question is the corner of the universe in which human history unfolds itself" (Elster, *Explaining Technical Change*, 56). Elster informs us that "sociodicy" was coined by Raymond Aron.

100. On Marx's critique of the sociodicy of "vulgar political economy," see Elster, "Marx et Leibniz," *Revue Philosophique* 173 (April 1983): 171–74.

labor has no evil consequences. For example, speaking of the division of labor between the town and the country, Smith says: "The gains of both are mutual and reciprocal, and the division of labour is in this, as in all other cases, advantageous to all the different persons employed in the various occupations into which it is subdivided."[101] In a similar vein, Smith tells us that the evils of poverty are not really evil, since providence grants all men roughly the same "ease of body and peace of mind."[102] In these passages, Smith's providential optimism has preempted the need for a theodicy since, *ex hypothesi*, there is no evil in the world to be justified.

According to Elster, theodicies can be classified into two groups: those that view evil as the inevitable by-product of good and those that view evil as indispensable for realizing the good. "The breaking of the eggs does not contribute anything to the taste of the omelette; it just cannot be helped."[103] Adam Smith, where he acknowledges evil, treats it as an inevitable though unfortunate by-product of the division of labor: "His [a worker's] dexterity at his own particular trade seems, in this manner, to be acquired at the expense of his intellectual, social, and martial virtues." That Smith does not regard this evil as indispensable for realizing the benefits of the division of labor is evident from his proposals for the publicly funded education of all children as a remedy for the degradation of workers. Smith is looking for a way to make an omelette with less egg-breaking or, perhaps, a way to repair broken eggs.[104]

Marx's sociodicy is much more sinister. He argues that the evils of the division of labor are not just inevitable but that they are indispensable to economic progress. "In manufacture, in order to make the collective labourer, and through him capital, rich in social productive power, each labourer must be

101. Smith, *Wealth of Nations*, 3:1.376. Smith was certainly not the first to argue that the division of labor must benefit all parties. According to Turgot: "Everyone profited by this arrangement, for each, by devoting himself to a single kind of labour, succeeded much better in it" (*The Economics of A. R. J. Turgot*, ed. and trans. P. D. Groenewegen [The Hague: Martinus Nijhoff, 1977], 44).

102. "In ease of body and peace of mind, all the different ranks of life are nearly upon a level, and the beggar, who suns himself by the side of the highway, possesses that security which kings are fighting for" (Smith, *Theory of Moral Sentiments*, 4:1.10.185).

103. Elster, *Explaining Technical Change*, 56; and *Leibniz et la formation de l'esprit capitaliste* (Paris: Aubier Montaigne, 1975), 207.

104. See *Wealth of Nations*, 5:1.782. Smith's remedies for the division of labor prompted Marx's sarcasm: "For preventing the complete deterioration of the great mass of the people by division of labour, Adam Smith recommends education of the people by the State, but prudently, and in homeopathic doses" (*Capital*, 1:14.5.342).

made poor in individual productive powers." Marx displays here and elsewhere a curious desire to justify the exploitation of workers by arguing that whatever the workers lose in skill and dignity is somehow gained by society: "Intelligence in production expands in one direction, because it vanishes in many others. What is lost by the detail labourers, is concentrated in the capital that employs them."[105] Yet Marx offers no argument or evidence that there is a causal relation between the workers' loss of craft skills and the growth of capital's productive knowledge; still less does he show that the improvement of productive methods somehow necessitates the loss of craft skills.

We are clearly in the presence of an a priori sociodicy: Marxist providence (the laws of history) excludes the possibility that the suffering and degradation of workers could simply be a meaningless social loss.[106] Smith's suggestion that schooling serve as a remedy for the evils of the division of labor may be pathetic, since it does not contribute to the humanization of work, but at least he does not suggest that the degradation of workers is positively indispensable for economic progress. By the logic of Marx's sociodicy, efforts to protect the autonomy of workers and thereby enhance the dignity of work would serve only to retard historical progress toward ultimate liberation.[107] It is not clear, however, how stripping all workers of their productive skill and knowledge prepares them for the "free association of producers" of communism; indeed, one would think that such an association presupposes the productive skill of each individual member. Marx's sociodicy makes sense only on the assumption that the goal of history is not the humanization of work, but the liberation from work—in which case productive skills are indeed superfluous.

By assuming that automated technology will someday liberate men from work, Marx can make a plausible case that the detailed social division of labor is historically indispensable because it paves the way for automation. Marx's historical sociodicy was anticipated by Dugald Stewart, who argued

---

105. Marx, *Capital*, 1:14.3.324, 14.5.341.

106. Indeed, Marx insists that wasting the lives of millions of workers is indispensable for social progress: "It is only by dint of the most extravagant waste of individual development that the development of the human race is at all safeguarded and maintained in the epoch of history immediately preceding the conscious reorganization of society" (*Capital*, 3:5.2.88).

107. Marx actually found himself compelled by this logic to "say to the workers and the petty bourgeois: it is better to suffer in modern bourgeois society, which by its industry creates the material means for the foundation of a new society that will liberate you all, than to revert to a bygone form of society which, on the pretext of saving your classes, thrusts the entire nation back into medieval barbarism." Cited in Elster, *Making Sense of Marx*, 116–17.

that the evil of the division of labor would transform itself over time into social goodness: "The evil, though a real one while it lasts, naturally leads the way to its own correction, so as to render it probable that it is but a step in the progress of human improvement. . . . The ultimate tendency, therefore, of this process, is to substitute mechanical contrivances for manufacturing works, and to open a field for human genius in the nobler departments of industry and talent."[108] Although it is a historically contingent fact that the detailed social division of labor, by reducing labor to a few simple motions, promoted the introduction of machinery, Marx's sociodicy logically depends on there being a necessary relation between the technical division of tasks, the design of technology, and the social division of labor. The slippage of contingent social choice that derails his economic determinism, however, also derails his sociodicy.

When it came to the enterprise of justifying the evils of capitalism, Marx was much more resourceful and innovative than were the bourgeois apologists. For example, Marx was one of the first economists to defend capitalism by appealing to what Elster calls a "biodicy." In one extraordinary and disturbing passage, Marx ridicules Jean Sismondi's insistence that the dignity of the individual worker should take precedence over economic growth:

> Although at first the development of the capacities of the human species takes place at the cost of the majority of human individuals and even classes, in the end it breaks through this contradiction and coincides with the development of the individual; the higher development of individuality is thus only achieved by a historical process during which individuals are sacrificed; for the interests of the species in the human kingdom, as in the animal and plant kingdoms, always assert themselves at the cost of the interests of certain individuals, and it is this coincidence which constitutes the strength of these privileged individuals.[109]

Marx's turn to a biodicy may well have been caused by his reading of Darwin's *Origin of Species*, but the logic of this analysis represents a frightful muddle of Leibnizian theodicy and Darwinian evolution. From Leibniz's view that in providential history *"il faut reculer pour mieux sauter,"* Marx argues that in social history whole classes of people must be sacrificed in the short

108. Stewart, "Lectures on Political Economy," 330.
109. Marx, *Theories of Surplus Value*, 2:118. The *Origin of Species* appeared in 1859, whereas Marx wrote these manuscripts in 1862–63.

run for the long-term prosperity of humanity. To bolster his sociodicy, Marx claims that in natural history individual organisms are sacrificed for the survival of the species. However, since individual organisms are the unit of natural selection it makes no sense to argue, on Darwinian grounds, that individuals are sacrificed for the good of the species; on the contrary, according to Darwin, the fixity of the species is sacrificed for the good of individual survival. Marx's curious desire to justify the exploitation of workers as a necessary stage in economic history leads him to a bizarre distortion of biological theory. Perhaps Marx should have devoted his considerable talents less toward the justification and more toward the amelioration of the evils of the social division of labor.

Chapter 6

The Natural, Customary, and Stipulated Division of Labor in Classical Political Economy

From Natural Law to the Laws of Nature

As observed in chapter 2, the metaphor "natural law" is a condensed analogy between natural order and legal order; indeed, what makes this metaphor obscure is that it can imply several different analogies between nature and law. In the early modern period we find the development of a scientific natural law alongside the traditional moral natural law. These two conceptions of natural law reflect very different analogies between nature and law: in the Thomistic doctrine of natural law, God is to the moral order of human nature what a prince is to the legal order of society; in the modern scientific doctrine of the laws of nature, the minerals, plants, animals, and stars obey the laws of God just as men obey the laws of a prince. Because the metaphor "natural law" can imply either or both of these analogies, we find a profound confusion during the seventeenth and eighteenth centuries of the moral and the physical laws of nature. It was not until the nineteenth century that J. S. Mill distinguished clearly the normative or moral natural law from the descriptive or physical laws of nature. As Rulon Wells puts this distinction, if you break a moral law of nature, so much the worse for you; if you break a physical law of nature, so much the worse for that law.[1]

Aristotle carefully avoided any use of the term *law* (*nomos*) to describe the uniformities of nature; he, and natural scientists until the twelfth century,

---

1. See J. S. Mill, "Nature," in *Three Essays on Religion* [1874] (New York: Greenwood Press, 1969), 14–15; and Rulon S. Wells, "Thirdness and Linguistics" in *The Signifying Animal*, ed. Irmengard Rauch and Gerald F. Carr (Bloomington: Indiana University Press, 1980), 186.

used instead concepts such as causation, principle, and necessity. Aristotelians like Francisco Suárez, for example, argued into the seventeenth century that the use of the term *lex* to refer to the order of nature "is therefore strictly metaphorical, since things which lack reason are not, strictly speaking, susceptible to law, just as they are not capable of obedience."[2] Suárez's logic here may be impeccable, but some of his contemporaries were arguing to the contrary that inanimate beings are quite literally subject to the laws of nature. Interestingly, the very notion that nature is governed by laws emerged prior to the discovery of those laws by seventeenth-century physicists. Scientists like René Descartes, Galileo, Johannes Kepler, and Isaac Newton discovered "laws" of nature because they had already begun to think of nature as lawful. The concept of the laws of nature is not the product of, but the precondition for, modern physics.[3] Ever since Newton referred to the "axioms or laws of motion," however, natural scientists and philosophers alike have for the most part ignored the problematic assumptions inherent in the notion of the "laws of physics," such as: Is the order of nature really analogous to a legal code? Who stipulated these laws? What does it mean to obey a law of physics? How can natural laws evolve? Are new laws stipulated to replace old laws? C. S. Peirce, by contrast, argued that the only way to account for the evolving uniformities of the natural world is to describe the behavior of atoms, planets, and molecules in terms of the acquisition of habits.[4] Nonetheless, the analogy between natural order and legal order continues to escape critical scrutiny: we are not likely to be speaking soon of the habits of planetary motion.

The prominence of the concept of the physical laws of nature seems inversely proportional to the prominence of Aristotelian philosophy. Although the term *law* appears frequently in the natural philosophy of the twelfth-century Platonists of the school of Chartres, the most systematic use of the term

2. Francisco Suárez, *De Legibus ac Deo Legislatore* [1612], in *Selections from Three Works*, ed. J. B. Scott (Oxford: Clarendon Press, 1944), 1:1.2. Aquinas had said that the law in which irrational creatures participate *non potest dici lex nisi per similitudinem*. See *Summa Theologiae*, ed. Thomas Gilby (Cambridge: Blackfriars, 1964), 1–2, Q. 91, art. 2. In one place, Aristotle does use the term *nomos* to refer to the order of nature, when he comments that the Pythagoreans take numbers to be the laws of nature (*Cael.* 268a10).

3. John R. Milton shows that the conception of the laws of nature was present in Bacon, Hooker, Calvin, and Melanchthon before the scientific revolution. See "The Concept of the 'Laws of Nature,'" *European Journal of Sociology* 22 (1981): 173–98.

4. C. S. Peirce, *The Collected Papers of Charles Sanders Peirce*, ed. Charles Hartshorne and Paul Weiss (Cambridge: Harvard University Press, 1960), 6.12 and 1.409.

is found in the optics of Roger Bacon. Indeed, Roger Bacon's use of the term *lex* to describe physical phenomena is remarkable because it was so rare in the midst of the thirteenth-century revival of Aristotle.[5] Still, it is not until Francis Bacon that we see the explicit rejection of Platonic and Aristotelian "form" in favor of "law" to describe the order of nature. Bacon tells us that instead of seeking to define the forms of things we should seek to discover the laws of things: "The form of heat or the form of light, therefore, means no more than the law of heat or the law of light."[6] And, says Bacon, since these laws of nature reflect the inscrutable will of God, they can be discovered only by induction and experiment—not by syllogistic deduction. What makes Bacon's treatment of the laws of nature so remarkable is that he even distinguishes the moral from the physical laws of nature. He says that the "laws of heaven and earth" are discovered by reason, sense induction, and argument whereas the "law of conscience" is "an inward instinct."[7]

These new theories of the physical laws of nature were bound to have a profound influence on the treatment of the moral laws of nature. Indeed, despite Bacon's attempt to demarcate a frontier between the two, the early modern development of both the moral and the scientific conception of natural law was accompanied by considerable confusion between them. The moral natural law was subjected to the experimental methodology of scientific investigation while the scientific laws of nature were assumed to be morally good. Thus where "natural price" in Thomism refers to the price consistent with the moral natural law, in physiocracy it refers to the price consistent with the observed uniformities of the market—indeed, with a market equilibrium that is assumed to be morally good.[8]

5. For many medieval examples of the use of the term *lex* in natural philosophy, see Jane E. Ruby, "The Origins of Scientific 'Law,'" *Journal of the History of Ideas* 47 (July–September 1986).

6. Francis Bacon, *Novum Organum*, 2.17. M. B. Foster sees this transition from the conception of nature as rational form to that of law as the essential contrast between ancient and modern science. "To both of these, to form as well as to law, we apply the same term 'the universal,' and we thereby obscure to ourselves the great difference between them" (*The Political Philosophies of Plato and Hegel* [Oxford: Clarendon Press, 1935], 111).

7. Bacon, *The Advancement of Learning*, 2:25.3.

8. "Whatever the process of intellectual development may have been, by the seventeenth century, 'law of nature' had come to include two disparate notions, moral laws and scientific laws. Bacon, Newton, and Locke—as well as many of their contemporaries—used the terms natural law in their scientific sense, regularly and with no apology for depending on an analogy, or worse, a strained analogy. Indeed, within the framework of the view that the universe and

Classical and medieval treatments of natural law were based on a critical appropriation of tradition—both traditions of practice and traditions of reflection. For Roman jurists, the law of nature was most clearly discerned in the common customs of the nations, based on the view that what is universal must be natural; ever since, the *ius gentium* and the *ius naturale* have been closely intertwined. For Christian jurists, natural law was to be found both in the common customs of the nations and in the tradition of philosophical reflection on natural law from Antiphon to Suárez. Natural law theory never followed tradition blindly but instead relied on the critical scrutiny of tradition in the light of reason. Beginning with Francis Bacon, however, the modern science of nature rejected this appeal to tradition in the discernment of natural law: truth was now said to be discovered entirely by empirical observation in the light of individual reason.

The confusion of the moral with the physical laws of nature is evident in the fact that as soon as scientists rejected tradition as a basis for discerning the physical laws of nature, philosophers began to reject tradition in the discernment of the moral laws of nature as well. Thomas Hobbes, for example, followed Galileo by adopting a radically new method of inquiry. Just as Galileo used thought experiments to discover the natural laws of physical motion by isolating physical bodies from all extraneous influences, so Hobbes constructs his own thought experiment to discover the laws of human motion by isolating human bodies from all extraneous social influences in a "state of nature."

This same profound shift of method is most evident in the natural law theory of John Locke. The fusion of the moral and the scientific law of nature during this period is well illustrated by Locke's doctrine:

> Once it has been granted that some divine power presides over the world . . . and all creatures in their obedience to his will have their own proper laws governing their birth and life; and there is nothing in all this world so unstable, so uncertain that it does not recognize authoritative and fixed laws which are suited to its own nature—once this has been granted it seems proper to ask if man alone has come into this world entirely outside some Jurisdiction, with no law proper to him, without plan, without law, without a rule for his life."[9]

---

everything in it is dominated by one omnipotent God, no apology was needed" (William Letwin, *The Origins of Scientific Economics* [London: Methuen, 1963], 174).

9. John Locke, *Questions Concerning the Law of Nature* [1664–82], trans. and ed. Robert

Once we grant that the universe is governed by the physical laws of nature, says Locke, we must also grant that man is governed by a moral natural law. And to add to the confusion, this moral natural law is discovered by the same methods as the physical laws of nature.

Locke's discussion of how the moral natural law is discovered reveals his profound break with the Thomistic conception of natural law. Locke tells us that the natural law is not inscribed in the minds of men, that it cannot become known to us by tradition, and that it cannot be known from the consensus of mankind. If natural law cannot be discerned from these sources, then how can it be discerned? Sense experience in the light of individual reason, says Locke, is the only method for arriving at knowledge of the physical or moral law of nature. Indeed, Locke tells us that only by first discovering the physical laws of nature ("once the mind has carefully and exactly weighed the machine of this world") can we then discover the moral law appropriate to human nature.[10] That Locke insists upon the same canons of inquiry for arriving at knowledge of both the physical and the moral laws of nature reveals his fusion and confusion of them.

In the economic theories of Locke and his contemporary William Petty, we find the transition from a moral to a physical conception of natural law. Locke applied his new scientific notion of natural law to the question of usury: "The first thing to be considered is, 'Whether the price of the hire of money can be regulated by law?' And to that I think, generally speaking, one may say, it is manifest it cannot."[11] Locke's treatment here of the question of usury is a radical departure from the moral natural law tradition. Instead of considering the views of various authorities on the question or the universal customary restrictions on usury, Locke simply observes that the price of money is subject to its

Horwitz, Jenny Strauss Clay, and Diskin Clay (Ithaca: Cornell University Press, 1990), Q. 1, 95–97. After thus informing us that every entity in the universe is subject to natural law, Locke subsequently tells us that the law of nature is not binding on brute animals (Q. 9). Of course, if we distinguish the physical from the moral natural law, then it makes sense to say that brutes are subject to the former but not to the latter.

10. On Locke's rejection of individual conscience as a source of natural law, see *Questions Concerning the Law of Nature*, Q. 4; on Locke's rejection of tradition, see Q. 3; on Locke's rejection of the *consensus mundi*, see Q. 7. On Locke's endorsement of scientific method for arriving at natural law, see Q. 5: "Can Reason arrive at a knowledge of the law of nature through sense experience? It can."

11. Locke, "Essay on Interest and Value of Money" [1692], in J. R. McCulloch, *The Principles of Political Economy* (London: Alex. Murray and Son, 1870), 221.

own "natural law" and therefore cannot be morally regulated any more than can the laws of motion. Similarly, William Petty treated the generation of wealth not in terms of the moral natural laws governing the market (the Scholastic doctrines of just prices and wages) but in terms of the physical laws of nature: "Labour is the Father and active principle of Wealth, as Lands are the Mother."[12] Here the generation of wealth is ascribed to the physiology of labor (the program of British political economy) and to the fertility of the soil (the program of physiocracy).[13] In neither case, interestingly, is the production of wealth ascribed to specifically social institutions.

During this transitional period in the history of economic theory we find some remarkable fusions of moral and scientific concepts. In a physiocratic pamphlet we read: "Natural laws are either physical or moral. I am here taking physical law to mean the regular course of all physical events in the natural order which is self-evidently the most advantageous to the human race. I am here taking moral law to mean the rule of all human action in the moral order conforming to the physical order which is self-evidently the most advantageous to the human race."[14] Here even the physical laws of nature are said to be advantageous to the human race. Indeed, we often find two claims explicitly made that are glaringly incompatible: the first is that the laws of nature are good and therefore ought to be obeyed; the second is that we could not disobey the laws of nature even if we would. Thus Petty tells us that many matters now governed by law ought to be governed by nature, but he also speaks of "the vanity and fruitlessness of making Civil Positive Laws against the Laws of Nature."[15] Econo-

12. For Petty, nature is both the cause of wealth, and the standard of value: "All things ought to be valued by two natural Denominations, which is Land and Labour; that is, we ought to say, a Ship or garment is worth such a measure of Land, with such another measure of Labour" (*The Economic Writings of Sir William Petty* [1676–90], ed. Charles Henry Hull [Cambridge: Cambridge University Press, 1899], 1:44, 68).

13. Marx is thus further justified in calling Petty the father of modern political economy. Terence Hutchison disagrees: "Nor, moreover, do we accept Marx's conception of 'classical' political economy as beginning with Petty, and running on through Locke, Hume, Steuart, Quesnay, Smith, James Mill and Ricardo, down to 1830—that is, until just before Marx himself took up the subject" (*Before Adam Smith* [Oxford: Basil Blackwell, 1988], 3).

14. See Ronald L. Meek, ed., *The Economics of Physiocracy* (London: George Allen and Unwin, 1962), 53.

15. Petty, *Economic Writings of Sir William Petty*, 1:48, 243. Letwin comments on the first of these claims: "From the standpoint of social science, as it developed during the century after Locke, the most important result of this fusion of ideas, which bracketed scientific laws with moral precepts, was that the goodness originally attributed to the latter was now imputed to the former" (*Origins of Scientific Economics*, 174).

mists often point to the way in which trade barriers are undermined by smuggling to illustrate the impossibility of disobeying the natural laws of the market. The moral natural law tradition held that civil law ought to be consistent with natural law but recognized that civil law often deviated from natural law; the scientific conception of natural law holds that civil laws cannot possibly violate natural laws. Our economists often insist on both of these principles.[16]

Economics as Social Physics and Physics as Nature's Economics

Scientific economics began as a branch of the moral natural law theory of the seventeenth-century Spanish Jesuits, but in French physiocracy and in British political economy, economic theory increasingly adopted a physical conception of the laws of nature. Still, as Philip Mirowski shows, economics became social physics in part because physics already saw itself as nature's economics.[17] Although it prided itself on its rejection of Aristotle, early modern physics was profoundly teleological in structure. Just as Aristotle had insisted that nature makes nothing in vain, modern physicists argued that nature economizes in its expenditure of motion and energy.

For example, the employment of the calculus of maxima and minima in modern physics reflects the view that nature economizes. Leibniz first developed this calculus to describe the rationality by which the "divine entrepreneur" had allocated scarce resources to create a world with the maximum net goodness; God, he says, created the world with the mathematical structure of constrained maximization. According to Jon Elster, Leibniz's mathematical physics does not reflect but rather anticipates the rationality of a capitalist economy.[18] It has always been known that merchants seek to buy low and sell high, but the notion that they seek to maximize revenue and minimize costs is the product of neoclassical economics. Smith, as we saw in chapter 5, argues that capitalists seek to maximize the physical quantities produced by minimiz-

16. The physiocrats, however, seem to acknowledge that positive laws can deviate from natural law: "The host of contradictory and absurd laws which nations have successfully adopted proves clearly that positive laws are often apt to deviate from the immutable rules of justice and of the natural order which is most advantageous to society." Cited in Meek, *Economics of Physiocracy*, 45.

17. See Philip Mirowski, *More Heat than Light* (Cambridge: Cambridge University Press, 1989).

18. See Jon Elster, *Leibniz et la formation de l'esprit capitaliste* (Paris: Aubier Montaigne, 1975), 26 and 34.

ing the task of each worker. J. S. Mill, following Nassau Senior, describes the fundamental law of economics as the desire of every individual to obtain the maximum of wealth with the minimum of labor.[19] But it was not until neoclassical economics adopted the calculus of constrained maximization, of extremal and variational principles, that the notions of economic maximization and optimization achieved precise formulation. What is chiefly of interest here is the origin of these mathematical principles in a view of nature as economizer.

The most influential exposition of nature's economy was P. L. M. Maupertuis's principle of least action (1744): according to this principle, all motion in nature follows the path of least action—that is, motion seeks to minimize the product of time and distance.[20] Maupertuis argues explicitly that God created nature in such a way that all natural phenomena are "produced" by "saving" on the "expense" of action.[21] Leibniz may well have anticipated Maupertuis in the formulation of this principle since Leibniz, like Maupertuis, argued that God applied the calculus of maxima and minima in creating the world to realize the greatest good with the least expense.[22] In any event, it is widely agreed that the principle of least action has been one of the most fruitful generalizations in the history of science—in part because, like the conservation of energy, the principle has admitted a variety of theoretical interpretations. Indeed, the principle of natural economy lives on as the foundation of the Lagrangian formulation of quantum mechanics.[23] So if the economists began to turn to physics, the physicists had also begun to turn to economics.

19. Nassau Senior, *An Outline of the Science of Political Economy* (London: W. Clowes, 1836), 26; J. S. Mill, *Essays on Some Unsettled Questions of Political Economy* (London: John W. Parker, 1844), 137–38.

20. P. L. M. Maupertuis's definition of action: "*Lorsqu'un corps est porté d'un point à un autre, il faut pour cela une certaine action: cette action dépend de la vitesse qu'a le corps, et de l'espace qu'il parcourt; mais elle n'est ni vitesse ni l'espace pris séparément.*" Maupertuis's definition of least action: "*Lorsqu'il arrive quelque changement dans la Nature, la quantité d'action, nécessaire pour ce changement, est la plus petite qui soit possible.*" See *Maupertuis*, ed. Emile Callot (Paris: Marcel Rivière, 1964), 65 and 58.

21. Thus Maupertuis calls action "*la vraie dépense de la Nature . . . que la Nature épargne dans le mouvement de la lumière*" in *Maupertuis*, 65–66. Callot describes least action as the principle of general economy or least cost.

22. For a discussion of the relation of Leibniz to Maupertuis, see Martial Gueroult, *Leibniz* (Paris: Aubier-Montaigne, 1967), 216 and 222.

23. In the eighteenth century, Leonhard Euler and Joseph-Louis Lagrange developed the principle of least action in the context of the rational mechanics of *vis viva* (kinetic energy). In the nineteenth century, least action was linked to the conservation of energy: action was now defined as the

One of the most important points of convergence between economics and physics was the nineteenth-century definition of "work" as the transference of energy from a force to a body. The concept of work in rational mechanics, defined as the product of force times distance, was developed as a measure of energy expended in a process; for example, the energy consumed by a steam engine could be measured by the work it performed. Gradually, however, physicists like Julius Mayer, James Joule, Hermann Helmholtz, and William Thomson began to realize that thermal, chemical, and electrical phenomena were all interconvertible with mechanical work. The principle of the conservation of energy held that in the conversion of electrical, thermal, and chemical energy into mechanical work, energy was neither created nor destroyed but merely changed form.[24] The conservation of energy was thought to reflect divine economizing: God designed nature so as to minimize the expenditure of energy.

The science of "energetics" was an attempt to unify the physical sciences by treating heat, light, electricity, and magnetism as different but interconvertible manifestations of energy. Helmholtz defined all of these forms of energy in terms of the capacity to do work: "In a mechanical sense the idea of work has become identical with the expenditure of energy." Helmholtz's term for the work capacity of machines was *Arbeitskraft*, which, of course, became Marx's term for labor power. Marx uses this term in the physical sense of labor as an abstract expenditure of energy apart from any consideration of the moral purpose or even the skill of the workman.[25] Marx believed that by destroying the diverse skills of the various craft traditions, the detailed division of labor in capitalist production had reduced the specificity of concrete

---

product of time and energy. In the twentieth century, least action has been defined as Planck's Constant. See Jerome Fee, "Maupertuis and the Principle of Least Action," *Scientific Monthly* 52 (1941); and Claude Cohen-Tannoudji et al., *Quantum Mechanics* (New York: John Wiley, 1977), 2:1494–95.

24. "Leibniz had argued that living force, measured by the product of the mass and the square of the velocity, was conserved in mechanical processes" (P. M. Harman, *Energy, Force, and Matter* [Cambridge: Cambridge University Press, 1982], 36).

25. On the origins of Marx's *Arbeitskraft* in Helmholtz's physics, see Anson Rabinbach, *The Human Motor* (New York: Basic Books. 1990), 72–81. In his definition of a day's labor power, Marx cites William Grove (who popularized energy physics): "The amount of labour which a man had undergone in the course of 24 hours might be approximately arrived at by an examination of the chemical changes which had taken place in his body, changed forms of matter indicating the anterior exercise of dynamic force" (*Capital*, vol. 1 [1867] [New York: International Publishers, 1967], 17.3.493n).

labor to an abstract labor power—the mere expenditure of human energy in a few repetitive motions. Just as energy physics was establishing the theoretical equivalence of human, animal, and mechanical work, so capitalist production was establishing the practical equivalence of human and mechanical labor by substituting machinery for human labor.

Marx's mature theory of human labor as "man's metabolism [*Stoffwechsel*] with nature," which seems to appeal to biology, is actually based on the popular energy physics of the 1850s.[26] Indeed, the origins of Helmholtz's energy theory lie in his early research on the physiology of animal metabolism: animals could generate heat from the oxidation of foodstuffs only if the energy of food could be converted into heat energy. Helmholtz was profoundly influenced by Justus von Liebig, whose work on animal metabolism depended upon the principle of the indestructibility and transformability of energy. Marx's theory of human labor as "man's metabolism with nature" reflects the assumptions of energy physics about the convertibility of energy from foodstuffs to human work and from raw materials (coal or wood) to mechanical work.[27] Moreover, Marx insists that labor understood as metabolism is "an eternal nature-imposed necessity" that is "independent of all forms of society." Labor, in short, is to be understood not in terms of the moral natural law but in terms of the physical laws of nature.

Because Marx saw no alternative to the homogenization of labor through the destruction of all craft-specific skills, he begins in the *Grundrisse* to define labor not as the "life expression" but as the "force expenditure" of the worker. The attempt to humanize labor makes sense only if labor is understood in terms of the moral personality of the worker; if labor is understood as a necessary expenditure of energy, then the task is not to humanize but to minimize that expenditure. I am not suggesting that Marx's study of energy physics in

26. Marx describes labor as man's metabolism with nature many times in *Capital* (1:1.2.50, 7.1.173, 179), though *Stoffwechsel* is often translated as "exchange of matter." Alfred Schmidt agrees that "metabolism" is Marx's mature theory of labor, but he sees it as an appeal to biology: "Marx used new and in part peculiarly biological metaphors, of which the expression 'metabolism,' used throughout *Capital*, seems finally to have been chosen as the best formulation" (*The Concept of Nature in Marx*, trans. Ben Fowkes [London: NLB, 1971], 80).

27. Marx does not tell us where he got his term *Stoffwechsel*. Schmidt and Rabinbach suggest Jacob Moleschott, although Marx does not cite him; perhaps we should consider Justus von Liebig, whom Marx does cite frequently in *Capital*. On Helmholtz's relation to Liebig, see Harman, *Energy, Force, and Matter*, 41; on Marx's relation to Liebig, see Schmidt, *Concept of Nature in Marx*, 281n.

the 1850s caused him to shift his concern from emancipation through labor to emancipation from labor. For one thing, we saw in chapter 5 that Marx calls for the abolition of labor in his earliest writings of the 1840s. Marx's turn to energy physics was not the cause but the consequence of a failure of moral imagination; because he could not imagine a more humane organization of labor, he simply used the physics of his day to articulate the age-old reduction of labor to technical and natural necessity.[28]

Marx's turn to energy physics also helps to explain the discrepancy of his alternative theories of capitalist rationality. In some places Marx says that the rationale of modern production is the minimization of labor time; in other places he says that it is the minimization of energy expenditure. What he seems to have been seeking to formulate is the principle of least action, which was interpreted by energy physics to mean that all natural processes seek to minimize the product of both time and energy.[29] In short, capitalist rationality in production is but a special case of the rationality of nature; despite the fact that the market distorts this rationality, says Marx, the capitalist economy in production reflects the economy of nature.

Nature and the Division of Labor in Smith

Naturalism, as we saw in chapter 2, takes two different forms: something can be causally determined by nature and something can be analogous to nature. That Smith has creatively combined these two modes of naturalism is evident in his insistence that all natural and moral explanation refer to both efficient and final causes. At the center of Smith's economic theory is an elaborate analogy between the moral economy and the "economy of nature": in both cases individual organisms pursue means as if they were ends, while the invisible hand guides these means to the ultimate ends of nature. Thus, says Smith, the final causes of every natural organism, "the two great purposes of nature," are "the support of the individual and the propagation of the species"; the effi-

28. Indeed, many social scientists still use energy physics to define human labor. In *Social Anthropology of Work*, ed. Sandra Wallman (London: Academic Press, 1979, 4), we read: "Work is the application of human energy to things."

29. In the "Grundrisse," Marx says that "all economy is a matter of economy of time" (*Collected Works*, vols. 28–29 [New York: International Publishers, 1987], 28:109); in *Capital*, vol. 3 [1894] (New York: International Publishers, 1967), 48.3.820, he says that the rationale of production is "least expenditure of energy." The science of minimizing the expenditure of both time and energy in human labor came to be known as Taylorism.

cient causes of these organisms are the instincts for food and sex, which bring about the final purpose.[30] The "director of nature" has so ordered things that although food and sex are only means to the end of nature, humans and other animals pursue these means as if they were ends, and by doing so they promote the propagation of the species.

> The oeconomy of nature is in this respect exactly of a piece with what it is upon many other occasions. With regard to all these ends which, upon account of their peculiar importance, may be regarded, if such an expression is allowable, as the favourite ends of nature, she has constantly in this manner not only endowed mankind with an appetite for the end which she proposes, but likewise with an appetite for the means by which alone this end can be brought about, for their own sakes, and independent of their tendency to produce it.[31]

In other words, the displacement of goals operates in such a way that in the economy of nature organisms tend to treat efficient causes as if they were final causes; fortunately, providence ensures that this displacement leads to the realization of the final cause or goal of behavior. And since the displacement of goals is at work in the moral as well as in the natural economy, any explanation of social institutions must also refer to both efficient and final causes. "This division of labour, from which so many advantages are derived, is not originally the effect of any human wisdom, which foresees and intends that general opulence to which it gives occasion. It is the necessary, though very slow and gradual consequence of a certain propensity in human nature which has in view no such extensive utility; the propensity to truck, barter, and exchange one thing for another."[32] Here the efficient cause of the division of labor is the natural instinct to truck, barter, and exchange; the final cause is the

30. On Smith's view of the relation of efficient to final causes as an example of the "displacement of goals," see *The Theory of Moral Sentiments* [1759], ed. D. D. Raphael and A. L. Macfie (Oxford: Oxford University Press, 1979), 2:2.3.87.

31. Ibid., 2:1.5.77. Smith continues: "Thus self-preservation, and the propagation of the species, are the great ends which nature seems to have proposed in the formation of all animals. . . . Hunger, thirst, the passion which unites the two sexes, the love of pleasure, and the dread of pain, prompt us to apply these means for their own sakes, and without any consideration of their tendency to those beneficent ends which the great Director of nature intended to produce by them."

32. Adam Smith, *The Wealth of Nations* [1776], ed. R. H. Campbell, A. S. Skinner, and W. B. Todd (Oxford: Oxford University Press, 1979), 1:2.25.

prosperity of the human community. But even though exchange is but a means to the division of labor and prosperity, we treat it as an end in itself. Luckily, nature or providence has arranged things so that this displacement of goals leads to the common good.

Smith was well aware that social institutions are the product neither of human nature alone nor of deliberate human stipulation; but rather than look to the genealogy of custom, Smith relies on divine stipulation to direct the natural sentiments toward optimal social arrangements. Social institutions are then the joint product of human nature and divine stipulation; that is, of nature as efficient cause and Nature as final cause. And since Smith tells us that our natural sentiments are planted in us by the Author of Nature, even human nature is stipulated by God. The shortcomings of the circle of interdefinability are especially evident here: by defining human nature in terms of divine stipulation, Smith collapses the distinction between the order of nature and the order of stipulation—a collapse typical of the Enlightenment equation of nature and God. "When by natural principles we are led to advance those ends, which a refined and enlightened reason would recommend to us, we are very apt to impute to that reason, as to their efficient cause, the sentiments and actions by which we advance those ends, and to imagine that to be the wisdom of man, which in reality is the wisdom of God."[33] Smith's important insight that social institutions are not the product of the stipulation of a human lawgiver leads him to conclude that such institutions reflect the order of divine stipulation. The market, for example, creates an order to human exchange that certainly was not deliberately stipulated; but instead of suggesting that market relations embody customary patterns of exchange, which are shaped by legal stipulation, Smith argues that the market embodies the trans-historical efficiency of providential design. In the end, for Smith there is but one type of order—the order of deliberate stipulation, whether divine or human.

Smith's view that social institutions are the product of natural sentiments harmonized by divine reason makes it difficult for him to account for the diversity of human institutions across time and space. "That order of things which necessity imposes in general, though not in every particular country, is, in every particular country, promoted by the natural inclinations of man." If, however, all humans have the same natural inclinations, and all are subject to the same providential displacement of goals, then all humans should have

---

33. Smith, *Theory of Moral Sentiments*, 2:2.87

identical social institutions. Smith acknowledges that this would indeed be the case "if human institutions had never thwarted those natural inclinations."[34] In other words, custom and stipulation play only a negative role in social life by thwarting nature; they do not shape natural potentialities. Smith's reductive naturalism is especially evident here in his view that the moral sentiments are the product of nature alone; custom and law can thwart but not shape the natural moral sentiments.[35]

Smith thus believes that the division of labor is natural but in a roundabout fashion: the propensity to truck and barter, which gives rise to the division of labor, is a natural instinct. However, as we saw in chapter 2, ever since Plato social theorists have ascribed the division of labor to nature in a more direct fashion: innate differences in natural aptitude are usually said to determine the division of labor. Smith's critique of this commonplace is justly famous: "The very different genius which appears to distinguish men of different professions, when grown up to maturity, is not upon many occasions so much the cause, as the effect of the division of labor." Smith here raises the problem of ascribing causation to an observed correlation: a person's aptitude may correlate to his role, but we are still left with the question of the direction of causation. Melvin Kohn and Carmi Schooler's careful study of the relation of jobs to personality shows that although personality does shape the choice of jobs, the job also shapes the personality.[36] Smith's cautious language is certainly consistent with Kohn and Schooler's findings that aptitude is both the cause and the effect of specialization.

The ancient rhetoricians rightly held that aptitude is the joint product of nature, habit, and education. Unfortunately, Smith, in a passage that makes use of our three categories, insists upon resorting to the Sophistic antithesis of nature and convention: "The difference between the most dissimilar characters, between a philosopher and a common street porter, for example, seems to arise not so much from nature, as from habit, custom, and education."[37] Do not habit and education cultivate natural dispositions?

34. Smith, *Wealth of Nations*, 3:1.377.

35. As Jacob Viner says: "I have found not even a casual reference in *The Theory of Moral Sentiments* to the moral sentiments being influenced by changes in the physical or political environment or of their being different in different countries or at different stages of history" (*The Role of Providence in the Social Order* [Philadelphia: American Philosophical Society, 1972], 84).

36. Melvin Kohn and Carmi Schooler attempt to measure the reciprocal effects of personality on job and job on personality in *Work and Personality* (Norwood, N.J.: Ablex Publishing, 1983).

37. Smith, *Wealth of Nations*, 1:2.28. Smith here closely approximates Aristotle's trichotomy in the *Nicomachean Ethics*: nature (*physis*), custom (*ethos*), and teaching (*didakē*).

Smith's critique of Plato has led most commentators to insist that Smith entirely rejects any appeal to natural aptitude in his account of the division of labor. Schumpeter was thinking of Smith when he wrote of Plato: "This [Plato's] recognition of innate differences in abilities is worth mentioning because it was so completely lost later on."[38] Since every treatment of the division of labor in the history of European literature—with the possible exception of Rousseau—refers to innate differences in abilities, Schumpeter's comment is rather bizarre. Jacob Viner comments on Schumpeter's view: "I know of no one of consequence except Adam Smith who failed to point out as one of the services of division of labor that it enabled tasks to be assigned in accordance with aptitudes. (Even Adam Smith's failure was not a complete one)."[39]

As Viner suggests, even Smith could not resist the pull of the pervasive appeal to innate differences in ability to explain the division of labor. Speculating on the historical origin of specialization, Smith says: "In a tribe of hunters or shepherds a particular person makes bows and arrows, for example, with more readiness and dexterity than any other."[40] Since, in Smith's example, all hunters make bows and arrows, the superior dexterity of one bowmaker cannot initially be the result of training, but must be based on natural aptitude. But how plausible is Smith's scenario as an account of the origins of the division of labor? Despite its commonsense appeal, Smith's account contradicts the findings of contemporary economic anthropology. In primitive societies, specialization is a function of sex and clan rather than individual aptitude; indeed, can we even say about modern society that sex and family background have no bearing on one's occupational role?

38. Joseph Schumpeter, *History of Economic Analysis* (New York: Oxford University Press, 1954), 56.

39. Jacob Viner, *The Long View and the Short* (Glencoe, Ill.: Free Press, 1958), 352. Edwin Cannan accepts the view that Smith ignored the role of natural aptitude: "And he not only omitted but actually denied the existence of the advantage which is got by sorting persons out among different kinds of labour according to their natural qualities" (*A Review of Economic Theory* [London: P. S. King and Son, 1929], 96).

40. Smith, *Wealth of Nations*, 1:2.27. We find a similar comment in the *Lectures on Jurisprudence* [1762–66], ed. Ronald L. Meek, D. D. Raphael, and P. G. Stein (Oxford: Oxford University Press, 1978), 493: "In a nation of hunters, if any one has a talent for making bows and arrows better than his neighbors he will at first make presents of them, and in return get presents of the game."

The Division of Labor in Society and in the Firm

Marx's most significant contribution to the theory of the division of labor is his emphasis on the distinction between the firm and society. Marx shows that the division of labor within a firm proceeds on a very different basis from the division of labor across the whole of society. Marx calls the division of labor within a firm "technical" because, as we saw in chapter 5, he views it as merely the product of technical reason; he calls the division of labor across society "social." In his account, Marx says that the technical division of labor is stipulated by the capitalist whereas the social division of labor is simply natural. Indeed, as we shall see, Marx ends up arguing, on grounds of the economy of nature, that because the technical division of labor within a firm is efficient it must be natural. Marx does not provide, any more than did Smith, a genuinely social theory of the division of labor: both Smith and Marx offer explanations of the division of labor that refer to nature and to stipulated design but never to the collective and habitual traditions of custom.

Marx emphasized his distinction between the firm and society in response to Smith's confusion of them. Smith argues that the division of labor arises from a natural propensity to exchange and is then coordinated by exchange. It is curious, then, that Smith uses pin-making to illustrate this claim, since the division of labor in the pin factory is not coordinated by exchange. As Ugo Pagano says, "The man who draws the wire does not *sell* it to the man who straightens it, and the latter does not *sell* the straightened wire to the man who cuts it."[41] In the second chapter of the *Wealth of Nations*, however, Smith finds a much more appropriate illustration of his claim that the division of labor presupposes the propensity to exchange. Here he describes a tribe of hunters and shepherds in which each individual specializes in the production of one commodity in order to exchange goods with other individuals. Smith seems to have confused the market-coordinated division of labor in society with the planning-coordinated division of labor within a firm.

Exchange, in other words, is only one possible basis for the division of labor. Smith's misunderstanding of the relation of exchange to the division of labor reflects, in part, his poor understanding of biology. Smith argues that just as one does not see brute animals exchange goods, so one does not see them divide their labor. However, ever since the Italian economist Mechiorre Gioria argued that social specialization is common among many species of animals,

41. Ugo Pagano, *Work and Welfare in Economic Theory* (Oxford: Basil Blackwell, 1985), 8.

it has been clear that exchange is only one means of coordinating the division of labor.[42] Moreover, as Marx points out, one need not look to insect societies in order to criticize Smith's view that exchange is a necessary condition for the division of labor: "In the primitive Indian community there is social division of labour, without production of commodities. Or, to take an example nearer home, in every factory the labour is divided according to a system, but this division is not brought about by the operatives mutually exchanging their individual products."[43] Both a customary caste hierarchy and a pin factory are examples of a division of labor that is not coordinated by exchange. Indeed, Marx goes so far as to reverse Smith's causal argument. Far from exchange being a necessary condition for division of labor, the division of labor is a necessary condition for exchange.

Despite these confusions, Smith does see a difference between the firm and the society: he describes the division of labor in a firm as a microcosm of the social macrocosm. "The effects of the division of labour, in the general business of society, will be more easily understood, by considering in what manner it operates in some particular manufactures."[44] Smith here makes the important point that the perspicuity of the division of labor in a firm greatly promotes reflective awareness of the division of labor in society; and since such reflection is a precondition for stipulation, the firm is the major historical vehicle for bringing the customary division of labor to deliberate stipulation. Marx attacks Smith's doctrine of the microcosm by arguing that the firm and the society "are only *subjectively* different matters for him, not *objectively*. In the first case one sees the division at a glance, in the second case one does not."[45] Marx's distinction here between merely "subjective" and really "objective" differences is unfortunate in view of the historical fact that the subjective perspicuity of the division of labor in the

42. According to Smith's sociobiology: "In almost every other race of animals each individual, when it is grown up to maturity, is entirely independent" (*Wealth of Nations*, 1:2.26). On Gioia's 1815 critique of Smith, see Pagano, *Work and Welfare in Economic Theory*, 11. Kenneth Arrow uses contemporary sociobiology to criticize Smith: "Smith apparently is not aware of the possibility that the interaction and cooperation of human beings or animals can be achieved by means other than the market." See "The Division of Labor in the Economy, the Polity, and Society," in *Adam Smith and Modern Political Economy*, ed. Gerald P. O'Driscoll (Ames: Iowa State University Press, 1979), 157.

43. Marx, *Capital*, 1:1.2.49.

44. Smith, *Wealth of Nations*, 1:1.14.

45. Marx, "Economic Manuscript of 1861–63," in *Collected Works*, vol. 30 (New York: International Publishers, 1988), 268. Marx makes the same point in *Capital*, 1:14.4.335.

firm helped managers bring about far-reaching and objective transformations of the division of labor.

Still, Marx is justified in his view that Smith's microcosm-macrocosm model blurred some important distinctions between the firm and society. Indeed, Smith's use of the expression "division of labor" to refer indifferently to the firm or to society leads to some profound shortcomings in his doctrine. At the center of Smith's defense of capitalism is the view that the market promotes natural liberty and natural equality by coordinating human activity without domination and coercion. In Smith's "nation of shopkeepers" each person is equally free to truck, barter, and exchange: "Every man thus lives by exchanging, or becomes in some measure a merchant."[46] This system of natural liberty whereby each individual plies her or his own trade is appropriate only to a world of small independent producers whose social relations are mediated by the market. But Smith refuses to acknowledge the important differences between labor divided by the invisible hand of the market and labor divided by the visible hand of the manager. "What takes place among the labourers in a particular workhouse, takes place, for the same reason, among those of a great society. The greater their number, the more they naturally divide themselves into different classes and subdivisions of employment."[47] Is there no difference in the autonomy, liberty, and power of workers whether they are divided by a manager in a factory or divide themselves into trades? How can every man be a merchant if he is subject not just to the market but to the authority of a master? Smith can include the manufacturing division of labor in his system of natural liberty only with the fiction that detail workers "naturally divide themselves" into specialties.

Marx distinguishes the firm from society only to reduce the customary and stipulated division of labor in society to the natural differences of sex, age, and ability. From *The German Ideology* to *Capital* we find Marx simply repeating Thomas Hodgskin's arguments about the physiological basis of the division of labor in society.[48] Speaking of the sexual division of labor, Hodgskin says:

46. Smith, *Wealth of Nations*, 1:4.37.

47. Ibid., 1:8.104.

48. See Marx, "The German Ideology" [1846], in *Collected Works*, vol. 6 (New York: International Publishers, 1976), 44: "There develops the division of labour, which was originally nothing but the division of labour in the sexual act, then the division of labour which develops spontaneously or 'naturally' by virtue of natural predisposition." Confer "Economic Manuscript of 1861–63," 292: "It exists originally in the family, where it emerges spontaneously from physiological differences, differences of sex and age." Confer *Capital*, 1:14.4.332: "Within a family,

"This primary division of labour springs from sexual difference of organization, it has its foundation in the difference of our physical constitution. . . . The aptitude of the sexes for different employments is only an example of the more general principle, that every human being, by the circumstances of age, health, bodily or mental powers, is better adapted than another to some particular occupation."[49] Such naturalism is only to be expected from a man who insisted that political economy is not a political but a natural science. What is surprising is that Marx adopted Hodgskin's theory without reservation. Although every division of labor makes use of natural powers, the particular natural power selected is almost always a function of custom and stipulation. Yet Marx never refers to the general role of custom in shaping the division of labor nor to the particular genealogy whereby certain groups become customarily associated with certain tasks.

The absence of a concept of custom also undermines Marx's theory of the stipulated division of labor within the firm. Rather than seeing capitalist stipulation of the division of labor as reflecting in large part particular customary hierarchies of sex and class, Marx usually describes this stipulation simply as "technical"—as the disembodied application of science. Marx does acknowledge, however, that the authority structure of the firm reflects traditional hierarchies: "the factory code in which capital formulates, like a private legislator, and at his own good will, his autocracy over his workpeople . . . The place of the slave-driver's lash is taken by the overlooker's book of penalties."[50] In general, Marx acknowledges the customary and political dimension of the authority structure in production but not of the productive division of labor itself.

Although Marx calls the division of labor in a firm "technical," he reductively explains it in terms of nature. Arguing from the principle of natural economy, Marx insists that the stipulated division of labor in production is efficient because it is based on the objective natural aptitudes of individual workers.[51]

---

and after further development within a tribe, there springs up naturally a division of labour caused by differences of sex and age, a division that is consequently based on a purely physiological foundation."

49. Thomas Hodgskin, *Popular Political Economy* (London: Charles Tait, 1827), 112. Not only is Hodgskin the first economist to discuss the sexual division of labor, but he correctly points out that it is common to all societies.

50. Marx, *Capital*, 1:15.4.400.

51. "After manufacture has once separated, made independent, and isolated the various operations, the labourers are divided, classified, and grouped according to their predominating qualities . . . their natural endowments are . . . the foundation on which the division of labour is built up" (ibid., 1:14.3.330).

As usual, Marx displays too much confidence in the efficiency of the capitalist mode of production: as we saw in chapter 1, a century of industrial psychology has been unable reliably to link individual aptitude to job performance. Men, women, and children are generally assigned to tasks based on customary views of their roles, not on measures of individual aptitude.

Marx's radical naturalism is well illustrated by his use of energy physics to describe the division of labor in a firm: he argues that the division of labor within a firm efficiently exploits labor power (*Arbeitskraft*) just as the engineering sciences exploit natural powers (*Naturkräfte*). "We saw that the productive forces resulting from co-operation and division of labour cost capital nothing. They are natural forces [*Naturkräfte*] of social labour. So also physical forces [*Naturkräfte*] like steam, water, etc., when appropriated to productive processes, cost nothing."[52] Through the division of labor, then, the capitalist exploits labor power just as he exploits steam power: he converts the energy (*kraft*) of the worker and the energy of steam into mechanical work. The division of labor, for Marx, belongs not to political but to natural science.

That Marx's theory of the difference between the firm and society was inspired by Smith is most evident in his discussion of the difference between degree and kind. Smith often speaks of the "division" and "subdivision" of labor in a way that seems to correspond to the distinction between society and the firm.[53] In this view, the division of labor in society becomes subdivided in the firm; this seems plausible since detail labor is found within a workshop or office, but not as a separate trade or occupation. Marx criticizes Smith's view that the division of labor in society and that in the firm differ only in degree, saying they differ "also in kind." Since it is a basic Hegelian-Marxist tenet that differences of degree become differences of kind, Marx's emphasis here on the distinction between degree and kind is ironic. Perhaps the Hegelian dialectic of degree and kind helps to explain why Marx sometimes reverts to Smith's emphasis on a difference in degree: "Manufacture, in fact, produces the skill of the detail labourer, by reproducing, and systemically driving to an extreme within the workshop, the naturally developed differentiation of trades which it found ready to hand in society at large."[54]

---

52. Ibid., 1:15.2.365.
53. See Smith, *Wealth of Nations*, 1:8.104; 2 (intro.): 277; and 3:1.376.
54. Marx, *Capital*, 1:14.4.334, 14.2.321.

Neither Smith nor Marx can accurately characterize the distinction between the firm and society because neither is able to escape the superficial distinction between degree and kind. With our Aristotelian logic of progressive hierarchy, however, we can see that the division of labor in the firm presupposes the division of labor in society while bringing it to reflection and synoptic perspective. The division of labor within a firm does not necessarily differ in degree or in kind from the division of labor in society: it differs in the way that law differs from custom or grammar differs from speech.

Marx, Darwin, and the "Physiological Division of Labor"

At the end of the nineteenth century, Kuno Fischer argued that Darwinism was merely the logical outcome of the Hegelian notion of development: "That which Hegel had begun as a thinker, Darwin had completed as an empirical investigator." Ernst Cassirer, however, rightly observed that Darwinian evolution and Hegelian development (*Entwickelung*) have almost nothing in common.[55] Hegelian development, like Aristotle's *entelecheia*, is an unfolding of potentiality into actuality. The *telos* of the development is already present at the beginning. Moreover, for Hegel, it is not nature but culture (*Geist*) that is the locus of development. Darwinian evolution, by contrast, is genuinely historical: the path of development cannot be anticipated but must be reconstructed retrospectively. Strictly speaking, Darwinian evolution is not "evolution," since the word means precisely an unfolding of that which is already there; Darwin himself refers to natural history as "descent with modification."

Marx was the first bridge between Hegel and Darwin. Lewis Feuer argues that Marx's use of the term *Entwickelung* shifts from the *Contribution to the Critique of Political Economy* to *Capital*: "The connotation of *Entwickelung* has changed from that of a Hegelian sense of development in 1859 into a Darwinian mode of evolution in 1873. In other words, the language and method of Marx have become 'biologized.'"[56] Feuer is right about Marx's language but wrong about his method. Because Marx never grasped the logic of Darwinian

55. For Ernst Cassirer's discussion of Fischer, see *The Problem of Knowledge*, trans. Charles W. Hendel (New Haven: Yale University Press, 1950), 171.

56. Lewis Feuer is comparing the language of the 1859 *Preface* to the "Afterword to the Second German Edition" of *Capital*. See "Marx and Engels as Sociobiologists," *Survey* 23 (1978): 110–11. Feuer's use of the term *sociobiologists* to describe Marx and Engels is absurdly anachronistic: sociobiology is the application of neoclassical economics to Darwinian biology. Marx did not even grasp Darwinism, let alone neoclassical economics!

natural selection, he was able only to dress up Hegel's logic in the garb of Darwin's biology. Thus the encounter of Hegel and Darwin in Marx's thought generates a host of conceptual tangles: Hegel is Darwinized, Darwin is Hegelianized.[57] Marx's confusion of Hegel's development and Darwin's evolution, because it effaces the intrinsic logic of both concepts, leads him to bad biology and worse social theory.

Friedrich Engels recommended Darwin's *Origin of Species* to Marx in a letter of December 12, 1859; a year later, Marx wrote to Engels of the *Origin*: "This is the book which, in the field of natural history, provides the basis for our views."[58] Marx's misplaced enthusiasm for Darwin cannot be ascribed to the influence of Engels—quite the opposite. Engels, who knew much more science than Marx, rescued Marx from the worthless pseudoscience of Pierre Tremaux. Marx wrote to Engels that Tremaux's work "represents a very significant advance over Darwin" because Tremaux interprets natural history teleologically: "Progress, which Darwin regards as purely accidental, is essential here on the basis of the stages of the earth's development."[59] Even after Engels heaped ridicule on Tremaux, Marx insisted that Tremaux was right to emphasize the influence of the soil on racial and cultural evolution.[60] That the mature Marx could fall prey even briefly to such pseudoscientific naturalism reveals his poor grasp of the elemental logic of Darwinian biology.

What is the relation of the radical humanism of the early Marx to the naturalism of the mature Marx? Perhaps his humanism prepared the way for his naturalism by erasing the important distinction between natural order and customary order. Marxist humanism reduced nature to custom by insisting that human industry had transformed nature into its own image. In the *German Ideology*, for example, Marx argues that nature "is not a thing given

57. As Jean Hyppolite puts it (with considerable understatement): "There is in Marx's thought, as it comes through Hegel and Darwin, a certain ambiguity" (*Studies on Marx and Hegel*, trans. John O'Neill [New York: Basic Books, 1969], 129).

58. See Karl Marx and Friedrich Engels, "Letters," in *Collected Works*, vols. 40–42 (New York: International Publishers, 1983–87), 40:550 and 41:232.

59. Marx to Engels, August 7, 1866, in "Letters," 42:304–5. Marx begins this letter with his assessment of Tremaux: "In spite of all the shortcomings that I have noted, it represents a very significant advance over Darwin." What makes Tremaux superior to Darwin is his explicit natural teleology; yet, according to Terence Ball, "Marx clearly admired and agreed with Darwin's having finished off teleology in the natural sciences." See "Marx and Darwin: A Reconsideration," *Political Theory* 7 (November 1979), 474.

60. See Marx and Engels, "Letters," 42:320–23.

direct from all eternity, remaining ever the same, but the product of industry and of the state of society." Marx insists throughout his early work that through human labor nature becomes something recognizably human.

Nonetheless, just because man has transformed pristine nature (or at least corner of nature called earth) does not mean that man has transformed the laws and processes of nature; indeed, man can transform nature only through the laws of nature. The order of natural processes remains distinct from the order of custom and stipulation. Marxist humanism, by blurring the distinction between nature and custom, prepared the way for Marxist naturalism; reducing nature to custom made it all the easier to then reduce custom to nature. Indeed, the young Marx sees no difference between humanism and naturalism: "Thus society is the complete unity of man with nature—the true resurrection of nature—the accomplished naturalism of man and the accomplished humanism of nature." Marx's early equation of humanism and naturalism left him vulnerable to pseudoscientific naturalism: "Natural science will in time incorporate into itself the science of man, just as the science of man will incorporate into itself natural science: there will be one science."[61] Although one cannot rule out the possibility of such a unified science in the fullness of time, attempts at a shotgun marriage have not been promising.

In a letter of December 7, 1867, Marx instructed Engels how to review *Capital*: "When he [Marx] demonstrates that present society, economically considered, is pregnant with a new, higher form, he is only showing in the social context the same gradual process of evolution that Darwin has demonstrated in natural history."[62] Here Marx ascribes the teleological unfolding of Hegel's concept of development to Darwin's concept of evolution: Darwin, however, wrote in his notebook the famous rule "never say higher and lower." Instead of learning from Darwin that history does not have the prospective order of growth but the retrospective order of genealogy, Marx makes Darwin into the champion of progress. Marx never abandoned his teleological view that the study of capitalism provides the essential concepts for the study of all

61. Karl Marx, "Economic and Philosophic Manuscripts of 1844," in *Collected Works*, vol. 3 (New York: International Publishers, 1975), 298 and 304.

62. Marx and Engels, "Letters," 42:494. Feuer argues that Darwin's uniformitarianism led Marx to the notion that the evolution to socialism would be gradual and cumulative. See "Marx and Engels as Sociobiologists," 112. If so, this is ironic, since Darwin's uniformitarianism is now under attack by advocates of "punctuated equilibrium" in natural evolution: nature may be much more revolutionary than Marx thought! Thus the hazards of the slavish imitation of natural science.

previous economic systems: "The anatomy of man is a key to the anatomy of the ape."[63] Or, as Marx puts it in *Capital*: "The country that is more developed industrially only shows, to the less developed, the image of its own future."[64]

When we turn to Marx's theory of the division of labor, Darwin's influence is unmistakable. Throughout *Capital* we find an analogy between the division of labor and the differentiation of species, between specialization and speciation.[65] Marx tells us that the different kinds of useful labor may be "classified according to the order, genus, species, and variety to which they belong in the social division of labour."[66] Indeed, in many contexts, Marx employs the biological term for the differentiation of labor (*Unterscheidung*) instead of the usual term for the division of labor (*Teilung*). "Castes and guilds arise from the action of the same natural law [*Naturgesetz*] that regulates the differentiation of plants and animals into species and varieties, except that, when a certain degree of development has been reached, the heredity of castes and the exclusiveness of guilds are ordained as a law of society (*gesellschaftliches Gesetz*)."[67] Where Marx in some places associates natural selection with market competition, here, curiously, he associates natural selection with castes and guilds—the opposite of market competition. Moreover, Marx is not content with simply suggesting an analogy; he is clearly arguing that natural selection is the cause of the specialization of trades. Yet castes and guilds serve precisely to prevent the competition between individuals that is a precondition for natural selection.

Just as the classical political economists believed that the economy is natural, so Darwin believed that nature was economical. Darwin cites Goethe with approval: "In order to spend on one side, nature is forced to economise on the other side."[68] It is well known that Darwin's (and Alfred Wallace's) discovery of natural selection was inspired by their reading about the struggle for survival in the political economy of Malthus; what is less well known is

63. Marx, "Grundrisse," 28:42. Marx's quip about anatomy is doubly mistaken: first, because evolution is not an unfolding in which the later reveals the earlier; second, because the ape is not man's ancestor but his cousin.

64. Marx, *Capital*, "Preface to the First German Edition," 1:19.

65. For a recent attempt to develop the same analogy, see H. S. Houthakker, "Economics and Biology: Specialization and Speciation," *Kyklos* 9 (1956).

66. Marx, *Capital*, 1:1.2.49.

67. Ibid., 1:14.2.321.

68. See Charles Darwin, "Origin of Species" [1859], in *Darwin: A Norton Critical Edition*, ed. Philip Appleman (New York: W. W. Norton, 1970), chap. 5.

the role of Smith's theory of the division of labor in biological theory. A leading French zoologist, Henri Milne-Edwards, seems to have read Smith's tale of the pin factory; he argued that because of the "law of natural economy" there is a highly specialized "division of physiological labor" within organisms. He said that the body of an organism resembles a workshop (*atelier*) in which the organs are specialized detail workers: "In the creations of nature, just as in the industry of men, perfection is obtained mainly through the division of labor."[69] Milne-Edwards classified species on the basis of the degree of the physiological division of labor: the "higher" the species, the greater the specialization of organs.

Darwin was so impressed with Milne-Edwards's principle that he was surprised at the rarity of the sexual division of labor among plants: "No naturalist doubts the advantage of what has been called the 'physiological division of labour'; hence we may believe that it would be advantageous to a plant to produce stamens alone in one flower or on one whole plant, and pistils alone in another flower or on another plant."[70] In this case, Darwin was led astray by the analogy between a workshop and an organism. Darwin observed that the reproductive tasks of most plants are divided between pistil and stamen; he then concluded that there must be some general tendency for plants to divide into male and female. Darwin assumed with the political economists that the "social" division of plants must logically follow from the technical division of reproductive tasks. Yet the "social" division of plants into male and female is extremely rare; nor do plants exhibit a general tendency toward an increasing social division.

Despite the dubious value of the concept of the division of labor in biology, Marx appeals to Darwin's use of the physiological division of labor to help explain the development of productive technology. Since *organa* are literally tools, Marx models the development of specialized technologies on the development of specialized organs. "Darwin has interested us in the history of Nature's Technology, i.e. in the formation of the organs of plants and animals which organs serve as the instruments of production for sustaining life. Does not the history of the productive organs of man, of organs that are the material basis of all social organization deserve equal attention?"[71] Marx's appeal

69. See Henri Milne-Edwards, *Introduction à la zoologie générale* [1853] (New York: Arno Press, 1981), 35. On Milne-Edwards's relation to Adam Smith and to Darwin, see Camille Limoges, "Milne-Edwards, Darwin, Durkheim and Division of Labor," in *The Relations between the Natural and the Social Sciences* (Princeton: Princeton University Press, 1992).

70. Darwin, "Origin of Species," chap. 4.

71. Marx, *Capital*, 1:15.1.352n.

to the physiological division of labor only obscures what is distinctive about human technology. Although every animal of the same species has the same organs, human technologies vary widely over time and place. This is because animals have an unmediated relation to nature: their organs are the product of the direct relation between the organism and its natural environment. Human technologies have a mediated relation to nature: our technologies are shaped by specific customs and social interests. Marx often reduces human technology to natural physiology: "Technology discloses man's mode of dealing with Nature, the unmediated [*unmittelbar*] process of production by which he sustains his life."[72] Yet as we saw in chapter 5, because our technical relation to nature is mediated by custom and stipulation, technologies disclose our social relations as much as they disclose our relations to nature.[73]

Marx argues that modern technology is efficient because it is designed with the same functional principles as are natural organs. "The manufacturing period simplifies, improves, and multiplies the implements of labour, by adapting them to the exclusive special functions of each detail labourer." Marx glosses this observation with a quote from Darwin to show that natural selection, like industry, works to create organs whose forms are determined solely by their function. "As long as the same part has to perform diversified work, we can perhaps see why it should remain variable, that is, why natural selection should not have preserved or rejected each little deviation of form so carefully as when the part has to serve for some one special purpose. In the same way that a knife which has to cut all sorts of things may be of almost any shape; whilst a tool for some particular purpose must be of some particular shape."[74] Here we can see the hazards of the analogy between natural organs and human tools—both for biology and for social theory. Darwin argues that just as human tools are designed to fit their functions, so organs

72. Ibid. "In the section of *Capital* where he deals with technology and the transformations of man's forces and relations of production, he speaks about the invention of tools, machinery, and machine-tools like a Darwinian. He considers these inventions an extrapolation of a natural technology" (Hyppolite, *Studies on Marx and Hegel*, 129).

73. In one place, Marx does suggest that technology is an index of social relations: "Instruments of labour not only supply a standard of the degree of development to which human labour has attained, but they are also indicators of the social conditions under which that labour is carried on." As to just what these instruments signify about social relations Marx never tells us. Moreover, if instruments are indicators of social relations, then industry has a mediated relation to nature—something Marx often denies. See *Capital*, 1:7.1.175–76.

74. Darwin, "Origin of Species," chap. 5, cited by Marx in ibid., 1:14.3.323n.

are designed by natural selection to fit their functions. Marx then cites Darwin to argue that just as natural selection adapts form to function, so modern industry designs tools for their specialized functions.

Yet although functionalism makes sense as an explanation of the intentional human adaptation of means to ends, natural selection does not design structures to match functions. As Darwin realized in his later book on orchids (1862), natural selection does not design organs at all but merely tinkers with inherited parts that previously had served different functions: "Thus throughout nature almost every part of every living being has probably served, in a slightly modified condition, for diverse purposes, and has acted in the living machinery of many ancient and distinct specific forms."[75] Thus by the time Marx turned to Darwin to prove that technical functionalism is natural, Darwin had already abandoned strict functionalism. By rejecting functionalism, Darwin was able to develop a profoundly historical concept of evolution in which the morphology of an organism could be explained only as the product of a specific genealogy. Darwinian evolution reflects the genealogical order of custom more than the functional order of design.

Human Nature and Society in Marx: From Species Being to Collective Laborer

The paradox of social life is that we must submit to society in order to be free, we must be dependent on the collectivity in order to become autonomous: in short, the individual is only a part of the social whole while he or she transcends that whole. This paradox, unfortunately, is usually reduced to the cliché of "the individual versus society": either society is said to be prior to the individual or the individual is said to be prior to society. But no dialectical play of these concepts will do justice to our paradox.

Jacques Maritain makes a useful distinction between our being *individuals* who are subordinate to the social whole and our being *persons* who transcend the claims of any human institution.[76] I will propose a different approach to

75. Darwin, *On the Various Contrivances by Which British and Foreign Orchids Are Fertilized by Insects* [1862], cited in S. J. Gould, *The Panda's Thumb* (New York: W. W. Norton, 1980), 26. As Gould puts it: "Orchids were not made by an ideal engineer; they were jury-rigged from a limited set of available components."

76. See Jacques Maritain, *The Person and the Common Good*, trans. John J. Fitzgerald (New York: Charles Scribner's Sons, 1947).

this question. In the realm of the customary, each individual is subordinate to the whole: customs are collective rituals in which we merely participate. We are vehicles for customs—think of language—because we absorb them unknowingly. Customs transcend us in time because they were here before us and will outlive us; and customs transcend us in space because we never exercise more than a small part of any customary practice. Nonetheless, each individual has the power, through reflection, to bring a part of the customary order to synoptic stipulation. Our power to affirm or reject deliberately certain customary norms and to stipulate new norms is the basis for our transcendence of the customary social order. Stipulation makes social custom, to some modest extent, the vehicle of individual design. But just as stipulation always presupposes custom, so an individual's transcendence of society presupposes that individual's subordination to society.

Whether Marx was an individualist or a collectivist has long been in dispute: did Marx see socialism as a vehicle for individual fulfillment or did Marx see the individual as a vehicle for the social good? There is evidence in Marx for both views—showing that Marx was caught in the same sterile dialectic of the individual versus society as his commentators. At the root of Marx's inability to grasp the relation of the individual to society is his theory of human nature. What Marx terms "man's social nature" turns out to be an analogy between human nature and society that utterly effaces the distinction between them. As we shall see, a good illustration of the weakness of Marx's social theory is his complete inability to grasp the elemental role of the division of labor in creating social solidarity.

Marx's theory of human nature is best illustrated by his concept of man as a species being (*Gattungswesen*). Marx adopted the term from Ludwig Feuerbach; if we are to understand the concept of species being, however, we must turn to Aquinas's doctrine of angels.[77] According to Aquinas, every angel is a species being because angels have no matter to individuate them: each angel is the exemplar of the species. The perfection of the species of angels is fully preserved in each angel. Yet because humans are individuated, says Aquinas, the perfection of the human species requires the differentiation of persons: in short, no human individual can ever be the exemplar of the species.[78] The

77. I owe this insight to my teacher Dermot Brendan Moran.

78. As Aquinas says: "If then the angels are not composed of matter and form . . . it is impossible that there should be more than one angel in a species" (*Summa Theologiae*, 1, Q. 50, art. 4). The gloss on this passage reads: "Each angel in and by himself realizes the fullness of his angelhood; no single man can realize the fullness of humanity."

human community achieves goodness and solidarity through cooperation based on social differentiation.

Marx's philosophical anthropology is but a secular version of Aquinas's angelology. The old saw that "communism would work only if men were angels" turns out to be quite literally true: "Man is a species-being, not only because in practice and in theory he adopts the species . . . as his object, but—and this is only another way of expressing it—also because he treats himself as the actual, living species; because he treats himself as a universal and therefore a free being."[79] Marx's individual person, like Aquinas's individual angel, is the exemplar, the microcosm, of the entire species: "Man's individual and species-life are not different" because man "is a being that treats the species as its own essential being, or that treats itself as a species-being."[80] Anything that differentiates one person from another, in Marx's view, estranges man from his essence as a universal or species being. Each individual is potentially the perfection of humanity. In short, everything that distinguishes human beings from angels is the source of alienation.

Clearly, the division of labor differentiates individuals; therefore it estranges us from our essential human nature. "The division of labour is the economic expression of the social character of labour within the estrangement."[81] Far from being a source of solidarity, it pits the individual against society: "The division of labour also implies the contradiction between the interest of the separate individual or the individual family and the common interest of all individuals." In communist society, therefore, when man fully realizes his human nature as a species being, there will no longer be any division of labor: one will "hunt in the morning, fish in the afternoon, rear cattle in the evening, criticise after dinner, just as I have a mind, without ever becoming hunter, fisherman, shepherd, or critic."[82] This ideal species being, whose activity encom-

79. Marx, "Economic and Philosophic Manuscripts of 1844," 275.

80. Ibid., 299 and 276.

81. Ibid., 317. Division of labor, for Marx, is alienation: "'Division of labour' seems on the face of it to be a totally different idea from 'self-alienation' or 'alienated labour.' On closer analysis, however, it turns out that the transition is essentially a metamorphosis of one and the same basic idea." Robert C. Tucker, *Philosophy and Myth in Karl Marx* (Cambridge: Cambridge University Press, 1961), 185.

82. Marx, "German Ideology," 46–47. Louis Dumont observes that in "German Ideology," species being (*Gattungswesen*) has become common essence (*Gemeinwesen*), but with no real change of meaning. Thus Dumont asks "why the replacement of man's universal essence (*Gattungswesen*) by man's social essence (*Gemeinwesen*) did not develop the implications and soci-

passes the entire division of labor in society, is himself a microcosm of society. He has no need of society; he is his own society. Marx's ideal society is thus a society of one.[83]

Marx never fully abandoned his view of man as a species being; indeed, this view of human nature motivates Marx's lifelong attack on the social division of labor. Marx's hostility to human individuation in the division of labor is especially evident in his critique of craft production. Because a craftsman is a specialist, his expertise estranges him from his universal human essence: "What characterises the division of labour inside modern society is that it engenders specialties, specialists, and with them craft-idiocy."[84] Marx, who in the *Communist Manifesto* attacks capitalist production because it "holds no interest for the worker," here attacks craft production because it holds great interest for the worker. The reason why Marx did not see any "trade-off between breadth and depth," as Elster puts it, is that for a species being all specialization is alienation.[85] Thus it is no surprise that Marx cites Hegel's comment with approval: "By well educated men we understand in the first instance, those who can do everything that others do."[86] Someone who can do everything others do is precisely someone with no need of society—either a beast or a god, as Aristotle said.

If Marx makes every individual a self-contained society, then it is not surprising that he also describes society as an individual. "If the whole society were considered as a single individual, necessary labour would consist of the sum of all the particular functions of labour which are made independent by the division of labour. The single individual would have to spend, e.g. so much time for agriculture, so much for industry, so much for trade, so much for the production of instruments."[87] This logical inversion of the species

---

ological insights one could have hoped for." See *From Mandeville to Marx* (Chicago: University of Chicago Press, 1977), 145.

83. "The Individual has here his apotheosis; he has become a society in himself. Society, insofar as it transcended the individual, has simply gone; there is no social whole left, no collective ends apart from the ends of the individuals" (Dumont, *From Mandeville to Marx*, 137).

84. Marx, "The Poverty of Philosophy" [1847], in *Collected Works*, vol. 6 (New York: International Publishers, 1976), 190. Nor did Marx believe that craft-idiocy was limited to modern society: "Every medieval craftsman was completely absorbed in his work, to which he had a complacent servile relationship" ("German Ideology," 66).

85. See Jon Elster, *Making Sense of Marx* (Cambridge: Cambridge University Press, 1985), 90.

86. Hegel, *Philosophy of Right*, par. 187 (addition), cited in Marx, *Capital*, 1:14.5.34n.

87. Marx, "Grundrisse," 28:450.

being is the collective laborer (*Gesammtarbeiter*). Where the species being is an individual microcosm of society, the collective laborer is the social macrocosm of the individual. Imagine, says Marx, the whole society or the whole factory as one individual. Where the individual species being realized his social nature by encompassing the entire division of labor in society, the collective laborer is the personification of the group to which individuals radically subordinate themselves. Individuals thus realize their social natures only as organs of the collective laborer: "When the labourer co-operates systematically with others, he strips off the fetters of his individuality and develops the capabilities of his species." Before, the social division of labor was a fetter on the individual species being; now individuality is a fetter on the social division of labor. The same division of labor that frustrated the social nature of the species being becomes the very affirmation of the social nature of the collective laborer: "The reason of this is that man is, if not as Aristotle contends, a political animal, at all events a social animal." Man then becomes a social being because society is an individual being. Marx returns to the familiar topos of the pin factory and proceeds to describe the division of labor as the various activities of a single individual: "The collective-labourer, with one set of his many hands armed with one kind of tools, draws the wire, with another set, armed with different tools, he, at the same time, straightens it, with another he cuts it, with another, points it, and so on."[88]

We cannot simply regard the collective laborer as a literary conceit, because this concept has profound implications for Marx's theory of the division of labor. As we saw in chapter 5, Marx often ignores the coordination costs intrinsic to the social division of labor—now we can see why. If the social unity of production is modeled on the psychological unity of individual activity, then coordination vanishes as a problem. Production by an individual worker is integrated by his skill: coordination is a function of psychology, not sociology. Speaking of a team of bottle-makers, Marx says: "These five detail workers are so many special organs [*Sonderorgane*] of a single working organism [*einzige Arbeitskorper*] that acts only as a whole, and therefore can operate only by the direct cooperation of the whole five."[89] Thus the collective laborer plays a crucial role in Marx's strategy of explaining the division of labor in terms of human nature rather than in terms of custom or stipulation.

88. Marx, *Capital*, 1:13.312, 13.309, and 14.3.326.
89. Ibid., 1.14.3.328.

Indeed, in the collective laborer Marx brings together both reductive strands of his thought: the social division of labor is at once technically efficient and natural. "The collective-labourer now possesses, in equal degree of excellence, all the qualities requisite for production, and expends them in the most economical manner, by exclusively employing all his organs, consisting of particular labourers, or groups of labourers, in performing their special functions."[90] The collective laborer is also at the center of Marx's sociodicy, since "the deficiencies of the detail-worker became perfections when he is part of the collective-labourer." In other words, the degradation of labor in the modern factory only appears to be evil; when seen in the context of the overall productivity of the factory, what seems evil is actually good. Once again, we see Marx's strange faith that the impoverishment of individual workers is a necessary condition of the productivity of the firm. And Marx gives his sociodicy a historical turn: through the emergence of the collective laborer, capitalism is unknowingly bringing about communism. By freeing the worker from the "fetters of his individuality," capitalism realizes man's true social nature.

In the transition from the species being to the collective laborer we see the fundamental unity of Marx's thought. For one is the microcosm and the other the macrocosm of the same Platonic analogy between the individual and society. The development of Marx's thought reflects neither a fundamental rupture nor a simple continuity: the species being of the young Marx is inverted into the collective laborer of the mature Marx. This inversion leads to two implausible views of the division of labor. In the case of the species being, the social division of labor simply negates man's social nature by alienating man from man; in the case of the collective laborer, the social division of labor affirms man's social nature by negating his individuality. In the first we find total disintegration and in the second total integration. What we need instead is a theory that accounts for how social solidarity is created through social differentiation: "The division of labor unites at the same time that it opposes; it makes the activities it differentiates converge; it brings together those it separates."[91]

At a deeper level, of course, the problem lies with the analogy between the individual and society. Since it was Plato who developed the famous analogy between the division of labor in society and the division of labor in the human

90. Ibid., 1.14.3.330.

91. Emile Durkheim, *The Division of Labor in Society* [1893], trans. George Simpson (New York: Free Press, 1964), 276.

soul, Marx's collective laborer is thus a throwback to the Platonic analogy between the tripartite soul and the tripartite city. Aristotle, however, explicitly rejected this analogy between society and the individual; Aristotle insisted that a society could never have the unity of the individual soul. For social custom has more diversity and complexity than an individual will ever encompass; at the same time, individual stipulation has more unity and clarity than social custom will ever achieve. There is thus an undeniable pathos in the hope of Plato and Marx that society will realize the unity of the individual while the individual will realize the wealth of society.

The Natural Economy of Robinson Crusoe

Who is the species being of the *German Ideology*—the one who hunts, fishes, rears cattle, and criticizes all in the same day—if not Robinson Crusoe? After all, Crusoe himself said that "every Man may be in time Master of every mechanical Art."[92] There can be no doubt that Crusoe is the exemplar of Marx's view of human nature—the original species being. Indeed, far from being peculiar to Marx, Defoe's fictional character has played a prominent role in the economic imagination from Adam Smith to Paul Samuelson. What makes Robinson Crusoe so irresistible to classical, neoclassical, and Marxist theorists?

Robinson Crusoe represents not the commencement but the culmination of liberal theorizing about the "state of nature." A "state of nature" is a thought experiment that is designed to discover the rational essence of social obligation and distributive justice beneath the irrational sediment of custom and law. In terms of experimental design, the state of nature functions to isolate natural justice and natural right by controlling for custom and for law. When it comes to the question of distributive justice, however, the state-of-nature experiment of John Locke does not control sufficiently for intervening variables. Locke's labor theory of property, for example, holds that in the state of nature, every man is entitled to the fruits of his labor: each is the rightful owner of all that he appropriates. But since Locke sees the state of nature as a viable society of free and equal economic agents, each man in the state of nature must have a wife. If so, her labor is a precondition for his; so already

92. Daniel Defoe, *Robinson Crusoe* [1719], ed. Michael Shinagel (New York: W. W. Norton, 1975), 55.

we have a sexual division of labor, social cooperation, and the quandary of distributive justice. Insofar as there is any social division of labor, wealth is jointly produced and cannot be neatly assigned to individual laborers. As a theory of distributive justice, Locke's state of nature is incoherent even as a thought experiment because of poor experimental design.

Daniel Defoe, by creating Robinson Crusoe, made a major contribution to liberal social theory by taking the state of nature to its logical conclusion: the individual as a microcosm of society. Robinson Crusoe neatly solves the problem of distributive justice because in his one-man economy there is absolutely no social division of labor, at least until Friday arrives. As an exercise in state-of-nature theorizing, Robinson Crusoe is far superior in experimental design to Hobbes's or Locke's state of nature. For Defoe alone has controlled for all of the relevant variables by totalling isolating Crusoe from the social division of labor. Because of the logical simplicity of its experimental design, Crusoe's one-man economy has been a constant source of theorizing about the actual economy. Indeed, Robinson Crusoe has decisively replaced the traditional state of nature as the starting point of liberal economic theory.[93]

In his *Lectures on Jurisprudence*, Adam Smith attacks theories based on the state of nature: "It in reality serves no purpose to treat of the laws which would take place in a state of nature, or by what means succession to property was carried on, as there is no such state existing."[94] But this attack does not prevent Smith from making considerable use of the state of nature in his own theory. Smith frequently appeals, for example, to Locke's theory that labor is the source of property in the state of nature: "In that original state of things, which precedes both the appropriation of land and the accumulation of stock, the whole produce of labour belongs to the labourer. He has neither landlord nor master to share with him."[95] This link between labor and property, however, is plausible only if there is no social division of labor: "in that rude state of society in which there is no division of labor, in which exchanges are seldom made, and in which every man provides every thing for himself."[96] That Smith is oblivious to the fundamental role of the sexual division of labor is

93. Even contemporary liberal political theory treats Crusoe as the exemplar of the state of nature. See Robert Nozick, *Anarchy, State, and Utopia* (New York: Basic Books, 1974), 185.

94. Smith, *Lectures on Jurisprudence*, 398.

95. Smith, *Wealth of Nations*, 1:8.82.

96. Ibid., 2 (intro.):276.

evident in his view that there has been or indeed could be a society with no division of labor. Smith's man in the state of nature may not have to share his produce with a landlord or master, but he will surely have to share with his wife and children. Since even the most primitive production requires the cooperative labor of the whole family, how is the contribution of each member to be measured? The dilemma of distributive justice is inescapable. Smith never quite grasps that the "whole produce of labour belongs to the labourer" only in the case of Robinson Crusoe because he truly has no one to share with him.

Just as Smith attacks the "state of nature" only to make use of it, so Marx attacks "Robinsonades" only to make use of Crusoe: "Individuals producing in a society—hence the socially determined production by individuals is of course the point of departure. The individual and isolated hunter and fisherman, who serves Adam Smith and Ricardo as a starting point, is one of the unimaginative fantasies of the 18th century."[97] Marx's claim here that he will adopt a social rather than an individual point of departure has led many commentators into believing that Marx delivers on this promise.[98] But as we saw with the concepts of the species being and the collective laborer, Marx often explains social institutions by analogy to the individual.[99] For example, Marx jumps directly from Crusoe's economy to the communist economy: "All the characteristics of Robinson's labour are here [in communism] repeated, but with this difference, that they are social, instead of individual." So communism is Crusoe writ large whereas Crusoe is communism writ small.

Marx even turns to Robinson Crusoe to illustrate the labor theory of value.

> Since Robinson Crusoe's experiences are a favourite theme with political economists, let us take a look at him on his island. . . . All the relations between Robinson and the objects that form this wealth of his own creation, are here so simple and clear as to be intelligible without exertion. . . . And yet those relations contain all that is

97. Marx, "Grundrisse," 28:17.

98. Thus Shlomo Avineri tells us that "Marx cannot accept on principle any economic theory that starts with an individualistic model of human existence or behaviour. . . . Marx argues that as an explicatory model the 'Robinsonade' is fallacious and misleading" (*The Social and Political Thought of Karl Marx* [Cambridge: Cambridge University Press, 1968], 82).

99. Louis Dupré recognizes the relation of Marx's theory to liberal state-of-nature theory: "Marx's position on the social condition of man comes dangerously close to the eighteenth-century natural right theory, according to which man is by nature an individual being—he comes to live in society only to remedy the accidental limitations of his individuality" (*The Philosophical Foundations of Marxism* [New York: Harcourt Brace and World, 1966], 227).

essential to the determination of value. . . . In spite of the variety of his work, he knows that his labour, whatever its form, is but the activity of one and the same Robinson, and consequently, that it consists of nothing but different modes of human labour.[100]

That Marx can use Crusoe to illustrate the labor theory of value reveals the absence of a genuinely social theory of value in Marx. Instead of defining value by the social processes of communication and exchange, Marx defines value as the transference of energy that occurs when a force is applied to a body. In Marx's physics of labor power, an agent doing work is losing energy to the body on which the work is done; value is a measure of this transfer of energy. The labor theory of value, then, is a theory of the transference of energy from labor power (*Arbeitskraft*) to a commodity, from what Marx calls "living labor" (*vis viva*) to "dead labor" (*vis mortua*).[101] Because of the principle of the conservation of energy, the quantity of socially necessary energy expended by the worker is equivalent to the value of the commodity. Just as heat, electricity, and work are but different modes of energy, so Crusoe's activity, "whatever its form," is "nothing but different modes of human labour." Value, for Marx, is not determined by our relations to persons but by our relations to natural objects: Crusoe's relations to his productions, says Marx, "contain all that is essential to the determination of value."

Indeed, Robinson Crusoe's economy seems to reflect both Marx's objective labor theory of value and the neoclassical theory of value as subjective utility. According to Marx, Crusoe knows the value of his productions because "his stock-book contains a list . . . of the labour-time that definite quantities of those objects have, on average, cost him." Value is equal to the amount of energy (measured by labor time) that is crystallized in artifacts. Neoclassical economists, by contrast, argue that different types of labor are of different subjective value to Crusoe, just as different types of commodities are of different subjective value to a consumer. And just as a consumer allocates his scarce resources to different commodities in order to maximize his subjective utility, so Crusoe allocates his scarce time to different branches of production.[102]

100. Marx, *Capital*, 1:1.4.81–83.

101. On Marx's treatment of the relation of living labor to dead labor as the relation of *vis viva* (kinetic energy) to *vis mortua* (potential energy), see Mirowski, *More Heat than Light*, 181.

102. Robinson Crusoe is used to illustrate economic rationality in the works of W. S. Jevons, Karl Menger, Philip Wicksteed, Eugen Böhm-Bawerk, Alfred Marshall, Knut Wicksell, Lionel Robbins, and Paul Samuelson.

Despite these radically different notions of what constitutes value, Marx and the neoclassical economists are in full agreement that Robinson Crusoe is the exemplar of economic rationality, the true *homo oeconomicus*. Marx insists that "necessity itself compels him to apportion his time accurately between his different kinds of work," whereas neoclassical economists insist that rationality compels him to allocate his time optimally between competing uses. The real Crusoe, unfortunately, was neither a Marxist nor a neoclassical economist: "But my Time or Labour was little worth, and so it was as well employ'd one way as another."[103]

How is it that Defoe's hero became the very prototype of *homo oeconomicus*? Because Robinson Crusoe personifies the pervasive reduction of productive labor to technical efficiency and to nature. Instead of moral relations to persons, Crusoe has only technical relations to nature: indeed, Crusoe's production is unique because it has a technical but not a social division of labor. Moreover, having been extricated from society, Crusoe's behavior is thought to reflect pure natural reason without the distortions of historically specific customs: his lone economy is the economy of nature.

103. Defoe, *Robinson Crusoe*, 55.

Epilogue
Self-Realization at Work

When Aristotle says that to become a good person we must make use of nature, habit, and reason, he is saying that excellence, whether moral or intellectual, involves what would later be called "self-realization." Excellence or self-realization are essentially by-products of certain activities: in the course of learning a foreign language or learning to play chess, for example, we cultivate our natural powers into skillful habits, we exercise those habits in complex ways, and we deliberately modify our habits to meet the challenges of new situations. Self-realization is of considerable moral concern because the exercise of complex skills promotes the happiness and well-being that constitute human flourishing.

Because self-realization is so central to human flourishing we need to consider more precisely what self-realization means, what kinds of work foster self-realization, and what ought to be done to create more opportunity for self-realization in work. Jon Elster describes self-realization in terms of Aristotle's two-stage model of the actualization of potential: the abilities of an individual, he says, must first be developed and then be deployed. "Being able to (learn to) speak French is a condition for knowing how to speak French, and this, in turn, is a condition for speaking French."[1] As a model of human excellence, however, Aristotle's potency-act model is radically inferior to his nature, habit, and reason model. Because it omits the role of rational reflection, the potency-act model of self-realization applies to the exercise of brute animal habits as much as to specifically human self-realization. Human excellence

1. See Jon Elster, "Self-Realization in Work and Politics," *Social Philosophy and Policy* 3 (Spring 1986): 102. All citations of Elster below are from this essay. Elster admits that his model of self-realization is Aristotelian, but he does not tell us what makes it so. His model is Aristotelian because its two stages correspond to the passage from *dynamis* to *hexis* and from *hexis* to *energeia* (see *DA* 417a21ff).

(or self-realization) requires the capacity for reflective modification of our habits in accordance with rational ideals. Indeed, Elster's emphasis on the human capacity for "self-paternalism"—that is, our capacity for deliberately changing our habitual preferences—is an acknowledgment of the centrality of rational stipulation in any model of human self-realization.

What activities lend themselves to self-realization? Aristotle often says that whereas moral and political action shapes the agent, productive work shapes only the product; Aristotle thus seems to eliminate work from the sphere of self-realization. Ever since Hegel and Marx, however, it has been well understood that work shapes the character of the worker: work, in other words, lends itself to self-realization. Elster usefully provides a description of self-realizing activities that cuts across Aristotle's distinction between action and production. An activity lends itself to self-realization, he says, if it is directed to an external goal, if it can be performed more or less well, and if it is of enough complexity to be a challenge.

What kinds of work provide a mode of self-realization? Elster says that working a lathe lends itself to self-realization but not working on an assembly line. The latter, he says, is mere drudgery that does not lend itself to self-realization "because it very soon becomes trivial or boring." This makes sense, but is there a more theoretically precise way to distinguish challenging work from drudgery? We saw in the Prologue that Aristotle defines work as the unity of conception and execution; on Aristotelian grounds, then, we can say that work is a mode of self-realization only if it respects the integrity of conception and execution. First, merely to carry out the instructions of another person contradicts the autonomy inherent in the notion of *self*-realization. Autonomy requires not just that we have the liberty to choose what kind of work to pursue, whether carpentry or teaching, but also that we have some discretion about how to perform our work.[2] Second, the actualization of one's potential, implicit in the notion of self-*realization*, depends upon a dialogue between conception and execution; the success or failure of any complex activity requires that we reflect on the interaction between an idea and its realization. What counts as a good idea will depend upon the means of execution, and what counts as a good execution depends upon the quality of

2. Elster limits the "freedom of self-realization" to the choice of "which of one's abilities to develop," by which he means the choice of a particular job or career. See "Self-Realization in Work and Politics," 101.

the idea. As John Ruskin says: "It is only by labour that thought can be made healthy, and only by thought that labour can be made happy, and the two cannot be separated with impunity."[3]

If moral and intellectual excellence involve self-realization, then the detailed division of labor, Taylor's scientific management, and automated technology are all developments that should be of moral concern because they have all tended to shatter the integrity of work as the unity of conception and execution. Whereas the skilled crafts and the professions are characterized by the acquisition of considerable knowledge and skill through a long apprenticeship, a great deal of clerical and manual labor is characterized by the divorce of conception from execution: managers and engineers do the thinking, while blue-, pink-, and, increasingly, white-collar workers do the executing. We have seen that the use of the division of labor and of technology to turn work into monotonous drudgery is not a technical or natural necessity, but is the result of a complex constellation of moral and political choices; there is a variety of alternative patterns for designing jobs and deploying technology equally compatible with economic efficiency.

If there are various divisions of labor that promote self-realization without sacrificing economic efficiency, then why is the scope for self-realization so limited in the contemporary economy? And what moral and political choices could advance the prospect for self-realization in work? Some have argued that every person has a moral "right" to meaningful work, that is, work promoting self-realization. Since every right imposes a duty, the right to meaningful work imposes a duty on government to guarantee access to such work. "How can a government not intervene," asks Adina Schwartz, "when it is indeed possible to restructure industrial employment so that all persons' jobs foster instead of stunt their autonomous development?"[4]

The difficulty with claiming a right to meaningful work is that the definition of what constitutes meaningful work is vague. I have defined meaningful work in terms of the unity of conception and execution because this unity is rooted in the natural structure of the human personality. But human nature is itself vague until it becomes specified by particular customs and stipulations. The unity of conception and execution has taken, and will con-

3. Ruskin, *The Stones of Venice*, vol. 2 (London: Smith, Elder, and Co., 1853), chap. 6.
4. Adina Schwartz, "Meaningful Work," *Ethics* 92 (July 1982): 646.

tinue to take, a great variety of different forms depending upon the technical requisites of work, the varying aptitudes of individual workers, and evolving customary expectations about work. It is much easier to determine that conception and execution are divorced than to judge how, once divorced, they can be rejoined. Rights are effective only when they require the performance of specific duties; a right to meaningful work would not impose such a specific duty. Moreover, even where one can specify what constitutes meaningful work in a given context, it is not clear that government is the appropriate agent for restructuring industry. Redesigning the content of jobs is fraught with hazards even where workers and managers cooperate enthusiastically—such experiments are so often sabotaged by either labor or management. But for government to somehow mandate the restructuring of a firm's jobs in order to protect a vague right to meaningful work is a recipe for disaster.

Government should be concerned with the distribution of meaningful work not because of a putative right to such work but simply because meaningful work is so fundamental to human happiness and well-being. How should government go about the business of enhancing the opportunities for self-realization in work? The obstacles to self-realization are so deeply rooted in the institutions of our economy that only profound changes in the ownership and control of industry can create the opportunity for greater access to meaningful work. Government can play a significant though indirect role supporting institutional change in our economy—change that might well be desirable even apart from its role in helping to create meaningful jobs.

Here, of course, we can only mention some of the obstacles to self-realization and only suggest some possible strategies for overcoming them. Louis Putterman lists some plausible reasons why most firms do not offer greater scope for self-realization in work as a way to compete for workers: first, because of chronic unemployment, competition among firms for limited workers is the exception, and competition among workers for limited jobs is the rule; second, even if employers did compete for workers, they would not know what aspects of job design to change, since often the only signal they receive about workers' preferences is the decision to accept or leave a job; third, managers and capital owners may have an interest in maintaining their own power within firms, both for its own sake and because they believe it necessary in order to protect their share of the firm's earnings; and finally, workers are habituated to accept routine and monotonous jobs.[5]

I will briefly describe some possible strategies for overcoming these obstacles, beginning with the final one—which in some ways is the most confounding. The psychological habituation of workers to degrading work is indeed a powerful obstacle to the transformation of work, as can be seen in the fact that most labor-management agreements confer on management sole responsibility for determining the methods, processes, and means of production. So deep-seated are these customary expectations about the content of work that even when workers have the power to humanize labor through collective bargaining or through outright ownership, they often do not.[6] Elster argues that the lack of desire for self-realization is not so much the cause as the effect of the paucity of opportunities for self-realization; workers reduce their desire for meaningful work because they have so few opportunities to enjoy it. Moreover, because the mastery of a complex skill requires an arduous and unrewarding initial effort, says Elster, "the fact that many people do not desire challenging work does not mean that they would not 'prosper' in it, once they got over the initial hurdles." In the liberal professions, a long and arduous apprenticeship is accepted for the sake of the rewards of challenging work; the same could be true of the mechanical arts.

The habituation of workers to degrading work—rooted in the customary expectation that managers do the thinking while workers do the executing— is a profound obstacle to moral self-realization. Nevertheless, through reflection on these customary preferences, and through what Elster calls "self-paternalism," we, as individuals and as a society, can take steps to change our preferences. John Ruskin eloquently describes the transformation of individual moral attitudes required for the possibility of self-realization at work:

> We are always in these days endeavoring to separate the two; we want one man to be always thinking, and another to be always working, and we call one a gentleman, and the other an operative; whereas the

---

5. See Louis Putterman, *Division of Labor and Welfare* (Oxford: Oxford University Press, 1990), 161.

6. Even in industries with strong unions, labor contracts cede all control over the organization of labor to management. See Harley Shaiken, *Work Transformed* (New York: Holt, Rinehart and Winston, 1984), 4. Perhaps the most successful worker-owned companies in the world are part of the Mondragon Cooperatives; they employed Taylorist methods of production until a strike signalled the need for change.

workman ought often to be thinking, and the thinker often to be working, and both should be gentlemen, in the best sense.[7]

An illustration of Ruskin's point can be seen in the contrast between union and nonunion electricians. Electrical work involves both the creative work of diagramming the circuits and the monotony of pulling wire through walls. Union electricians working as a team will usually rotate the jobs so that no one is stuck only pulling wire; a team of nonunion electricians, by contrast, will usually have one master electrician who only diagrams and a team of unskilled workers who only pull wire. The union electricians have acknowledged a fundamental moral duty: respect for the self-realization of others demands that we do not slough off all routine tasks to them. We all make many decisions during the workday either to do our own routine tasks or to get someone else to do them; yet few of us acknowledge the moral dimension of such mundane choices.

Since individual preferences about the content of work are largely the product of the institutional environment, the transformation of individual attitudes must be supported by the creation of new social institutions. A useful criterion for evaluating a set of economic institutions is to consider which institutions make it easiest for us to respect the self-realization of our fellow employees. By describing three institutional changes in order of increasing magnitude, we will gauge the immensity of the challenge facing those who would promote self-realization in work. These three institutional strategies—collective bargaining, workplace democracy, and the diffusion of engineering knowledge—form a hierarchy in the sense that each strategy can build on the prior one.

A minimal prerequisite for self-realization at work is a strong and progressive union. Economists have shown that union-sponsored grievance and arbitration procedures provide workers with their only real voice for suggesting improvements in job design.[8] Otherwise, a worker's only signal about job dissatisfaction is his or her decision to quit, which, as Putterman points out, pro-

---

7. Ruskin, *Stones of Venice,* vol. 2, chap. 6.

8. According to Richard B. Freeman and James L. Medoff, "collective rather than individual bargaining with an employer is necessary for effective voice at the workplace," because without union protection workers risk losing their jobs. Providing workers with a voice at the workplace promotes equity as well as efficiency. "If management uses the collective bargaining process to learn about and improve the operation of the workplace and the production process, unionism can be a significant plus to enterprise" (*What Do Unions Do?* [New York: Basic Books, 1984], 8 and 12).

vides little useful information to managers. Moreover, a union must be committed to the principle that the design of jobs and the deployment of technology are legitimate issues for collective bargaining. To this end, the International Association of Machinists and Aerospace Workers has proposed a "Technology Bill of Rights" to require that automation be deployed to enhance skill and to expand the responsibility of workers, rather than to destroy skill and to contract workers' responsibility.[9] Such a bill of rights, by making the organization of work a matter of political negotiation, forces workers to reflect on customary preferences and perhaps to develop new preferences for challenging work. The use of collective bargaining to address the issues of job design and the deployment of technology represents a significant break with the existing custom of ceding all such decisions to management.

Worker ownership and control of a company is a more radical strategy, offering greater potential scope for self-realization in work. Nor is this strategy incompatible with the first: in many cases unions are the vehicle for establishing worker ownership. In such "self-governing enterprises," all decisions about the division of labor and the deployment of technology are potentially subject to democratic decision-making. Although many utopian visions have been attached to the idea of workplace democracy, experience shows that worker self-government does not usually generate a demand for radically new methods of organizing work—so strong is the force of custom.[10] Nonetheless, although workplace democracy is not a sufficient condition for advancing the dignity of work, it may be a necessary one. Because every employee has a voice in the firm's governance and a stake in its welfare, workplace democracy vastly reduces the conflict between employees and employers, in turn reducing the chances that the organization of work will reflect management's desire for power over workers. For example, a self-governing firm is less likely to be willing to sacrifice productivity in the short run in order to solidify the authority of management in the long run.[11] Indeed, there are several

9. The three main provisions of this bill of rights are: "1) New technology must be used in a way that creates or maintains jobs. 2) New technology must be used to improve the conditions of work. 3) New technology must be used to develop the industrial base and improve the environment." See Shaiken, *Work Transformed*, chap. 8.

10. "Such evidence as we now have does not, I think, warrant high hopes for huge changes in attitudes, values, and character from greater democracy at work" (Robert A. Dahl, *A Preface to Economic Democracy* [Berkeley: University of California Press, 1985], 98).

11. For examples of firms that deploy technology in a way that reduces productivity and increases managerial power, see Shaiken, *Work Transformed*, 113-20.

examples of successful experiments in job design that were sabotaged by managers who feared the loss of their prerogatives.[12] Where conception and execution have long been divorced there is likely to be considerable opposition to a remarriage. Worker-owned cooperatives, such as the Mondragon Cooperatives in Spain, however, have shown a significant willingness to experiment with the design of jobs and the deployment of technology. Self-governing firms thus offer the best long-term possibility that the "technical" issues of the organization of labor will become subject to political debate, reflection, and experimentation.

Ultimately, however, the integrity of conception and execution cannot be restored without reducing the gulf between engineers and workers. Workplace democracy may well be necessary, but it is not sufficient. "The worker can regain mastery over collective and socialized production only by assuming the scientific, design, and operational prerogatives of modern engineering; short of this, there is no mastery over the labor process." Harry Braverman thus argues that without some knowledge of modern engineering the worker remains a captive of experts, a tool of management—even if the experts and managers are democratically elected. How can workers assume the prerogatives of modern engineering? Braverman suggests a combination of formal polytechnical education with lifelong opportunities for specialized job training. With rapidly changing processes and products, a traditional one-time apprenticeship will not be adequate except in relatively stable trades like carpentry, plumbing, and electrical work.[13]

Recent economic and technological developments, however, may pose some real opportunities for bridging the gap between workers and engineers. First, with the saturation of markets for mass-produced goods and the growing demand for specialized designer products in advanced industrial nations,

12. At a General Foods plant in Topeka, Kansas, the detailed division of labor was abolished in 1971 and productivity improved significantly. But *Business Week* reported in 1977 that its democratic division of labor had "been eroding steadily" because of "indifference and outright hostility from some GF managers." "The problem," *Business Week* noted, "has been not so much that the workers could not manage their own affairs as that some management and staff personnel saw their own positions threatened because the workers performed almost too well. . . . Personnel managers object because team members made hiring decisions. Engineers resented workers doing engineering work." For more details, see Schwartz, "Meaningful Work," 641–46.

13. For Harry Braverman's vision of worker-engineers and his critique of workplace democracy, see *Labor and Monopoly Capital* (New York: Harper and Row, 1984), 444–45.

manufacturing may become increasingly organized around the principles of flexible specialization as opposed to rigid mass production. The high-technology cottage industries that manufacture such specialized goods depend on the fusion of conception and execution among highly skilled craftsmen and designers.[14] As the rapidly changing demand for such specialized goods as women's high-fashion apparel, scientific instruments, and electronic components grows, so too should the demand for workers with the engineering expertise to accommodate frequent shifts in production runs. Second, the microelectronics revolution has made computer technology the basis of most manufacturing and service industries. Mastery of computer skills now means mastery of many productive processes. A solid understanding of computer circuitry and programming would equip a young person for challenging and creative work in industries ranging from the production of specialty steels to data-base management. With microcomputers, for example, it is now feasible for operators of automated machine tools, and other automated machines, to do their own on-site programming. Therefore, general computer skills combined with specialized training for particular productive processes would go far in giving workers in most industries scope for imagination and innovation at work.

Even if we find the goal of eliminating engineering as a separate occupation to be utopian, we might agree with Braverman that workers' ability to exercise imagination and autonomy at work, their ability to experience the pride of craftsmanship, will be directly proportional to their knowledge of productive materials and processes. In medicine, for example, doctors are able to make use of medical engineering without compromising their autonomy only if they understand the design, capacities, and use of the relevant technologies—otherwise they are at the mercy of engineers. Engineering knowledge alone enables workers to conceptualize tasks: to program their own computers, to draft their own layouts, to diagram their own circuitry.

Aristotle's model of self-realization grew out of the Athenian tradition of rhetorical education (*paideia*); rhetorical excellence was thought to require natural aptitude, practice, and knowledge. Since Athenian democracy prided

14. "Where Fordism calls for the separation of conception from execution, the substitution of unskilled for skilled labor and special-purpose for universal machines, I will argue that specialization often demands the reverse: collaboration between designers and skilled producers to make a variety of goods with general-purpose machines" (Charles Sabel, *Work and Politics* [Cambridge: Cambridge University Press, 1984], 194).

itself as "rule by argument," self-realization in democratic politics demanded the diffusion of rhetorical *paideia*. Later, Thomas Jefferson would insist on the importance of widespread education for a political democracy; he feared that if the mass of people did not have the requisite knowledge they would be manipulated by their leaders. Advocates of economic democracy ought to consider what kind of knowledge is required by workers if they are to avoid being manipulated by managers.[15] Indeed, technical knowledge may well be of greater importance to economic democracy than to political democracy. In the workplace, perhaps, the devil is truly in the detail. Self-realization in the economy of the future will require a new *paideia*, a radical empowerment of workers through the diffusion of engineering knowledge. The full exercise of moral freedom in the workplace requires not just the liberty to choose but also the knowledge to create the alternatives of choice.

15. Dahl says that one assumption of any democratic assocation is that the whole body of citizens (the *demos*) shall decide which issues the *demos* is qualified to decide for itself, and which issues the *demos* will delegate to experts. He does not consider what kinds of knowledge may be necessary for workers to make this determination. See *Preface to Economic Democracy*, 58.

Index

Ackrill, J. L., 90, 91, 96*n26*

Action (*praxis*), 13, 14; governed by moral reason, 85, 87, 88, 92, 102, 110; distinct from production, 87–93, 94–95, 96, 97, 98, 99–100, 102, 109, 110–12; means-end relation, 88–89, 94, 97–99, 100–101, 111; political, 92–93; process/activity distinction, 93–95, 96, 97; act of mind and moral act, 95, 96–97; and theory, 95–96; principle of least action, 195, 198

Activity (*energeia*), 99; distinct from process, 93–95, 96, 97, 98

Actuality (*energeia*): distinct from potentiality, 93, 94, 95, 129, 132–33, 208, 225; theory and, 96; moral reason as, 106

d'Alembert, Jean Le Rond, 156

Alston, William, 48*n5*

Anaximander, 117–18

Anthropology, 40, 55, 74, 131–32, 202, 216

Antigone (Sophocles), 140, 141

Antiphon, 13, 47, 51, 114, 191

Arendt, Hannah, 13, 14, 34, 88, 144*n2*, 177

Aristotle: theories of justice, 2, 5, 99, 128, 129, 140; theory of production, 5, 87; theory of human flourishing, 5–6, 46, 225–26, 233; on unity of conception and execution, 8, 87, 226; explicit and implicit logic, 11, 12, 85, 86; exclusion of moral reason from production, 12, 13, 34, 91; on division of labor, 12, 24–25, 56–57, 143; and teleology, 12–13, 51, 88–89, 98, 116, 125, 142; economy of nature doctrine, 12–13, 143, 194; on technical reason in production, 34, 43*n61*, 85, 88, 92, 143; doctrine of hypothetical necessity, 36,

103–4; on human as social animal, 40; on technology as slave, 41, 164; on the polis, 46, 124, 127; nature, custom, stipulation trichotomy, 46–47, 50, 53, 54, 59, 81, 86, 115, 117, 119, 120–22, 127; custom as "second nature," 51, 52, 80, 85–86, 116, 130, 132, 142; custom as "unwritten law," 51, 52, 80, 116, 117, 130, 139, 142; use of analogy and metaphor, 51, 52, 116–17; on natural law, 52, 85–86, 117, 119, 139, 141–42, 188–89, 190; analysis of souls, 53, 119; on slavery, 57, 111, 113, 124; on learning, 69, 79; influence on classical political economy, 85–86, 143–44; distinction of moral and technical reason, 86, 87–88, 92–93, 103–10, 178; action, production, contemplation trichotomy, 87, 90–91; distinction of action and production, 87–92, 94, 98–99, 101, 110–12, 177, 226; use of syllogism, 89, 104; archery analogy, 89, 107–8; on politics, 92–93, 144; on economics, 93; distinction of process and activity, 93–97, 98; on virtues, 99, 105; and nature/convention dichotomy, 113, 116, 119; on education, 115, 121, 130, 131; analogy of art and nature, 116, 117, 125–26; analogy of nature and law, 117, 118–19; on custom and habit, 118, 119, 130–34; logic of progressive hierarchy, 119–21; on nature, 123–29; on stipulation, 130, 135–36, 137–42; on reason (*logos*), 135, 136; modern physics and, 194; on individual and society, 217, 220

Aron, Raymond, 183*n99*

Arrow, Kenneth, 158*n29*, 163*n43*